★ ★ ★ ★ CONTROLLING REGULATORY SPRAWL

Recent Titles in
Contributions in Political Science
Series Editor: Bernard K. Johnpoll

International Dynamics of Technology
Ralph Sanders

Party Politics in Israel and the Occupied Territories
Gershon R. Kieval

The Strange Career of Marihuana: Politics and Ideology of
Drug Control in America
Jerome L. Himmelstein

French Communism in the Era of Stalin: The Quest for Unity
and Integration, 1945–1962
Irwin M. Wall

North Korea in Transition: From Dictatorship to Dynasty
Tai Sung An

The Harmonization of European Public Policy: Regional Responses
to Transnational Challenges
Edited by Leon Hurwitz

The Press and the Rebirth of Iberian Democracy
Edited by Kenneth Maxwell

Domestic Policy Formation: Presidential-Congressional
Partnership?
Steven A. Shull

Communications Policy and the Political Process
Edited by John J. Havick

Abortion: A Case Study in Law and Morals
Fred M. Frohock

The State as Terrorist: The Dynamics of Governmental
Violence and Repression
Edited by Michael Stohl and George A. Lopez

Minority Rights: A Comparative Analysis
Jay A. Sigler

★★★★CONTROLLING REGULATORY SPRAWL

PRESIDENTIAL STRATEGIES FROM NIXON TO REAGAN

HOWARD BALL

Contributions in Political Science, Number 105

GREENWOOD PRESS
Westport, Connecticut • London, England

Library of Congress Cataloging in Publication Data

Ball, Howard, 1937–
    Controlling regulatory sprawl.

    (Contributions in political science, ISSN 1047-1066 ;
no. 105)
    Bibliography: p.
    Includes index.
    1. Administrative agencies—United States.
2. Administrative procedure—United States.   3. Trade
regulation—United States.   4. Presidents—United
States.   5. United States—Politics and government—
1945–   . I. Title. II. Series.
JK469 1984   353'.075   83-8541
ISBN 0-313-23525-2 (lib. bdg.)

Library of Congress Catalog Card Number: 83-8541
ISBN: 0-313-23525-2
ISSN: 1047-1066

First published in 1984

Greenwood Press
A division of Congressional Information Service, Inc.
88 Post Road West
Westport, Connecticut 06881

Printed in the United States of America

10 9 8 7 6 5 4 3 2 1

TO
my actress, Sue
my dreamer, Sheryl
my vet, Melissa, and
my love, Carol

Contents

Figures and Tables

Preface

Numerous scholars, administrators, and politicians have expressed great concern about the recent efforts of the White House to assume greater control over the federal regulatory bureaucracy by providing direction and oversight to the careerists managing the federal agencies. These critics, along with a hostile Congress, have argued that the various regulatory control actions taken by the Nixon, Ford, Carter, and Reagan administrations have deprived midlevel managers in the federal agencies of "significant policymaking discretion."[1] Generally these critics argue that the presidential efforts are unconstitutional actions in violation of the separation-of-powers concept.

There are others, myself included, who strongly believe that federal managers of regulatory agencies should operate with a diminished expectation of power over the direction of national goals and policies, and that national political actors, especially the President, should act aggressively and continuously to ensure that this diminution comes to pass.

At issue is the fundamental question of accountability in a democratic political system. Federal agency managers understand this to mean "answerability and willingness to take responsibility for the broad principles and initiatives set forth by the President."[2] But practical experience has led the White House to develop mechanisms to ensure that the regulatory agencies are indeed acting in a manner consistent with national policy as established by the Congress and the President.

Congress cannot, and will not, develop the ability to oversee their surrogates, generally due to "poor congressional leadership and factional discipline."[3] The federal courts do not have the necessary jurisdictional capability to deal with this essentially "political question." The President and his political appointees heading the federal agencies must become the critical linkage between the policy formulated by the Congress and the White House and its actual implementation by the federal administrative managers. The executive branch political leadership must coordinate and direct the federal bureaucracy in order to "transform the shadow of the policy into the substance of the program."[4]

The President and his political appointees must balance agency concerns and actions in light of the national agenda that the incumbent is responsible for developing and implementing. Without this type of supervision and control over agency policymaking by the President, there is no assurance that the chief executive and career civil servants (his subordinates) will be moving on the same track relative to national goals and priorities. Without such oversight, the outcome is an insidious transfer of power to nonelected policymakers and a "stunning loss of governmental accountability."[5]

This book examines the character of the shift of power from political policymaking to administrative policymaking and the consequences of this development in American politics over the past three decades. After discussing reasons for the inability of the national legislature to deal with the problem of regulatory sprawl, the book examines the nature of presidential power and the basic strategies and tactics (procedural, substantive, personnel) available to the President in the effort to lead the federal bureaucracy. Finally, the book examines the specific strategies of the presidencies of Richard Nixon, Gerald Ford, Jimmy Carter, and, especially, Ronald Reagan.

Although all four presidents were different in terms of style, personality, and policy orientations, all four have seen the problem of regulatory control by the White House "in remarkably similar terms."[6] All have tried to walk "the fine line between continual oversight and arbitrary intervention."[7] Their administrations attempted to oversee federal agency activity through personnel control, deregulation, reorganization efforts, and forms of centralized review of agency actions by voluntary and mandatory oversight machinery.

This last strategy, oversight of agency activity from within the White House, is the most radical of the tactics developed by the White House, especially the Reagan administration's effort to use the Office of Management and Budget (OMB)'s Office of Information and Regulatory Affairs (OIRA) as a formal "preclearer" of all major federal executive agency regulatory proposals. (Chapter 5 focuses on the nature of the controversy that develops, over the toxic chemical labeling standard in this case study, between OMB and the adversely affected federal agency — the Occupational Safety and Health Administration [OSHA].)

The President is obligated to "take care that the laws be faithfully executed." The President, in this regard, must "properly supervise and guide their [executive department agency managers'] construction of the

statutes under which they act to secure that unitary and uniform execution of the laws which Article II of the Constitution evidently contemplated in vesting general power in the President alone."[8] Neglect of this
enduring, continuing responsibility will ultimately allow the "professional crowd in Washington to smother the President."[9]

The President cannot let this happen; the oath of office requires the
incumbent to pursue strategies, in the face of heavy criticism and condemnation, that enable the White House to have the final word on major
regulatory policies that affect national economic and social life. The
occupant of the White House must assume the final responsibility for
those agency decisions that will have a major impact on our nation. To
allow federal regulatory managers to act in an unchecked manner is to
court constitutional disaster.

NOTES

1. Kathryn Newcomer and Glenn Kamber, "Changing the Rules of Rulemaking," 11 *Bureaucrat*, Summer 1982, p. 12.

2. Warren Lasko, "Executive Accountability: Will SES Make a Difference,"
9 *Bureaucrat*, Fall 1980, p. 4.

3. Robert Gilmour, "Congressional Oversight," 10 *Bureaucrat*, Fall 1981,
p. 18.

4. Richard P. Nathan, *The Plot That Failed: Nixon and the Administrative
Presidency*, New York: John Wiley and Sons, 1975, p. viii.

5. Gilmour, "Congressional Oversight," p. 18.

6. George Eads, testifying before Dingle Committee Hearings on *The Role of
the OMB in Regulatory Control*, March 1981, p. 38.

7. Ibid.

8. *Meyers v. United States*, 272 U.S. 52 (1926).

9. Richard Neustadt, *Presidential Power*, rev. ed., New York: John Wiley and
Sons, 1980, p. 26.

Acknowledgments

Many people have assisted me in the development of this book. Staff members on the congressional committees that have been involved in substantive examinations of the role of the White House in regulatory reform have been extremely helpful, in particular Rick Grawey, on the staff of the House Subcommittee on Manpower and Housing, Government Operations Committee. Anonymous officials in OMB and OSHA gave me needed assistance at critical times, as did personnel in the General Accounting Office.

Jane Simpson was extremely valuable to me in bibliographic work on the manuscript. Barbara Sessions did an outstanding job typing the manuscript. I appreciate the assistance of both women very much.

I have had a number of discussions with academic peers, at professional meetings and in numerous offices and coffee shops, on this matter of regulatory oversight. I wish to thank all of them, especially Phil Cooper, Georgia State; Tom Lauth, University of Georgia; Lee Fritschler, Brookings Institution; Jerry Gabris and Ed Clynch, Mississippi State; and Bob Gilmour, University of Connecticut. There were many interesting conversations, some heated, on the question of managing the bureaucracy; I appreciated all these words—some more than others.

Finally, I want to acknowledge the love and support I have received from my wife, Carol, and from my daughters, Sue, Sheryl, and Melissa.

Abbreviations

AEI	American Enterprise Institute
APA	Administrative Procedure Act
CAB	Civil Aeronautics Board
CEA	Council of Economic Advisers
COWPS	Council on Wage and Price Stability
DOJ	Department of Justice
EIS	Economic Impact Statement
EO	executive order
EPA	Environmental Protection Agency
FCC	Federal Communications Commission
FEA	Federal Energy Administration
FMC	Federal Maritime Commission
FPC	Federal Power Commission
FTC	Federal Trade Commission
FY	fiscal year
GAO	General Accounting Office
ICC	Interstate Commerce Commission
IIS	Inflation Impact Statement
IRC	independent regulatory commission
MSDS	material safety data sheet
OIRA	Office of Information and Regulatory Affairs
OMB	Office of Management and Budget
OPM	Office of Personnel Management
OSHA	Occupational Safety and Health Administration
OSH Act	Occupational Safety and Health Act
PPM	parts per million
RARG	Regulatory Analysis Review Group

RIA	regulatory impact analysis
SEC	Securities and Exchange Commission
SES	senior executive service
USDA	United States Department of Agriculture
ZBB	zero based budgeting

★ ★ ★ ★ CONTROLLING REGULATORY SPRAWL

1

Controlling Regulatory Sprawl: Stage Setting

Often we didn't know where to put a program—in which agency—and we didn't particularly care where it went, we just wanted to make sure it got enacted.
—Joseph Califano, President Johnson's Domestic Adviser, 1964-1969

One department's watershed project threatens to slow the flow of water to another department's reclamation project downstream.
—Richard M. Nixon, 1970

There are too many agencies, doing too many things, overlapping too often, coordinating too rarely, wasting too much money—and doing too little to solve real problems.
—Jimmy Carter, 1978

In our democratic polity, the Congress and the White House form the core of the policymaking process. "Policy making is made up of several stages of decision making: problem identification; policy formulation; policy adoption; then implementation, evaluation, and, possibly, policy termination."[1] Once a problem has been identified—a very basic political process involving no fewer than five clusters of political actors: interest groups, agencies, subcommittee staffs, the President and his staff, and Congress—policy must then be formulated by the various actors in the political process. The actor's participation in this process will vary according to the type of policy determined to be appropriate to the problem. (Table 1 illustrates the various mixes in the policy formulation process.) Invariably, however, both the White House and the Congress, and the staffs who work in these institutions, are intimately involved in most types of policy formulation; democratic theory and practice call for their involvement.

Table 1
Political Relationships for Policymaking

Policy Type	Primary Actors	Relationship among Actors	Stability of Relationship	Visibility of Decision
Distrib- utive (1)	Congressional subcommittees and committees; executive bureaus; small interest groups	Logrolling (everyone gains)	Stable	Low
Protective regulatory (2)	Congressional subcommittees and committees; full House and Senate; executive agencies; trade associations	Bargaining; compromise	Unstable	Moderate
Redistrib- utive (3)	President and his appointees; committees and/or Congress; largest interest groups (peak associations); "liberals, con- servatives"	Ideological and class conflict	Stable	High
Structural	Congressional subcommittees and committees; executive bureaus; small interest groups	Logrolling (everyone gains)	Stable	Low
Strategic	Executive agencies; President	Bargaining; compromise	Unstable	Low until publicized; then low to high
Crisis	President and advisers	Cooperation	Unstable	Low until publicized; then gen- erally high

(1). Distributive policymaking is that policy that distributes goods and services to specific constituencies in the society.
(2). Regulatory policymaking includes those programs that limit various forms of activity—commercial and noncommercial. Regulatory policymaking may limit entrance into business or professions; set rates and routes; establish health and safety standards for the workshop; and so forth. It is, essentially, coercive.
(3). Redistributive policymaking aims at rearranging basic social and economic rewards, for example, the progressive income tax.

Table 1—*Continued*

		Influence of:		
President, Presidency, and Centralized Bureaucracy	Bureaus	Congress as a Whole	Congressional Subcommittees	Private Sector
Low	High	Low (supports sub-committees)	High	High (subsidized groups)
Moderately high	Moderate	Moderately high	Moderate	Moderately high (regulated interests)
High	Moderately low	High	Moderately low	High ("peak associations" representing clusters of interest groups)
Low	High	Low (supports sub-committees)	High	High (subsidized groups and corporations)
High	Low	High (often responsive to executive)	Low	Moderate interest groups, corporations)
High	Low	Low	Low	Low

Sources: Randall B. Ripley and Grace A. Franklin, *Congress, the Bureaucracy, and Public Policy*; Homewood, IL: Dorsey Press, 1980, pp. 22-23; and Phillip Cooper, *Public Law and Public Administration*, Palo Alto, CA: Mayfield Publishing Co., 1983, pp. 244-245.

It is in this intimate involvement with policymaking that both the Congress and the President come into direct and continued contact with the federal bureaucracy. For the national legislators, the federal agents and their agencies, created by Congress and directed to exercise delegated powers on behalf of the national legislature, are their surrogates. "Agencies," said the Supreme Court in 1961, "are creatures of Congress. . . . The determinative question is not what an agency thinks it should do but what Congress has said it *can* do."[2] These surrogates of the Congress should take cues from the legislators and their staffs in order to carry out the policy formulated in the political arena.

The President and his staff have maintained that, given the responsibility of the chief executive to "take care that the laws be faithfully executed," these administrative agents and agencies are under White House control and direction. The President staffs executive agencies with loyal supporters; names the chairpersons of the independent regulatory commissions; has general control over the budgeting and litigation that arises from agency activity; has limited impoundment authority; has reorganization powers; can intervene in regulatory matters; and has general informal powers.[3]

In recent years, especially since the Nixon administration (1969-1974), there has been a hard struggle between Congress and the President for control of the federal bureaucracy. "As a source of executive-legislative friction, it would be difficult to select an issue more deep-rooted than control of the bureaucracy. . . . Both have claims to a general supervisory power."[4] In recent decades, however, neither the Congress nor the President has done a substantive job in overseeing and controlling the federal bureaucracy. Lee Witter wrote in 1980 that "unless congressional oversight capability improves, bureaucracies created to administer legislation could readily go their own way, unchecked by the very people who created them."[5] During the Nixon administration, on the executive side, there was noncompliance with more than half of the President's orders, commands, requests, and directives to the executive branch in 1969-1970. For Presidents who have come into office in recent years, the federal bureaucracy is "the hated enemy yet it is a potential source of power and influence."[6]

One or both of these major political actors must be involved in effective leadership of the federal agencies. There are a wide variety of management techniques available to both the Congress and the President in order to ensure administrative accountability: the Administrative Procedure Act; OMB budget control; OMB legislative clearance; presidential appointment powers; senatorial appointment powers (advise and consent); Department of Justice (DOJ) lawsuit powers; and congressional definition of office and bureaus, definition of powers in the organic statute, determination of compensation for administrative agents, investigatory powers, appropriation powers, casework, nonstatutory controls, sunset legislation, sunshine legislation, and personnel policy and powers.[7] In June 1983, however, the U.S. Supreme Court invalidated the use by Congress of the legislative veto. In *Immigration and Naturalization Service v. Chadha* (1983), a seven-justice majority struck down the use of the legislative veto as written into Section 242 (c) (2) of the Immigration and Naturalization Act. By implication, the justices also invalidated over two hundred other statutes passed by Congress since 1932 that contained legislative veto provisions. Chief Justice Warren Burger concluded that while the legislative veto may be a "convenient shortcut; an appealing compromise," the Founding Fathers "ranked other values higher than efficiency," for example, the "checks and balances" and "separation of powers" concepts. Article I, concluded the Chief Justice, "erected enduring checks on each branch and to protect the people from the improvident exercise of power by mandating certain prescribed [Article I] steps," such as, bicameralism, presentment to present, presidential veto, and legislative override of presidential veto. These "step-by-step" procedures were "considered so imperative that the draftsmen took special pains to assure that these requirements could not be circumvented." The Court held that because the legislative veto short circuits these processes, it is an unconstitutional exercise of legislative power. The *Chadha* opinion will profoundly affect the manner in which the Congress will be able to constrain bureaucratic rulemaking.

Our democratic polity calls for effective administrative accountability by the elected officials. Subsequent segments of this book will examine the reasons for the growth of regulatory activity and power. Given regulatory sprawl in recent decades, America is now confronted with the consequences of a separation of administrative implementation of policy from governmental formulation of that same policy. According to Eugene Hickok and Gary McDowell,

Modern bureaucracy represents a challenge to good government because elected officials either are unable to direct and control the administrative process or they refrain from doing so. . . . [T]here is great harm in an administrative machinery detached from political leadership. Political leadership of the bureaucracy is necessary to ensure administrative responsibility.[8]

Good government, wrote Alexander Hamilton, is good administration; in a democracy, the political leaders, elected by the people, have to maintain this control over the federal bureaucracy. If there is a lack of effective oversight, by either the Congress or the President, there is an abdication of democratic responsibility by these elected agents.[9]

The problem of effective political leadership over the administrative process has grown to the crisis level as a result of the expansion of governmental activities in the domestic arena. There is an increase in administrative fragmentation, which leads to a diffusion of responsibility in the administrative governmental process.[10] For example, there are 100 federal human services programs administered by ten different departments and agencies; there are 77 housing programs administered by 15 agencies; and there are 60 transportation grant programs in the U.S. Department of Transportation and 25 other federal agencies.[11]

Although both Congress and the President are responsible for ensuring administrative accountability, this book focuses on the prospects of the President and his staff's controlling and directing administrative behavior through various management techniques because only through executive action can the federal bureaucracy be brought under control by elected actors. Congress does not have the capability, due to poor congressional leadership and factional discipline, for administrative control.

This fundamental question of how to hold administrative agents accountable to elected officials is perplexing and profoundly important. Robert Gilmour's perspective is gloomy. He perceives this "leadership crisis," especially in the Congress, to be one of "structural incapacity, not simply the personal inability of particular incumbents. . . . The outcome is a little appreciated yet stunning loss of governmental accountability." For example, Gilmour points out that congressional oversight authority "is fragmented into more committee and subcommittee units than ever before." The winners in this leadership struggle, then, are the agencies themselves.[12]

Regarding presidential oversight, federal Judge Henry J. Friendly has commented that the "spectacle of a chief executive [burdened with life and death issues, and so on] personally taking on the added task [of administrative regulatory review] is pure mirage."[13] It is my contention that the President—and his staff—is in a better position to assume the role of coordinator and balancer of executive agency action than is the Congress but that the confrontation between President and bureaucracy is ongoing and difficult.

Before examining these presidential efforts to ensure governmental accountability of federal agents and their agencies, it is important to examine the factors that have led to federal regulatory sprawl, fragmentation, and diffusion of responsibility within the federal executive agencies, as well as the independent regulatory commissions.

DEVELOPMENT OF REGULATORY SPRAWL

Why Regulate?

Federal regulations are those "rules or laws which impose government established standards and significant economic responsibilities on individuals or organizations outside the federal establishment," wrote President Gerald Ford's Domestic Council Review Group on Regulatory Reform in 1977.[14] Put another way, federal rules and regulations are "state-imposed limitations on the discretion that may be exercised by individuals or groups, which is supported by the threat of sanction."[15] Under certain defined conditions, the federal government can regulate particular markets that policymakers determine to be in need of artificial guidance. While we have a basic ideological commitment to the idea of the free market and to the concept of capitalism, throughout our history government has recognized the need to regulate; to protect emerging industries, to prevent monopolies from developing that would restrain free competition, to regulate for natural monopolies, and to protect the health, safety, and well-being of the workers, consumers, and citizens generally.[16]

Some basic justifications, then, for governmental tampering with natural market conditions and for governmental standards that evidently interfere with natural market conditions include the following:

1. Efficiency—for the free market leads to a less-than-optimum use of resources; competition fosters efficiency and the government must, in turn, enforce and protect competition through antitrust and antimonopolistic activities of organizations.

2. Externalities—social costs of organizational activity borne by persons external to the contractual arrangement among management, workers, and wholesalers; these can be positive or negative and therefore the need for government to set standards.

3. Equity—regulations by government necessary to ensure that contractual obligations are met by the parties.[17]

Although the theory called for the invisible hand of the marketplace to ensure competition, fairness, and equity, experience has led government to intervene in the marketplace. The national legislature has taken the lead in this regulatory activity. The Congress has, from time to time, delegated its legislative powers to various federal regulatory agencies in order to deal with these economic and, much later, social and environmental problems. In addition to directing executive department agencies to act in certain economic arenas, the Congress also created, beginning in 1887 (with the Interstate Commerce Commission), independent regulatory agencies, staffed by the President with general mandates for policymaking written by Congress.

Delegation and the History of Regulatory Activity

As the United States has developed into a major industrial power, the government has intervened more and more in the affairs of persons and

Table 2
Federal Executive Departments and Independent Agencies, 1981-1982

Executive Agencies

Departments
Department of Agriculture
Department of Commerce
Department of Defense
  Department of the Air Force
  Department of the Army
  Department of the Navy
  Department of Defense Agencies
    and Joint Service Schools
Department of Education
Department of Energy
Department of Health and Human Services
Department of Housing and Urban Development
Department of the Interior
Department of Justice
Department of Labor
Department of State
Department of Transportation
Department of the Treasury

Quasi-official Agencies

Legal Services Corporation
National Consumer Cooperative Bank
National Railroad Passenger Corporation
  (Amtrak)
Smithsonian Institution
United States Railway Association
United States Synthetic Fuels Corporation

**Independent Establishments and
Government Corporations**

ACTION
Administrative Conference of the
  United States
American Battle Monuments Commission
Appalachian Regional Commission
Board for International Broadcasting
Central Intelligence Agency
Civil Aeronautics Board
Commission on Civil Rights
Commission of Fine Arts
Commodity Futures Trading Commission
Community Services Administration
Consumer Product Safety Commission
Environmental Protection Agency
Equal Employment Opportunity Commission
Export-Import Bank of the United States

Farm Credit Administration
Federal Communications Commission
Federal Deposit Insurance Corporation
Federal Election Commission
Federal Emergency Management Agency
Federal Home Loan Bank Board
Federal Labor Relations Authority
Federal Maritime Commission
Federal Mediation and Conciliation Service
Federal Reserve System
Federal Trade Commission
General Services Administration
Inter-American Foundation
International Communication Agency
Interstate Commerce Commission
Merit Systems Protection Board
National Aeronautics and
  Space Administration
National Capital Planning Commission
National Credit Union Administration
National Foundation on the Arts
  and the Humanities
National Labor Relations Board
National Mediation Board
National Science Foundation
National Transportation Safety Board
Nuclear Regulatory Commission
Occupational Safety and Health
  Review Commission
Office of Personnel Management
Panama Canal Commission
Pennsylvania Avenue Development Corporation
Pension Benefit Guaranty Corporation
Postal Rate Commission
Railroad Retirement Board
Securities and Exchange Commission
Selective Service System
Small Business Administration
Tennessee Valley Authority
United States Arms Control and
  Disarmament Agency
United States International Development
  Cooperation Agency
United States International
  Trade Commission
United States Metric Board
United States Postal Service
Veterans Administration

Source: *United States Government Manual, 1981/1982* (Washington, D.C.: Government
Printing Office, 1981), pp. v-xvi.

organizations in the private sector. This "growth of governmental control is characteristic of industrial societies. In this country, regulation was the logical instrument."[18] How does the federal government get its job done? "From a strictly practical standpoint," wrote Kenneth Davis, the job "can best be performed through the administrative process."[19] Without the ability, time, and expertise to deal with the problems of a technological, highly complex society, Congress created regulatory agencies and delegated powers and responsibilities to these legislative surrogates. Many federal agencies were created (see table 2), in the words of the late House Speaker, Sam Rayburn, "to do what we don't have time to do."[20] By 1980, there were many dozens of administrative agencies, including the independent regulatory commissions, annually issuing 7,000 rules and policy statements, "including roughly 2,000 legally binding rules with significant impact on government or the private sector and over 150 with major economic effects."[21] There has developed "a shift in power from the elective to administrative [actors] which results in a loss of citizen's influence over government," wrote David Rosenbloom.[22]

This enlargement of agency activity has highlighted the basic question raised in this book: how to control and direct federal bureaucrats, not accountable to the citizenry in the ordinary political processes, who daily go about the policymaking task of reconciling and elaborating "lofty values into operational guidelines for the daily conduct of society's business."[23]

Congress is constitutionally responsible for developing public policy; in this effort it has authorized federal agencies to implement these public laws. "Agencies are not, like legislators, representative instruments. They are not created to formulate and express a will. Their essential duty is to carry out the will of the legislative body."[24] When the Congress first delegated powers to federal agencies to carry out its mandate, constitutional questions of the highest order were raised, and the U.S. Supreme Court, in the 1930s, declared two such congressional delegations unconstitutional.[25] While the judicial mandate since 1935 calls for legislative specificity—Congress must clearly define the character of the task assigned to an administrative or an independent agency—the reality is that the legislature continues to delegate broad powers to federal agencies. It still appears to be "delegation run riot" (the words of Justice Benjamin Cardozo, in the 1935 *Panama* case, which invalidated a congressional delegation). Thus, although the constitutionality of delegation may have been resolved, the policy and democratic theory dilemmas remain.

The major wave of regulatory activity came during the depression years. "A change in public philosophy took place during the New Deal [for] confidence in the power of the free market to achieve performance goals was very low in the face of the dismal record of the economic system in the depression."[26] It was during this period that the following regulatory agencies and policies were developed by President Franklin D. Roosevelt and Congress: National Industrial Recovery Act, Federal Communications Commission, Securities and Exchange Commission, Civil Aeronautics Board, Federal Deposit Insurance Corporation, Federal Home Loan Banking Board, National Labor Relations Board, and others.

The history of regulatory growth follows the basic pattern: Congress (or the President) identifies a problem and then, invariably, an agency is either created to deal with it extensively or an existing agency's scope of authority is broadened to include this new responsibility. Congress creates the agency or gives an existing one new powers but does "not tell the administrator or the staff of the agency what the time frame is or how much of a problem the congress thinks can be resolved through regulation."[27]

During the 1960s, for example, Ralph Nader's *Unsafe at Any Speed* and other consumer-environmental-oriented books and political action groups led to the era of consumerism.[28] National policymakers responded to these demands with the creation of such agencies as the Environmental Protection Agency, the Consumer Product Safety Commission, the National Highway Traffic Safety Administration, and the Occupational Safety and Health Administration, some in the executive branch and some newly created independent regulatory commissions.

These and other agencies were given an open-ended mandate to develop rules and regulations to deal with such problems as noise-air-water quality, toxic substances, product-related accidents, safety and health conditions in the workplace, and number and severity of automobile accidents. Administrators of these agencies found themselves "with a strong mandate, a mandate with little or no consideration for the cost."[29] These federal agencies went about their tasks with a vigor that triggered the regulatory counterreaction in the late 1970s.[30]

Congress thus established a pattern of creating specialized agencies to exercise delegated powers. In this activity, however, the national legislators created a "politically unrealistic" structure, one "poorly tailored to the aims of reform and destructive of the safeguards that traditionally serve to constrain delegations."[31] Congress has shifted power from elected to administrative agents. It has created a system of federal regulatory agencies, which has led to policy fragmentation, diffuseness, duplication, and carelessness, with little oversight by the very agency, the Congress, responsible for the immense growth of this federal regulatory sprawl.

Regulatory Sprawl: Fragmentation, Diffusion, Carelessness, Freedom

The "dangers of professional narrowness," wrote two scholars about the shifting of power to the federal bureaucrats, "are real ones. Deeply involved in a specific policy area day after day, [the agency-centered bureaucrat finds it difficult] to maintain a balanced outlook on his policy's importance relative to other systems."[32] Harold Bruff, who first discussed this problem in terms of "increasing regulatory sprawl,"[33] pointed out that the agency regulations of the 1970s have a tendency "to delve increasingly into highly complex and often controversial matters that affect broad segments of industry and the public."[34] This sprawl of regulatory activities has challenged the effectiveness of our constitutional system of checks and balances. In addition to the problems associated with the rapid growth of regulatory rulemaking, among them duplication and fragmentation, there is the problem of accountability and control and direction. Bruff and others are concerned about the former, structural, problems; they are, however, more concerned about the constitutional dilemmas.

Fragmentation

There are at least 75 federal agencies and over 164,000 federal employees in police or investigative work.[35] In 1982, there were 102 federal agencies (74 in the executive branch of the federal government; 28 independent regulatory commissions) regulating something or some persons.[36] Given the single-mission character of the bureaucratic environment, not many of the federal administrative managers are aware how their specific policy fits in with the larger picture. The world of the bureau chief is narrow; he or she develops working relationships with only those political actors important to his or her activity: congressional staff and congressional committee leaders, who provide appropriations and authorization, and interest groups, which have an intense interest in the activity of the federal agency; and the political bureaucracy in the White House (and the political appointees who are the agency manager's superiors). (See figure 1.) Operating without the "whole picture," the agency manager continues to act, for the most part, informally and with discretionary authority—even though his/her judgment is a major and difficult political one that has or could have a major impact on the larger society.[37] In this world of informal, discretionary, fragmented bureaucratic activity, without much oversight by Congress and without, until recently, any direction and control by the presidency, there developed practices that reflected the lack of political accountability: lack of thoroughness in agency investigations, lack of

Figure 1
Bureau Chiefs and Their World

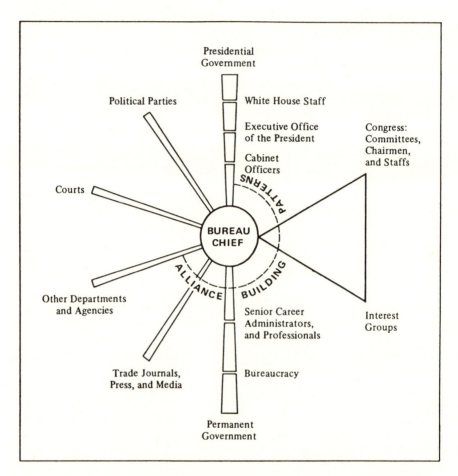

Source: James MacGregor Burns, J. W. Peltason, Thomas E. Cronin, GOVERNMENT BY
        THE PEOPLE: National, State, and Local Edition, 11th ed., © 1981, p. 432. Reprint-
        ed by permission of Prentice-Hall, Inc., Englewood Cliffs, N.J.

clarity in the presentation of findings, and lack of careful analysis of
supporting data.[38] Agencies developed policies that contradicted rules
developed by other federal groups; there was little effort made to
develop an awareness of what other agencies were doing in the same
area of policy formulation. Carelessness, lack of attention to details, and
lack of concern about costs and benefits were the consequences of the
growing "isolation and insulaton" of the federal bureaucracies.[39] A

federal bureaucracy had developed that was not responsive to the public's will and that produced rules with little care "to ensure that the rules were legally justifiable and will work in practice."[40]

Fragmentation and Iron Triangles

While the federal bureaucracy was growing and agencies were created willy-nilly, the ensuing fragmentation encouraged diffusion of responsibility and the growth of iron triangles.[41] The diffusion of authority created by fragmentation has led to the development of political subsystems consisting of the federal bureaucrats, congressional committee staff, and the representatives of interest groups controlled by the federal agency. These subsystems, occasionally called iron triangles (although they are not fixed or permanent and do change shape as influenced by outside forces), are essentially "open networks of policy specialists" in a given area (for example, consumer product safety regulation), who interact with each other in policy formulation.[42]

This creature of fragmentation poses practical dilemmas for the institutionalized presidency: the President, his counsellors in the White House, and his political appointees who staff the top positions in the federal executive agencies. John W. Gardner, a former Secretary of Health, Education, and Welfare, wrote of this problem, "Questions of public policy nominally lodged with the Secretary are often decided far beyond the secretary's reach by a trinity consisting of (1) representatives of an outside body, (2) middle-level bureaucrats, and (3) selected members of Congress—particularly those concerned with appropriations on behalf of their special interests."[43]

It is the President and his staff who are responsible for sketching the broad contours of national policy. The voters, it is stated, have given a mandate to the President to make substantial changes in public policy. Yet the President-elect faces a "pre-existing, entrenched relationship between the bureaus and the congressional committees and sub-committees."[44] This situation creates great difficulties for the President, especially when he tries to rearrange national priorities. "I under estimated the inertia or the momentum of the federal bureaucracy," stated a frustrated President Carter in 1978. "It is difficult to change," he concluded.[45]

Consequences: Freedom and the Constitutional Dilemma

The consequences of this recent expansion of regulatory activity are both political and normative. Politically, presidents have been strongly motivated, especially since the Nixon administration, to try to bring some degree of balance and coordination to the regulatory process. As Lloyd Cutler, one of President Carter's advisers, wrote in 1978:

Experts located in single-mission agencies cannot achieve balance and they should not be given that balancing function. . . . The only place to exercise this balancing function and to make someone accountable to the public for how it is exercised is to rest power in the President. At least the power to make the final decision on rule making should rest with the president in those cases in which he finds that what an agency proposed to do, or was failing to do, has a critical impact on achieving other major national goals.[46]

In addition to growing presidential concern about conflicts, duplication, waste, and general inefficiency and carelessness due to expansion and fragmentation, two other political factors have led to greater presidential (and, in a much less concerted and more episodic way, congressional) involvement in regulatory affairs. First is the growing concern about the financial costs of regulatory activity (both economic and social) "and their potential implications for efforts to restrain inflation and carry out traditional presidential economic management responsibilities."[47] Second, the executive branch has begun to develop management strategies for dealing with the sprawling federal bureaucracy in order to prevent a power vacuum. If the federal courts defer to agency actions (consistent with the 1946 Administrative Procedure Act's judicial review parameters) and if congressional oversight and other legislative strategies are not effective, then the President must "bolster these other checks and perform a coordinating, supervisory function that is not currently being discharged."[48]

These political consequences that have flowed from the growth of regulatory agency activity—regulatory sprawl—also raise the constitutional dilemma of how to control the activities of nonelected federal administrators in order to have some accountability for their actions. Michael Nelson has written about the "top-down" model for holding bureaucracy accountable to officials elected by the people—Congress and the President.[49] The problem, as Nelson and others view it, is that there are two actors involved, and the Constitution, in Articles I and II, does not provide clarity on who should be controlling.

Louis Fisher talks of two constitutional models that compete for control of the bureaucracy: the presidential model and the congressional model. The former model suggests presidential control of the federal bureaucracy because the President is chief administrative officer of the federal government. The President is head of a theoretically unified and hierarchical executive department and is capable of directing the activities and operations of agency personnel. It is the President "who serves to see that the 'laws be faithfully executed.' "[50] The congressional model stresses congressional supervisory power because that branch created the agencies, delegated the powers to its surrogates, and specified how the laws were to be implemented.[51]

Until recently, then, there has been a leadership crisis, which Gilmour and others have discussed. Given the conflicting models of control and the struggles between the President and Congress for control of the federal bureaucracy, the winners in this clash have been "the agencies themselves, their clientele groups, uncoordinated committees, individual members of congress, and the congressional staff."[52] Without effective economic or political control over the regulatory activities, the result will be the production of regulations that are not cost-efficient.

This crisis exacerbates the constitutional dilemma of accountability and control. Given the paralysis of the national legislature, recent (since 1969) presidential administrations have made attempts to fill the power vacuum and thereby deal with the constitutional dilemma of bureaucratic control and accountability. The federal bureaucracy must be held accountable for its actions. Congress has proved incapable of other-than-episodic general supervisory control of the federal bureaucracy.[53] The federal judiciary cannot, jurisdictionally and justiciably, deal with the broad contours of the accountability dilemma. It has fallen to the executive branch, to the President and his staff in the White House, especially the OMB, to deal with constitutional problems confronting our government. The freedom the federal agencies have had to develop policy through rulemaking has led to agency license and arbitrary discretion. This "stunning loss of governmental accountability," the ominous words of Gilmour, must be reversed by vigorous executive action. The question of paramount importance for the society is whether the executive branch can hold the regulators accountable.

THE EXECUTIVE RESPONSE

The problem of regulatory sprawl and governmental accountability is clearly perceived by the President and his staff. Since the late 1960s there has been an awareness, on the part of all Presidents and their staffs, of this political and constitutional dilemma. The next set of questions that they must confront is how to go about curbing, controlling, and holding accountable the federal regulators in the executive branch and in the independent regulatory commissions. What kinds of controls—personal, personnel, structural—will prove to be effective in this effort?

From the literature and from actual presidential initiatives, the primary control would seem to be structural.[54] The "leadership crisis" that writers discuss is one "of structural incapacity, not simply the personal inability of particular incumbents."[55] Moreover, since the

Nixon presidency, a basic assumption has existed: there are sufficient management tools available to the President and his top managers in the White House, along with the capability to restructure the administrative process through executive orders and reorganization plans, to give some coordination, direction, and balance to the federal bureaucracy. If this is indeed the case, the dilemma of governmental accountability can be resolved.

NOTES

1. Phillip Cooper, *Public Law and Public Administration*, Palo Alto, CA: Mayfield Publishing Co., 1983, p. 244. For a case study of the policymaking process, see Howard Ball, Dale Krane, and Thomas Lauth, *Compromised Compliance: The Implementation of the 1965 Voting Rights Act*, Westport, CT: Greenwood Press, 1982. See also Randall B. Ripley and Grace A. Franklin, *Congress, the Bureaucracy, and Public Policy*, Homewood, IL: Dorsey Press, 1980, pp. 212-213.

2. *CAB v. Delta Airlines*, 365 U.S. 316 (1961).

3. Note, "Delegation and Regulatory Reform: Letting the President Change the Rules," 89 *Yale Law Journal*, No. 3, January 1980, pp. 563-564.

4. Louis Fisher, *The Politics of Shared Power: Congress and the Executive*, Washington, D.C.: Congressional Quarterly Press, 1981, p. 117.

5. Lee F. Witter, "Legislative Veto," 9 *Bureaucrat*, No. 2, Summer 1980, p. 33.

6. George C. Edwards III, *Implementing Public Policy*, Washington, D.C.: Congressional Quarterly Press, 1980, p. 4. See also *The Malek Manual*, White House Personnel Office, 1970, in Frank J. Thompson, *Classics in Public Personnel Policy*, Chicago: Moore Publishing Co., 1979, p.84.

7. Fisher, *Politics*, pp. 75-76.

8. Eugene Hickok and Gary McDowell, "The Administrative Theory of the Constitution," paper presented at the 1981 Southern Political Science Association meeting, Memphis, TN, pp. 19, 20.

9. Alexander Hamilton, *The Federalist Papers*, #68, New York: New American Library, 1961, p. 414. "We may safely pronounce that the true test of a good government is its aptitude and tendency to produce a good administration."

10. Edwards, *Implementing Public Policy*, p. 137.

11. Ibid., pp. 134, 139-140.

12. Robert S. Gilmour, "Congressional Oversight: The Paradox of Fragmentation and Control," paper delivered at Southeast Conference of Public Administration (SECOPA), jackson, MS, October 1981 (also reprinted in 10 *Bureaucrat*, No. 3, Fall 1981, pp. 32-38), pp. 18-20.

13. Fisher, *Politics*, p. 173.

14. Lester M. Salamon, "Federal Regulation: A New Arena for Presidential Power," in Hugh Heclo and L. M. Salamon, *The Illusion of Presidential Government*, Boulder, CO: Westview Press, 1981, p. 169.

15. Alan Stone, *Regulation and Its Alternatives*, Washington, D.C.: Congressional Quarterly Press, 1982, p. 10

16. See, generally, Lloyd N. Cutler and David R. Johnson, "Regulation and the Political Process," 84 *Yale Law Journal*, No. 7, June 1975, p. 1396.

17. Stone, *Regulation*, pp. 65-125 passim.

18. White House, *Regulatory Reform: President Carter's Program*, Washington, D.C., 1980, p. 1.

19. Kenneth C. Davis, *Administrative Law and Government*, St. Paul, MN: West Publishing Co., 1975, p. 25.

20. White House, *Regulatory Reform*, p. 1.

21. Ibid.

22. David H. Rosenbloom, "Public Administrator's Official Immunity and the Supreme Court," 40 *Public Administration Review*, March-April 1980, p. 167.

23. Colin S. Diver, "Policymaking Paradigms in Administrative Law," 95 *Harvard Law Review*, December 1981, p. 393.

24. Fisher, *Politics*, p. 190.

25. *Panama Refining Company v. Ryan*, 293 U.S. 388 (1935) and *Schechter Poultry Corporation vs. U.S.*, 295 U.S. 495 (1935).

26. Stone, *Regulation*, p. 30.

27. John Snow, in Paul W. MacAvoy, ed., *Unsettled Questions on Regulatory Reform*, Washington, D.C.: American Enterprise Institute, 1978, p. 16.

28. Stone, *Regulation*, pp. 30-33.

29. Snow, in MacAvoy, *Unsettled Questions*, p. 16.

30. See A. Lee Fritschler, "The Changing Face of Government Regulation," paper delivered at Mississippi State University, November 1980, p. 6ff.

31. Note, "Delegation," p. 562.

32. Frank J. Thompson and Raymond G. Davis, "Personnel Reform: The Malek Manual Revisited," 6 *Bureaucrat*, No. 2, Summer 1977, p. 85.

33. See Harold H. Bruff, "Presidential Power and Administrative Rule-Making," 88 *Yale Law Journal*, No. 3, January 1979.

34. Ibid., pp. 451-452.

35. Edwards, "Implementing Public Policy," p. 139.

36. Salamon, "Federal Regulation," p. 169.

37. Cutler, in MacAvoy, *Unsettled Questions*, p. 28.

38. Les Garner, "Management Control in Regulatory Agencies," 34 *Administrative Law Review*, No. 3, Summer 1982, p. 474.

39. Elias Clark, "Holding Government Accountable," 84 *Yale Law Journal*, No. 4, March 1975, p. 743.

40. Bruff, "Presidential Power," p. 454.

41. Edwards, *Implementing Public Policy*, pp. 135-37.

42. Fisher, *Politics*, p. 190.

43. Thomas E. Cronin, *The State of the Presidency*, Boston, MA: Little, Brown, 1975, p. 90.

44. Ripley and Franklin, *Congress*, p. 51.

45. Ronald Randall, "Presidential Power vs Bureaucratic Intransigence," 73 *American Political Science Review*, No. 3, September, 1979, p. 795.

46. Cutler, in MacAvoy, *Unsettled Questions*, p. 28.

47. Salamon, "Federal Regulation," p. 149.

48. Bruff, "Presidential Power," p. 461.

49. Michael Nelson, "Holding Bureaucracy Accountable," paper delivered at

Southern Political Science Association meeting, Atlanta, GA, October 1982, pp. 2-3.

50. Fisher, *Politics*, p. 117.

51. Ibid.

52. Gilmour, "Congressional Oversight," p. 20.

53. Replying to my testimony (on the implementation of the Voting Rights Act by the U.S. Department of Justice since 1965) before the Subcommittee on Civil and Constitutional Rights of the House Judiciary Committee, Congressman Don Edwards (D-Cal), its chairman and a strong supporter of voting rights legislation, noted the lack of aggressive enforcement by both the Justice Department and the Federal Bureau of Investigation and said: "Certainly this committee could be faulted. We're supposed to have oversight jurisdiction on the operation of the Voting Rights Act. . . . Actually I didn't know [about southern jurisdictions' non-compliance with the Act] . . . and we'll have to ask them [DOJ and FBI] about that." *Extension of the Voting Rights Act*, Hearings before the Subcommittee on Civil and Constitutional Rights of the Committee on the Judiciary, House of Representatives, 97th Congress, 1st session, part 3, Washington, D.C., 1982, p. 2093.

54. Fisher, *Politics*, p. 170.

55. Gilmour, "Congressional Oversight," p. 20.

2

Curbing Regulatory Sprawl: Some Presidential Problems and Strategies

To attempt fundamental reorganization of the government is to take on a political fight almost impossible to win.

—John Whittaker

One of the enduring truths of the nation's capital is that bureaucrats *survive*.

—Gerald R. Ford

The coalition builders are a faceless glob of semi-permanent and semi-sovereign Washingtonians.

—Richard E. Neustadt

The presidency and the Congress are separated institutions sharing political power. The President is part of the legislative process (through policy formulation and use of the veto); the Congress is part of the administrative process (through delegation of authority to agencies and appropriation of funds).[1] The President and his senior White House advisers are the critical linkage between the policy formulated by the Congress and its actual implementation by the permanent bureaucracy. Congress does not have the will or the structural capability to ensure implementation of public policy. It does not fulfill its oversight function; consequently, unless the President and his staff act—continuously— there is no assurance that the policy formulated by the Congress is the policy implemented.[2] A brief illustration of this reality follows.

In 1978, Congress passed the Airline Deregulation Act. Section 43 of the act contained a special unemployment benefits and job-protection rights package for laid-off airline workers of airlines that suffer "major contractions" due to the deregulation of airlines. The section instructed the Civil Aeronautics Board (CAB) to establish rules to determine whether an airline's economic difficulties were due to the deregulation legislation. In those cases of economic hardships and worker layoffs attributed to the deregulation (as determined by the CAB regulations), the section instructed the U.S. Department of Labor to establish a special fund for the assistance of laid-off workers, including pilots, called the labor compensation fund; pay the moving expenses of workers who wish to relocate; and develop a first-hire-back regulation to enable laid-off workers, including airline pilots, to be hired back when economic conditions improved for the airlines.[3]

The statute was fairly clear and nondiscretionary. Section 43 stated, "Any rules and regulations which the Secretary [of Labor] deems necessary to carry out this section shall be promulgated within six months after the date of enactment of this section." But it was two years later, in July 1980, before the Department of Labor sent a notice of proposed rulemaking to the *Federal Register*. Its purpose was to find ways to determine whether deregulation was the cause of economic plight of an airline. And by January 1983, no one in the Department of Labor had written the federal regulations needed to implement the law calling for the labor compensation fund.

This regulatory lag, common to regulatory politics in the nations's capitol, is a situation that Congress cannot control and that the White House must try to ameliorate.[4] Craig Lindsey, a CAB official, suggested a reason for the delay in developing regulations that would implement section 43 of the Airline Deregulation Act: "People who were here then may not have seen this [section 43] as a priority at all, and that would not have surprised me."[5] An official in another agency also pointed to lack of high priority as the reason for a five and a half year delay on his agency's rulemaking. Regulatory inaction, he said, is "what happens to those kinds of questions."[6]

As a consequence of legislative inability to deal with this type of bureaucratic dilemma, the President must direct and coordinate federal regulatory agencies in order to "transform the shadow of the policy into the substance of the program."[7] If he does not do this difficult political task adequately, our system suffers a fundamental loss of governmental accountability. Absent direct and continuous action by the presidency over nonelected professionals, there is no elected unit of the federal government that can control, coordinate, balance, and coerce the federal bureaucracy. "Introducing balance and coordination in regulatory activities is what regulatory reform is designed to accomplish."[8] This balancing and coordinating task is probably the most important domestic reform activity of the modern presidency.

THE PRESIDENT AND THE BUREAUCRACY

Article II of the U.S. Constitution calls on the President to "take care that the laws be faithfully executed." The President must therefore develop regulatory reforms in order to ensure the proper implementation of policies formulated by the Congress and by the President. By developing these management tools, the President performs a fundamental coordinating, supervisory function.[9] How to gain this kind of control of the bureaucracy has become the major preoccupation for Presidents in recent years.[10] It has been an enormous responsibility for the President and his close aides and will grow even more burdensome in the future.

In his 1980 revision of his classic *Presidential Power*, Richard Neustadt noted that a major difference in Washington politics in the twenty years since the book's original publication has been the phenomenal growth of the "professional crowd," the "faceless glob of semipermanent and semisovereign Washingtonians" on the staffs of federal executive and regulatory agencies, congressional committees (3,000), personal staffs of legislators (10,000), and interest groups (15,000).[11] These federal employees and lobbyists are the core of the iron triangles. Neustadt, calling these policy groupings *issue networkers*—the permanent establishment in Washington—is greatly concerned about the growing fragmentation that they engender.

He calls for a "constructive tension" between the President (and his senior aides and a few department heads in the executive branch) and the middle levels of power that have developed in Washington in the past two decades.[12] If these permanent professionals in the federal regulatory agencies are narrow in scope, then the President and his staff must guide and balance the permanent bureaucracy, for only they can "rise above parochial interests, if and as they can, pursuing integrative goals, embodying the whole and taking the ultimate rap. As such, they are supposed to balance off the permanent establishment, indeed to guide it, give it an accountable, elective human cast to governance."[13]

The president must achieve this balancing and guidance; otherwise, wrote Neustadt, the "crowd might smother him." Our system of government has a fundamental need for a "lively presidency alongside [the permanent bureaucracy and their networks], with an independent popular connection," or else accountability in our democratic polity is jeopardized.[14]

Tension between the Presidency and the Bureaucracy

The typical relationship between the professional civil servant in the executive branch of the federal government and the president's White

House senior staff is not friendly.[15] Rich Williamson, President Reagan's administrative assistant for intergovernmental affairs (and the associate director of Reagan's Task Force on Regulatory Relief) has said of this struggle between the White House and the anonymous crowd in the federal agencies: "It's trench warfare day by day. On so many regulations, you're dealing with fourth and fifth level bureaucrats [GS 12-14s], most of them career people, who have seen presidents come and go and probably believe strongly in the regulations."[16] James C. Miller III, currently chairman of the Federal Trade Commission and recently executive director of the Reagan Task Force on Regulatory Relief, said, "We're trying to influence the behavior of the GS-13s and 14s who draft the rules and regulations."[17]

The objective of the President and his small group of senior advisers has been to try to influence the behavior of these federal agents, but as one commentator has written, leadership of agency actors "is a long-term proposition requiring considerable patience and dogged persistence."[18] This activity cannot be intermittent on the part of the President; continuously monitoring and controlling the federal bureaucracy is a political task of highest priority for occupants of the White House, but it is not an easy task. As a Nixon staff member wrote:

You cannot achieve management, policy or program control unless you have established political control. The record is quite replete with instances of the failures of program policy, and management goals because of sabotage by employees of the executive branch . . . because of their political persuasion and their loyalty to others rather than the executive that supervises them.[19]

Griffen Bell, President Carter's attorney general, discussed the techniques used by the federal bureaucracy to frustrate efforts by the Carter presidency to direct the implementation of public policy:

1. "Flooding" principle: Flood the political appointees with lengthy reports.
2. "Travel" technique: Keep the political appointees out of the office by encouraging travel away from Washington, D.C.
3. "Burying" principle: Sneaking some regulation past the political appointee by burying a proposal "deep in the innards of a long report."
4. "Leaking" principle: Distributing fragmented information to the press that would tend to embarrass the political appointee or extol the virtues of the federal bureaucrat.
5. "Cry politics" strategy: Employed when a key White House staff member inquires about a particular policy the agency is responsible for implementing.
6. "Play it safe" principle: Passing the buck to the political appointees in an agency when other pressures affect bureaucratic behavior.[20]

These principles and strategies might be somewhat exaggerated, but the attorney general made his point: federal managers have many ways to frustrate their political superiors in the agency and, in so doing, to block the efforts of the President to manage the executive branch of government effectively.

In this continuing struggle between the political members of the executive branch and the permanent bureaucracy, the President faces an entrenched policy triangle consisting of men and women, in the bureaus and on the subcommittees, who have worked together on policy formulation and implementation for many years.[21] The President, after all, is the newcomer and will hold office for at most eight years. Although the chief executive has the broad mandate from the voters, he must deal with career civil servants and their understanding of public policy needs, based on their values and on their interactions with the other units in the policy triangles that exist over time.

If the President views the entrenched bureaucracy with suspicion and concern, the institutionalized presidency—the President and his political appointees in the White House and in OMB—is not viewed sympathetically by most of the bureaucracy, "especially those at the operating level."[22] The presidency's centralizing tendency poses a threat to the stable triangular relationships that endure over time. Not having been an agency manager himself, the President cannot understand or appreciate the agency manager's "considerable concern about organizational essence, morale, and integrity."[23] Also, federal agency managers sincerely believe that they are caught between the "unrealistic demands and pressures from their executive branch superiors" and the pressures and demands of their more familiar, and realistic, clienteles.[24]

The reasons for this continual struggle between the presidency and the bureaucracy can be enumerated:

1. The tenure of the career civil servants.
2. Shortness of presidential administrations.
3. Institutionalized preexisting power relations among the federal agencies, congressional committees, and interest groups.
4. The federal bureaucracy's control of information and expertise.
5. Size of the federal bureaucracy—in terms of personnel and money.[25]

These kinds of reasons make it difficult for the President to control the way in which policies are implemented by the federal bureaucrats (if the policy is implemented at all by the managers) under these circumstances. President Carter said, "Before I became president, I realized that dealing with the bureaucracy would be one of the worst problems that I would ever have to face. It has been worse than I anticipated. Of all the steps that we can take to make the government more efficient and effective, reforming the civil service is the most important of all."[26] Nixon expressed his frustration more colorfully: "When a bureaucrat thumbs his nose, we're going to get him. . . . Demote him or send him to the Guam regional office. There's a way. Get him the Hell out."[27]

Regulatory reform efforts since the Nixon administration have attempted to deal with the conflict between a centralizing presidency and a decentralizing federal bureaucracy and its anonymous professional colleagues on congressional staffs and in the pressure groups.

Growth of the Independent Regulatory Commissions

The presidency's efforts to control and centralize the implementation of public policy, difficult enough to get a grip on within the executive branch agencies, are further compounded by the existence of dozens of independent regulatory commissions created by Congress since 1887.

Independent regulatory commissions (IRCs) have existed since the creation of the Interstate Commerce Commission (ICC) by the Congress in 1887. These creatures of the Congress, as they are often called, are hybrid political actors in our federal system in that they are isolated, structurally, from most of the operations of the executive branch of government.[28] Created by Congress to deal with public policy issues, such as antimonopoly, consumer protection, and stock transactions, independent of political influences, each commission has from five to eleven commissioners selected by the President, with the advice and consent of the Senate. The commissioners serve a set term, as determined by the Congress in the enabling legislation, during which the commissioner cannot be removed by the President except for cause.[29] There is a bipartisan cast of commissioners for there can be no more than a bare majority of commissioners from one party serving on the commission at any one time.

Given the development of special missions for these IRCs by the Congress in the organic statute that created the commission, these independent agencies draft regulations and rules, formal and informal, consistent with the organic statute, the U.S. Constitution, and the 1946 Administrative Procedure Act. In addition, the IRCs authorize enforcement of the regulations and adjudicate, with the assistance of the DOJ, in order to gain compliance with their rules and regulations.

The IRCs submit budgets to the OMB, although some submit their budgets concurrently to the Appropriations Committee in the Congress. By 1980, there were over forty such IRCs; the most prominent are the Federal Reserve Board, Consumer Product Safety Commission, Federal

Power Commission (FPC), Federal Communications Commission (FCC), Federal Energy Regulatory Commission, Interstate Commerce Commission (ICC), Nuclear Regulatory Commission (NRC), Securities and Exchange Commission (SEC), and Federal Trade Commission (FTC).

A number of mechanisms can be potential sources of control over IRC activities, although they have not really been very effective. Congress establishes the IRC's mission and theoretically has oversight responsibilities. The GAO is responsible for reviewing their information-gathering plans, and the OMB examines and revises IRC budget requests, subject to their adoption by Congress. The OMB also reviews recommendations for changes in the enabling legislation and, as a result of legislation passed in 1980, examines the IRCs paperwork requirements for the regulated constituencies to ensure a reduction in paperwork. The DOJ works with the staff of the IRCs to coordinate and conduct litigation when adjudication is necessary.[30]

There has been pervasive and continuous criticism of the IRCs. Five major presidential studies—the Brownlow Committee, 1937; the Hoover Commissions, 1949 and 1955; the Landis Report, 1960; and the Ash Report, 1971—have examined the characteristics of the IRCs and their relationship with the political branches of the national government, especially the executive branch. The conclusions reached varied from outright rejection of the concept of independent regulatory agency itself to suggestions for radical improvements in the structure of these agencies in order to get more meaningful regulations without waste and duplication.[31]

In its 1937 report, the Brownlow Committee stated that IRCs were a "headless, fourth branch of government, a haphazard deposit of irresponsible agencies and uncoordinated powers."[32] Its basic recommendation was that an increase in presidential control and coordination of administrative policy could come about only through abolition of the IRCs.[33] The first Hoover Commission report, focusing on "functions and administrative experience" and expertise, was mildly critical of the quality of staff personnel.[34] The second Hoover Commission report called for a reform of the IRCs through the formalization process; that is, it would have the IRCs develop their policy through formal adjudicatory hearings.[35] The Landis Report, developed for President-elect John F. Kennedy, called for a greater coordination of regulatory policy in the economic area by the presidency and improved staffing for the IRCs. The need, according to the report, was for the president to establish within the White House (the Executive Office) "several offices for coordination and development of policy in the areas of transportation, communication, energy, and an office of general oversight."[36]

When President Nixon's Ash Council's report on IRCs was made public, its recommendations had the flavor of President Roosevelt's Brownlow Committee report. The Ash report concluded that major IRCs—ICC, CAB, Federal Maritime Commission (FMC), FPC, FCC, SEC, and the FTC—"are not sufficiently accountable to the President and therefore are neither adequately supported nor effectively coordinated with national policy goals." In addition, the inherent deficiencies in the commission structure make the IRCs unable to respond quickly and effectively to economic and technological changes in the society. Finally, the Ash report criticized the role of IRC staff as well as the "overjudicalization" of the IRC process, which causes backlogs and higher costs.[37]

The Ash recommendations to Nixon paralleled the Brownlow report: put all IRCs under the control of a single administrator, serving at the pleasure of the President. This administrator would "assume coordination of regulatory matters with national policy goals, improve accountability to Congress and the executive branch and increase the probability of superior leadership for regulatory activities."[38] Consolidation of IRCs was also suggested. The ICC, CAB, and FMC were thought to form the core of a single transportation regulatory agency with a single administrator. Modification of the FCC was suggested, and a new administrative law court was recommended by the Ash Council to speed up the internal agency review of proceedings process.[39]

Presidents Roosevelt, Truman, Eisenhower, Kennedy, Johnson, and Nixon had commissions study the relationship between the presidency and the IRCs. The various conclusions struck a familiar note: problems of accountability and control. In sum, the criticism seems to point to the issue of accountability: the IRCs are not sufficiently politically accountable, to either the President or the Congress, and therefore are not responsive to the public interest, not coordinated with national policy, or concerned about the costs of their regulations.[40]

Since the Congress has not acted either to strengthen the power of the presidency or to use its own oversight powers more effectively, the White House is somewhat stifled in its efforts to improve the White House-IRC relationship. Its sole means of control are various management tools (OMB review, DOJ assistance), presidential persuasion, and the appointment process. As table 3 indicates, the Congress has not lessened its efforts to create new IRCs and major regulatory programs. As a consequence, the problem of controlling, coordinating, and directing the policies of the IRCs continues unabated. It will take the efforts of a skillful, determined, strong President and his senior aides to deal with this additional problem of regulatory control, if the person stays in office long enough to effectuate this balancing and guiding clerkship.[41]

Presidential Qualities Needed to Direct the Bureaucracy

Scholars on the presidency have focused on a number of personal characteristics that should assist the President in his efforts to ensure that the laws are faithfully executed. First, the implementation of policy by the presidency calls for effective communications between the presidency and the bureaucracy. The White House must clearly communicate the commitment of the President to implementation of a management program or to efforts to coordinate various regulatory agency activities and must also communicate this presidential thrust consistently. The permanent bureaucracy must know what the President wants to do, what he can do, and how much time and effort will be put into the presidential activity. This means that the President and his senior staff responsible for working with the permanent bureaucracy must devote considerable time (a major dilemma for the White House) to the formulation and implementation of various strategies to achieve this balancing and guidance of the federal agencies.[42]

The President has two essential sources of power in these efforts: formal, or external dimensions of power, and the internal dimension (his characteristic personal and political skills, his professional reputation, his prestige).[43] The formal powers of the President are those granted by the Constitution, statutes, and inherent powers of the institution itself. The President has the legitimate authority, through constitutional powers or statutory enactments, to appoint political supporters to executive branch agencies, to reorganize the Executive Office (with congressional approval), to issue executive orders, to develop management tools to control the federal bureaucracy through employment of the DOJ or the OMB, to control the budgetary process of federal agencies, to institute cutbacks and more. But these formal powers may prove to be ineffective if the internal dimensions of presidential power are not effectively employed by the incumbent.

The professional reputation of the President is based on the "impressions in the D.C. community about the skill and the will with which he puts [his formal powers] to use."[44] A president who is not perceived to be an effective leader will not succeed in efforts to use the formal powers he has to guide and oversee the permanent bureaucracy. In a study of the Carter administration's efforts to streamline the permanent bureaucracy, James Benze developed a list of personal and political characteristics assumed to be inherent in a strong chief executive and asked senior administrators in various federal agencies and IRCs about President Jimmy Carter's personal and political leadership skills. (See table 4.) Benze concluded that Carter's failure to curb regulatory sprawl was due to his personal deficiencies and poor professional reputation; he wrote,

Table 3
Major Regulatory Programs by Year of Birth, 1863–1975

Date	Economic & Industrial Regulation (Agency Responsible)	Social Regulation (Agency Responsible)
1863	Chartering and supervision of national banks (Comptroller of the Currency, Dept. of the Treasury)	
1887	Railroad regulation (Interstate Commerce Commission)	
1906		Food and drug production regulation (Food and Drug Administration, Department of H.H.S.)
1913	Supervision of Federal Reserve Banks and Members Banks (Federal Reserve System)	
1914	Preventing restraints of trade, unfair competition, and false labeling and advertising (Federal Trade Commission)	
1916	Regulation of offshore waterborne commerce (Federal Maritime Commission)	
1916	Regulation of import trade (U.S. International Trade Commission)	
1920	Licensing hydro-electric projects on navigable waters (Federal Energy Regulatory Commission)	

30

Year	Description (Agency)
1922	Regulating commodity futures trading (Commodity Futures Trading Commission)
1932	Supervision and insurance of savings and loan institutions (Federal Home Loan Bank Board)
1933	Supervision of non-member state banks; deposit insurance (Federal Deposit Insurance Corporation)
1933	Prevention of fraud in securities issuance (Securities and Exchange Commission)
1934	Radio/TV broadcast licensing (Federal Communications Commission)
1934	Regulation of security exchanges (Securities and Exchange Commission)
1935	Restructuring and regulation of public utility holding companies (Securities and Exchange Commission)
1935	Regulation of interstate wholesale electric traffic (Federal Energy Regulation Commission)
1935	Regulation of collective bargaining (National Labor Relations Board)
1935	Regulation of motor carriers (Interstate Commerce Commission)
1938	Regulation of civil commercial aviation (Civil Aeronautics Board)

Table 3—*Continued*

Date	Economic & Industrial Regulation (Agency Responsible)	Social Regulation (Agency Responsible)
1938	Regulation of interstate natural gas gas traffic (Federal Energy Regulatory Commission)	
1946	Regulation of civilian uses of atomic energy (Nuclear Regulatory Commission)	
1948		Certification of aircraft types and aircrew (Federal Aviation Administration)
1962		Air quality regulation (Environmental Protection Agency)
1963		Equal Pay Act (Equal Employment Opportunity Commission)
1964		Prevention of discrimination in employment (Equal Employment Opportunity Commission)
1965		Water quality regulation (Environmental Protection Agency)
1966	Safety regulation of motor carriers (Federal Highway Administration)	
1966		Safety regulation of railroads (Federal Railroad Administration)
1966	Safety and efficiency regulation of motor vehicles (Federal Highway Traffic Safety Administration)	

1967	Preventing age discrimination in employment (Equal Employment Opportunity Commission)	
1968	Full disclosure of credit terms ("Truth in Lending") (Federal Reserve System and Federal Trade Commission)	
1968	Regulate interstate firearms trade (Bureau of Alcohol, Tobacco, and Firearms, Treasury Department)	
1970	Promote uniformity of accounting among government contractors (Cost Accounting Standards Board)	
1970	Regulate occupational safety and health performance (Occupational Safety and Health Adm., Labor Department)	
1970	Supervise Federal credit unions (National Credit Union Administration)	
1970	Regulate postal rates and classifications (Postal Rate Commission)	
1970	Securing of environmental impact review of federal projects (Environmental Protection Agency)	
1972	Regulating safety of consumer products (Consumer Product Safety Commission)	
1972	Control of noise pollution (Environmental Protection Agency)	
1973	Regulating lawful trade in narcotic drugs (Drug Enforcement Adm., Justice Dept.)	

Table 3—*Continued*

Date	Economic & Industrial Regulation (Agency Responsible)	Social Regulation (Agency Responsible)
1973	Oil pricing, allocation, and import regulation (Economic Regulatory Administration, Energy Department)	
1973		Regulation of mine safety (Mine Safety and Health Administration, Labor Department)
1973		Employment of handicapped persons (Employment Standards Administration, Labor Department)
1974		Supervision of pension plans (Pension Benefit Guaranty Corporation)
1975		Transportation accident investigation; regulation of accident reporting (National Transportation Safety Board)

Source: A. Lee Fritschler, *The Changing Face of Government Regulations*, 1980, pp. 12-13.

"Carter was unable to convince the bureaucracy of the legitimacy of his management programs because he lacked the political skills to do so."[45] Although President Carter was keenly aware of the problem of regulatory sprawl and developed a fairly comprehensive management program in an effort to curb bureaucratic excess, in the end he was ineffective because he did not communicate his desires and his objectives well and because he was perceived as a weak chief executive. In sum, the President's formal powers must be accompanied by leadership skills, or the President will be unable to curb the federal agencies.

It is this continuous need to communicate, to bargain, to cajole, to use time effectively, to be flexible when necessary, to show self-confidence, to deal with the frustrations inherent in the political process, in a realistic way, that may enable a President to take hold of the permanent bureaucracy.[46] But these characteristics and the context in which they must be continuously employed emphasize the tenuousness of presidential power in our system of separated institutions sharing power.

President Truman once said of his successor in the White House, Eisenhower: "He'll sit here and he'll say, 'Do this!, Do that!'" *And nothing will happen.* Poor Ike—it won't be a bit like the Army. He'll find it very frustrating."[47] The point is that all Presidents have been frustrated by their inability to guide and move the sluggish federal bureaucracy easily.[48] The effective President is the one who uses his presidential persuasion, reputation, and prestige. Without the use of his personal and political skills, continuously and clearly, the President will confront a permanent professional Washington bureaucracy that does not comply with his more formal efforts to direct, guide, and coordinate federal regulatory activities.

In these terms, presidential power is contextual and relational. If the President is perceived by Washingtonians as a skillful person and is perceived by the general public (and the federal bureaucrats) as doing a fine job, then there is the possibility of successfully implementing management strategies that effectively direct the federal bureaucracy and control regulatory sprawl. If he lacks a strong reputation as leader and if his prestige is low, as former President Carter was perceived by Washington and by the public opinion polls, then efforts to curb the federal bureaucrats will fail.

President Carter's first major test on assuming the presidency in 1977 "was on a bill authorizing the President to address the problem of the federal bureaucracy—its complexity, its remoteness when people needed help, its intrusiveness when they wanted to be left alone, and its excessive regulation of the major industries to the detriment of consumers."[49] Although Carter developed a number of management

Table 4
Personal Characteristics and Political Skills of an
Effective President

	Seen as Important by Agency Staff	Found in Carter
Personal Characteristics		
Flexibility	77%	39%
Courage	84	37
Intelligence	83	47
Vision	84	17 (55% not found in Carter)
Self-confidence	85	46
Sincerity	66	65
Humor	30	15 (45% not found in Carter)
Vanity	21	29
Partisanship	50	30
Political Skills		
Ability to relate to Congress	96	4% (59% not found in Carter)
Ability to relate to staff	80	54
Ability to assess political realities	95	24
Ability to relate to interest groups	62	25
Ability to relate to press	72	32
Ability to relate to bureaucracy	69	5 (76% not found in Carter)
Skill in timing issues	85	15
Organizational skills	53	15
Ability to maintain public trust	94	28
Ability to avoid isolation	74	30
Ability to maintain image	67	20
Skill in shifting positions	65	15
Ability to sell programs	87	7 (57% not found in Carter)

Source: James G. Benze, Jr., "Presidential Management: The Importance of Presidential Skills, 11 *Presidential Studies Quarterly,* No. 4, Fall 1981, pp. 474-476.
Note: Questionnaires were mailed to 450 federal bureaucrats; 212 (48 percent) responded from the following federal agencies: Agriculture, Commerce, Energy, Health, Education and Welfare, Housing and Urban Development, Interior, Justice, Labor, Treasury, Transportation, and some IRCs (14 percent of total).

strategies using his formal powers, he never succeeded in winning his test with the federal bureaucracy, in part because of other dramatic political events that took him away from the regulatory control task but also in part because of how he was perceived by the professional elites who worked in executive branch agencies.

REGULATORY REFORM STRATEGIES OF THE PRESIDENCY

Since the Nixon presidency, the White House, through four administrations (Nixon, Ford, Carter, and Reagan), has used the formal powers and authority of the President in various ways to try to control and moderate the activities of the federal regulatory agencies. Regulatory reform by the presidency is the effort to ensure democratic accountability in the policy implementation phase of government. There is, however, a typology of regulatory reformers: traditionalists, restrictivists, and populists.[50]

The traditionalists are concerned about the regulatory agencies' abuses of economic power and the need to improve regulatory procedures, organization, and personnel. A great many presidential strategies are premised on this typology; they are efforts to introduce management controls in an attempt to reduce these perceived abuses of power by regulatory agencies. Restrictivists scorn governmental intervention in the economy and generally have "a distaste for controls." They want to develop strategies that strangle all regulatory initiatives, no matter how beneficial. The populists are strong supporters of regulatory activity that aids in achievement of social goals such as clean air and safe consumer products but are opposed to regulatory activity that aids the corporate sector.[51] Although all three types of regulatory reformers have appeared in the four administrations, the primary typology common to all four has been the traditionalist mode.

General Approaches to Regulatory Reform

There are at least four major presidential approaches to regulatory reform: substantive, procedural, structural, and personnel categories.[52] The substantive approach would incorporate changes in the fundamental organic statutes themselves. The White House might propose clarification of the goals of the National Environmental Protection Act and ask Congress to change the legislation. The President might ask the legislature to develop clear goals for the administrative agencies through changes in the organic statutes that created the agency or gave it substantive authority to act. Another substantive change would be in the area of deregulaton of certain areas of economic activity, such as interstate trucking and the airlines.

Procedural approaches to regulatory reform by the President would focus on the establishment or the improvement of procedures to encourage greater coordination among regulatory agencies, to lessen the paperwork burden on small businesses, or to improve the speed of agency responses to perceived needs.

The structural approach to regulatory reform would include the development of mechanisms for central review of regulations. A Bumpers-type amendment[53] would, if passed by Congress and signed into law by the President (not likely), use the federal courts' judicial review power in an oversight capacity. Until recently invalidated as a control mechanism by the U.S. Supreme Court, the legislative veto was another such structural mechanism that would, theoretically though not in reality, provide a central authority to oversee regulatory activity.[54] The efforts of the past three administrations to develop within the White House a central review mechanism to oversee regulatory activity is another example of structural reform. Still another general structural reform proposed by various administrations since the Roosevelt administrations (1933-1945) has been the repeated call for modification of the IRC's hybrid structure.

Changing the regulatory process to "inject particular types of considerations" into regulatory decision making on a systematic basis is a proposal that falls in the structural-substantive category.[55] The Reagan executive order of February 17, 1981, for example, added the cost-benefit analysis requirement and presentation by agency officials of regulatory impact analyses (of preliminary and final regulations proposed by the agency) to OMB's OIRA prior to their being published in the *Federal Register*. Presidents Ford and Carter added to the regulatory process less formal regulatory analysis and internal agency regulatory management review. All four administrations have discussed the possibility of a regulatory budget.

The personnel approach to regulatory reform, which clearly suggests that these different types of approaches to regulatory reform are not mutually exclusive, emphasizes the importance of careful presidential selection of persons to staff the many hundreds of senior political appointments in the executive agencies and in the IRCs. By improving the quality of the appointees and by constantly communicating to them the imperatives of presidential policy, there is the possibility of a redirection and greater coordination of agency activity.

Specific Strategies

Since the Nixon administration (1969-1974), a number of specific strategies have been employed, falling under the four general categories.

Substantive

Reorganizational Efforts

Presidential reorganization authority, subject to congressional approval, is "considered by many to be a useful tool for the president to use against the bureaucratic fiefdoms."[56] By redistributing influence in a particular policy field, the presidency can gain more effective control over the regulatory machinery. Both the Nixon and the Carter administrations made efforts to recognize the federal regulatory process in order to manage and coordinate the regulators better.

Deregulation

A fundamentally substantive strategy for reducing regulatory sprawl in a substantive area is to deregulate that field. Deregulation efforts made great headway during the Carter administration when a number of industries—chiefly airlines, trucking, banking, energy, railroads, telecommunications, natural gas—were freed of regulatory controls. If competition is present in the industry or if regulation has heavily burdened the industry, then deregulation may be an effective strategy of regulatory reform.

Procedural

The Carter administration, working with the Congress, made an effort to reduce the paperwork burden on, in particular, small businesses. At the urging of the presidency, the national legislature in 1980 passed the Paperwork Reduction Act and the Regulatory Flexibility Act. The OMB, in the former legislation, was empowered to review all requests made by governmental agencies (including the IRCs) for information and reports from businesses and individuals in an effort to reduce paperwork. The Regulatory Flexibility Act requires all agencies to review and revise regulations with respect to the economic impact on small business.[57]

Structural

Executive Orders

Presidents Ford, Carter, and Reagan used the executive order strategy in efforts to have the White House or other review groups examine major regulations and make recommendations for revising, modifying, or rejecting the regulation due to duplication, efficiency, and other reasons. Central review of discrete major regulations, and possible rejection of those not well developed, is the major goal of the various executive orders issued by the chief executives.

The OMB and Budgetary Controls

In a number of executive orders, especially the Reagan order of February 17, 1981, the OMB has been a major instrument in efforts at regulatory reform. Created in 1970, the OMB is the successor to the Bureau of the Budget (which had been placed in the Executive Office of the White House by legislation passed in 1939 by the Congress). Nixon's reorganization plan no. 2, introduced to Congress in March 1970 in response to the first of a number of Ash Council reports, called for the creation of a Domestic Council and the creation of the OMB. The former was needed for policy determination; the OMB would function as an executive management operation. In his message to the Congress transmitting the plan, Nixon wrote that the plan sought to establish an "Office of Management and Budget, which would be the President's principal arm for the exercise of his managerial functions. The Domestic Council will be primarily concerned with what we do; the OMB will be primarily concerned with *how* we do it, and *how well* we do it."[58]

Since congressional approval in July 1970, the OMB has become a major linchpin in presidential efforts to manage the regulatory process. A primary task is budgetary management of the "anarchical universe" of federal agency budgets.[59] This clearinghouse action of OMB helps the President retain some management control over agency activities by affecting the kind of resources an agency can receive. But as OMB director David Stockman stated, "The budget isn't something you reconstruct each year. The budget is a sort of rolling history of decisions. All kinds of decisions, made five, ten, fifteen years ago, are coming back to bite us unexpectedly."[60] Nevertheless, OMB has tried to develop and implement management tools such as Management By Objectives, (Nixon), Zero Based Budgeting (ZBB) (Carter), and Cost-Benefit Analysis (Reagan) in an effort to ensure that the President's policy objectives are carried out as much as they can be—given the politics of budget development and the fact that the OMB-developed budget must then be considered by Congress. However, the budget-creation process, while limited, incremental, and subject to the vicissitudes of the political process, is one "major means by which Congress and the President can attempt to influence the behavior of regulatory commissions."[61]

Regulatory Budget

Another structural device discussed in recent administrations is the regulatory budget. Essentially a framework for assembling the resource costs attributable to an agency's regulatory activities (including estimates of the costs incurred in carrying out and complying with the rules and regulations of federal agencies) and then placing a *limit* on additional agency costs permitted to be spent by an agency each year, the regulatory budget concept is quite radical.[62]

The device would force the regulatory agencies to focus on the costs of their regulations. These costs, direct and indirect, of regulatory practices are billions of dollars annually. The regulatory budget would get to the indirect costs generated by the regulations and borne by regulatees, individuals, and organizations in the private sector. Some estimates of these private sector costs in 1976 ran as high as $62 billion, with an "estimated cost of federal regulation in 1979 in excess of $100 billion . . . derived by extrapolating from prior years' data on the basis of the ratio of administrative costs to compliance costs."[63] These indirect costs of federal regulations, passed on to consumers, also may cause a dampening of industrial innovation, "causing a reduced flow of new and better products." One commentator has written, "Regulations which require industries to meet environmental standards utilizing certain pre-specified technologies reduce the incentive to develop more efficient and effective technologies as well as to implement measures other than technological ones that would reduce environmental damage."[64]

The regulatory budget would enable Congress to establish a cap on the costs of regulatory activities to the private sector, this sum to be allocated to the various regulatory agencies by the Congress, with major presidential participation in the process. OMB in 1978 actually developed and circulated proposed legislation that would have required each federal agency to "create a system capable of accounting for costs that their regulations impose on the private sector and other levels of government and to report these costs annually."[65] Under proposed plans developed by OMB, the annual budget transmitted to Congress would contain a regulatory budget for each agency. OMB or some other central agency would establish the standards and compile the regulatory budget information much as it does for the regular budgetary process.

The role "of the central regulatory budget authority would be that of overseer, enforcer, and promulgator of guidelines and standards to assure uniformity and adequacy of agency reporting procedures."[66] A major problem, pointed out by critics of this structural device to regulate the regulators, is that the formula as proposed does not take into account the potential benefits—health, safety, life—that flow from the regulations implemented by the federal agencies. Since the regulatory budget's figures are somewhat abstract, critics of the idea point to the mischief that such a device could foster: downward estimates to enhance some agency activity, budget brinkmanship, for example.[67] In any event, the regulatory budget concept is one much-discussed strategy in the continuing effort to find management tools that the President could use to control and direct the federal agencies.

Personnel

"Who you get *in* government directly affects what you get out of government."[68] Executive Office personnel and presidential appointees throughout the federal executive branch and the IRC's are critical linkages in the presidential effort to coordinate and manage the federal government. They serve as "links between the President and his programmatic ideas and the development of and implementation of these ideas in the bureaucracy."[69] Efforts have been made continuously by the President and his senior staff to appoint officials in agreement with basic presidential policy to staff the federal executive establishment—and to try to remove others who are not part of the presidential team.[70] Without political control in the executive agencies, wrote staff member Fred Malek to President Nixon, you cannot have management control of the agency.[71]

SUMMARY

Presidential efforts to control and coordinate the activities of the federal agencies have not gone unchallenged. Congress, always concerned about its powers and prerogatives vis-à-vis the President, is extremely wary about the possibility of the White House turning into an imperial presidency. In addition, congressional attitudes toward the federal regulatory agencies have attempted to assert the primary responsibility of the legislature to oversee the federal bureaucracy. The bureaucrats, after all, are surrogates of the legislature, and the Congress should be the political agency to monitor their activities.

The bureaucratic world, consisting of large numbers of anarchic policy triangles, has ways to avoid presidential efforts to control and monitor their activities. Perhaps the problem of controlling the federal bureaucracy is an insoluble one, with adverse consequences for the normative question of accountability. Before reaching this pessimistic conclusion, it is appropriate to review the efforts of the various administrations since 1969 to come to grips with the problem of regulatory sprawl and democratic accountability.

NOTES

1. Neustadt, *Presidential Power*, p. 26.
2. Nathan, *Plot*, p. 4. Robert S. Gilmour, criticizing the legislative veto as another abrogation by the Congress of its oversight responsibilities, wrote that "with the application of the legislative veto, Congress relinquishes its role as independent overseer in exchange for direct participation of its committees and staff in agency decisionmaking. Pointed accountability is inevitably lost in the bargain." ["Congressional Veto," p. 23]
3. Michael Wines, "Regulatory Writing in Washington—Making Days Stretch into Years," *National Journal*, November 13, 1982, p. 1938.
4. Ibid., p. 1937. See, for example, Ball et al., *Compromised Compliance*, which illustrates a six-year lag between passage of the 1965 Voting Rights Act and the

development of regulations (by DOJ) to implement the important preclearance section of the act (section 5).

5. Wines, "Regulatory Writing," p. 1940.

6. Ibid.

7. Nathan, *Plot*, p. viii.

8. Marvin H. Kosters and Jeffrey A. Eisenach, "Is Regulatory Relief Enough?" *Regulation*, March-April 1982, p. 27.

9. Bruff, "Presidential Power," p. 461.

10. Cronin, *State of the Presidency*, pp. 91-92.

11. Neustadt, *Presidential Power*, p. 213.

12. Ibid., p. 242.

13. Ibid., p. 241.

14. Ibid., pp. 241-242.

15. Aberbach and Rockman, "Clashing Beliefs," p. 456.

16. Neal R. Pierce and Jay Hamilton, "Flypaper Federalism," *National Journal*, September 12, 1981, p. 1636.

17. Antonin Scalia, "Deregulation HQ: An Interview on the New Executive Order with Murray L. Weidenbaum and James A. Miller, III," *Regulation*, March-April 1981, p. 18.

18. Charles Funderburk, *Presidents and Politics: The Limits of Power*, Monterey, CA: Brooks-Cole Publishing Co., 1982, p. 191.

19. *Malek Manual*, White House Personnel Office, 1970, in Thompson, *Classics*, p. 87.

20. Griffin B. Bell, *Taking Care of the Law*, New York: William Morrow and Co., 1982, pp. 52ff.

21. Ripley and Franklin, *Congress*, p. 57.

22. Ibid., p. 58.

23. Cronin, *State of Presidency*, p. 92.

24. Ripley and Franklin, *Congress*, p. 58.

25. James G. Benze, Jr., "Presidential Management: The Importance of Presidential Skills," 11 *Presidential Studies Quarterly*, No. 4, Fall 1981, p. 470.

26. Ibid., p. 472.

27. Aberbach and Rockman, "Clashing Beliefs," p. 457.

28. Fisher, *Politics*, p. 151.

29. See *Humphrey's Executor v. United States*, 295 U.S. 602 (1935).

30. Congressional Quarterly, *Federal Regulatory Directory, 1980-1981*, Washington, D.C.: CQ Press, 1980, p. 18.

31. See, generally, Norman C. Thomas, "Politics, Structure, and Personnel in Administrative Regulations," 57 *Virginia Law Review*, No. 6, September 1971, pp. 1035ff.

32. Ibid., p. 1053.

33. Ibid., p. 1037.

34. Fisher, *Politics*, p. 154.

35. Thomas, "Politics," pp. 1038-1039.

36. Ibid., pp. 1040-1041.

37. Glen O. Robinson, "On Reorganizing the IRAs," 57 *Virginia Law Review*, No. 6, September 1971, p. 933.

38. Thomas, "Politics," p. 1055.

39. Ibid., pp. 1055-1057.

40. Robinson, "On Reorganizing," p. 950.

41. Neustadt, *Presidential Power*, p. 241.

42. Cronin, *State of Presidency*, p. 98.

43. Neustadt, *Presidential Power*, pp. 164-167; see also Benze, "Presidential Management," pp. 473-477.

44. Neustadt, *Presidential Power*, p. 164.

45. Benze, "Presidential Management," p. 478.

46. Funderburk, *Presidents*, p. 188. "Separation of powers still remains the greatest check on presidential control of administration." Kenneth F. Warren, *Administrative Law in the American Political System*, St. Paul, MN: West Publishing Co., 1982, p. 48.

47. Neustadt, *Presidential Power*, p. 9.

48. Ronald Randall, "Presidental Power," p. 795.

49. Jimmy Carter, *Keeping Faith: Memoirs of a President*, New York: Bantam Books, 1982, p. 69.

50. Stone, *Regulation*, pp. 246ff.

51. Ibid.

52. See, generally, Randall, "Presidential Power"; Stephen Breyer, "Analyzing Regulatory Failure," *Harvard Law Review*, No. 3., January 1979; MacAvoy, *Unsettled Questions*; Timothy Clark, et al., *Reforming Regulation*, Washington, D.C.: AEI, 1980; Bruff, "Presidential Power;" and Note, "Delegation and Regulatory Reform."

53. Senator Dale Bumpers (D-Ark) has repeatedly introduced amendments to regulatory reform legislation that, essentially, would strengthen federal judicial review powers over agency actions by enabling federal judges to review without presuming the constitutionality of the regulation in question.

54. See Gilmour, "Congressional Veto."

55. Salamon, "Federal Regulation," p. 164.

56. Louis Fisher and Ronald C. Moe, "Presidential Reorganization Authority," 96 *Political Science Quarterly*, No. 2, Summer 1981, p. 314.

57. Laura Weiss, "Reagan and Congress Planning of Regulatory Machine Repairs," *Congressional Quarterly*, March 7, 1981, p. 412.

58. John H. Kessel, *The Domestic Presidency: Decisionmaking in the White House*, North Scituate, MA: Duxbury Press, 1975, p. 19.

59. William Greider, "The Education of David Stockman," *Atlantic Monthly*, December 1981, p. 39.

60. Ibid., p. 51.

61. Joseph Stewart, Jr., James E. Anderson, and Zona Taylor, "Presidential and Congressional Support for IRCs," 35 *Western Political Quarterly*, No. 3, September 1982, p. 319.

62. Clark, "Reforming Regulations," p. 3.

63. B. Ward White, "Proposals for a Regulatory Budget," 1 *Public Budgeting and Finance*, Autumn 1981, p. 48.

64. Ibid., p. 49.

65. Ibid.

66. Ibid., p. 52.

67. Ibid., p. 54.

68. G. Calvin MacKenzie, *The Politics of Presidential Appointments*, New York: Free Press, 1981, p. xx.

69. Ripley and Franklin, *Congress*, p. 5.

70. See *Meyers v. US*, 272 US 52 (1926); and Howard Ball, *No Pledge of Privacy: The Watergate Tapes Litigation, 1973-1974*, New York: Kennikat Press, 1977. During the course of the Watergate activities, Alexander Haig, one of President Nixon's senior staff, telephoned Elliot Richardson and William Ruchelshaus, attorney general and deputy attorney general, respectively, and asked them to fire Archibald Cox, the Watergate special prosecutor. Richardson resigned because "he could not execute ƒthe orders of the president"; Ruckelshaus was asked if he was prepared to do so. When the negative response was received, Haig stated, "Well, you know what it means when an order comes down from the Commander-in-Chief and a member of his team cannot execute it." Ruckelshaus immediately resigned. [Ball, *No Pledge*, pp. 41-42.]

71. See, generally, *Malek Manual*, in Thompson, *Classics*.

3

Presidential Efforts to Control the Bureaucracy: From Nixon to Carter, 1969-1981

We intend to begin a decade of government reform such as this nation has not witnessed in half a century. . . . That is the watchword of this Administration: Reform.

—Richard M. Nixon

The key to regulatory reform is not the wrecking ball; it is to pick up a mallet and apply a corrective tap.

—Gerald Ford

I came to Washington to reorganize a Federal Government which had grown more preoccupied with its own bureaucratic needs than with those of the people.

—Jimmy Carter

Recent presidential initiatives to centralize control of the federal regulatory agencies began with the Nixon administration (1969-1974). Nixon's efforts, however, stopped with the Watergate events that led to his resignation in August 1974. President Ford's administration had to cope with a surge of energy on the part of a Congress that attempted to limit the growth of future imperial presidencies. Jimmy Carter's administration was categorized as the outsider presidency; he was the first post-Watergate, non-"establishment" person to sit in the White House. All three men were concerned, in different ways, about what has been called the "demon" federal bureaucracy.[1] Their administrative efforts to curb regulatory sprawl took on different shades due to these differences of philosophy, style, and temperament and also due to outside political events that intervened and constrained each President's efforts to deal with the federal agencies.

Examining the regulatory reform strategies developed by these three Presidents and their senior staff illuminates two essentially different concerns. For President Nixon, the primary reason for dramatic efforts by his administration to direct and control the bureaucracy was to use the federal administrative machinery to implement public policies rejected by the national legislature. Frustrated by his inability to achieve basic policy goals through the Congress, policy goals that he considered consistent with the mandate he received from the voters in 1968, Nixon was urged to move to a top-down managerial strategy to achieve his programmatic objectives.

Presidents Ford and Carter, later in the decade, when the glaring problems of regulatory sprawl were more easily perceived, both developed strategies in an effort to ensure that policies formulated by the political policymakers were implemented in a timely, clearly understood, and cost-effective manner by the federal regulatory agencies. Both the Republican and the Democratic Presidents were primarily concerned about developing an executive management strategy toward the federal regulatory agencies that would ensure more efficient rulemaking and a greater degree of democratic accountability.

Consequently there are some differences between the Nixon strategy of ousting federal administrators who were not on the administration's team and the Ford and Carter efforts to develop management strategies only for those areas of regulatory activities that needed streamlining or reform. The differences, however, were in degree only; there is no real difference between Nixon's efforts to ensure obedience (on the part of career executives in executive agencies) to political executives in the agencies and the Carter effort to use the senior executive service (SES) to persuade senior career executives to go along with the policy initiatives of the agency secretary.

NIXON ADMINISTRATION'S
REGULATORY REFORM EFFORTS, 1969-1974

Traditional Politics

Richard Nixon was the first President in 120 years, since Zachary Taylor in 1849, to enter the White House confronting a Congress dominated by members of the other party. (In 1969, the U.S. Senate contained 57 Democrats and only 43 Republicans, and the U.S. House of Representatives had a similar 242 to 190 Democratic edge.) Further compounding the difficulties Nixon had with the legislature was the fact that there were only two men in the White House, Nixon himself and his counsel Bryce Harlow, who had experience and understanding of legislative politics and processes. (Nixon, moreover, had very little patience with, and no great interest in, the subject.) Given these facts, if Nixon's programs were to develop into public laws, there had to be a great deal of interaction and communication flowing between the White House and the Congress. Without staff who understood and were formerly part of the legislative process, the difficult task of getting policy through a legislature dominated by the opposition party was made nearly impossible during the first few years of the Nixon presidency. In his first year, Nixon "sent over forty domestic proposals to Congress; only two were passed."[2]

No action was taken by the Congress on a great number of major Nixon programs, among them manpower training, postal reform, revenue sharing, unemployment, the war on crime, unemployment insurance, welfare reform, anti-inflation efforts, and environmental programs. After expending this effort to develop legislation to achieve his policy objectives and, with a few notable exceptions, meeting with delay, inaction, or rejection, Nixon changed strategies. By the end of 1971, there developed in the White House the idea of the administrative presidency; the aim was to achieve Nixon's policy goals through the federal administrative structure.

Administrative Presidency Strategy

A basic assumption made by the Nixon White House, in particular, Nixon and top aides Robert Haldeman and John Ehrlichman, was that they would have to "take over the management of domestic affairs to achieve the Administration's major policy objectives."[3] A basic assumption was made that there were sufficient management tools available to the President and his top managers in the White House for this task. "When used adroitly," these management tools—personnel shifts; budget control, including impoundments and reductions; reorganization; regulatory reform—would enable Nixon to dominate the federal bureaucracy, "free from the glare of publicity, congressional control, and the awareness of the public."[4] Consequently, "more attention was paid to opportunities to achieve policy aims through administrative action, as opposed to legislative change, the former to be accomplished by taking advantage of the wide discretion available to federal officials under many existing laws."[5]

By late 1972, the new Nixon strategy was in place. The legislative agenda was reduced considerably, there were massive changes in White House personnel, and the effort to "take over the bureaucracy, and take on the Congress" began.[6] Use the federal bureaucracy to bring about domestic policy changes was the new Nixon theme. In his memoirs,

Nixon took note of his failure in 1969 "to fill all the key posts in the departments and agencies with people who were loyal to the President and his programs. Without this kind of leadership in the appointive positions, there is no way for a President to make any major impact on the bureaucracy."[7] To be successful in this second term, he had to put in place quickly the many political executives in the federal executive branch who would be surrogates for the President.

To accomplish this goal of using the federal bureaucracy to achieve policy goals, certain strategies developed: development of a counterbureaucracy in the White House; implementation of a New Federalism plan to weaken the power of lobbying representatives, bureaucrats, and congressional staff working in the capital; and organization plans to further these ends.[8]

Development of the Counterbureaucracy

The President, "constantly thwarted by the bureaucracy nominally under his command," had to create a counterbureaucracy.[9] If Nixon was not to be frustrated in his efforts to use the federal administrative machinery to implement his policies, he had to make sure that loyal staff were appointed to the major administrative agencies. He planned to do this by appointing men and women who were committed to the Nixon plans and by removing or transferring those federal bureaucrats who were not.

The Malek Report to Nixon clearly portrayed the strategy: political control of agencies precedes management, policy, or program control. By 1972, political appointees were placed in direct charge of major domestic program agencies. The appointees were politician-managers in line positions: "Nixon was trying to move the line between policy and administration closer to his office in the White House; in 1973 he could appoint 1500 to 2000 people as his agents at the top of the executive establishment of the federal government."[10]

The problem with appointing people who shared Nixon's policy and philosophic directions was that the administration might wind up with a group of mediocre persons staffing key regulatory agency positions. This may very well have been the intention of the White House. If a domestic policy is developed in the White House, then what is needed in the agency responsible for that domestic policy is a caretaker, not a policymaker. In developing and implementing this strategy, Nixon and his senior staff were looking for good political appointees, who would respond to the initiatives of the OMB, the Domestic Council, or the President by carrying them out quickly. At the core of this effort was the sacrifice of technical proficiency and knowledge for tight political and management control from the White House.[11]

The New Federalism Plan's Impact on Bureaucracy

One major policy thrust of President Nixon was his New Federalism. Said the President on August 8, 1969,

After a third of century of power flowing from the people and the states to Washington, it is time for a New Federalism in which power, funds, and responsibility will flow from Washington to the states and to the people. . . . This [New Federalism] is embodied in a package of four measures:

1) a complete replacement of the present welfare system;

2) a comprehensive new job training and placement program;

3) a revamping of the Office of Economic Opportunity; and

4) a start on the sharing of federal tax revenues with the states.[12]

While there were fundamental policy reasons for this Nixon initiative in domestic policy, the hoped-for impact on the federal bureaucracy was not overlooked.[13] Adoption of the New Federalism package would "weaken control of the permanent government in Washington."[14] A "third of a century of centralizing power and responsibility in Washington has produced a bureaucratic *monstrosity*, cumbersome, unresponsive and ineffective," stated Nixon. The New Federalism, by returning power to state and local governments, would—through this restructuring of regulatory programs through changes in the organic statutes—diminish the power of the federal regulatory agencies. For the President and his senior staff, this was an important consequence of the New Federalism.

Reorganization Efforts

As soon as he took office, President Nixon asked Roy Ash, president of Litton Industries, to chair an Advisory Council on Executive Management. During the first two years of the Nixon administration, the Ash council came up with a number of recommendations concerning IRCs and executive management, executive department reorganization, and suggestions for a more effective White House management of the federal bureaucracy. These plans for government reorganization, noted Nixon, were "sending seismic tremors through the federal bureaucracy."[15]

The major success came early in the Nixon administration with congressional approval in July 1970 of a major reorganization of the White House Office. Reorganization proposal no. 2 called for the creation of a Domestic Council and the conversion of the Bureau of the Budget into an enlarged Office of Management and Budget. The plan called for a Domestic Council (analogous, in policymaking terms, to the National Security Council) to develop centralized, coordinated national domestic policy, largely implemented "through administrative actions instead of asking for legislation."[16] The OMB was developed from a policy-neutral agency to a policy arm of the President in order to implement presidental domestic proposals through various controls over the federal bureaucracy. The plan was approved by Congress without much discussion. "With little debate, scant public attention and no great effort on his own part, Richard M. Nixon had effected a fundamental change in the very fabric of the federal government."[17]

There were other reorganization proposals presented to Congress by Nixon, including a 1972 proposal that would have collapsed eight existing executive department agencies into four superagencies—Departments of Natural Resources, Human Resources, Economic Affairs, and Community Development—but the 1970 reorganization was the only one that Congress approved.

Other Strategies

In addition to these basic efforts to gain domestic policy objectives through administrative actions and to reduce the size of the federal bureaucracy, Nixon employed more traditional methods available to a strong President.

In the effort to achieve domestic policy goals, Nixon unsuccessfully tried to impound funds appropriated by the Congress for various domestic programs.[18] In the effort to reform regulatory duplication, OMB's first formal effort at interagency regulatory review was developed in the Nixon period. Through an executive order issued in October 1971, OMB was to conduct a "Quality of Life" review process involving interagency coordination of proposed regulations in the health, safety, and environmental areas.

But these early strategies to use the regulatory process to achieve domestic policy goals, as well as to reduce its independence and its potency, came to a halt due to the public and legislative response to the events of Watergate. While the Nixon administration's plans, with the notable exception of the 1970 reorganization that created the Domestic Council and the OMB, failed, the problem of accountability for public policy actions in a democracy remained.

PRESIDENT GERALD FORD'S
EFFORTS AT REGULATORY REFORM, 1974-1976

President Ford's perception of the problem of regulatory sprawl and the ensuing dilemma of democratic accountability was not inconsistent with that of other chief executives. Carelessly written regulations have a damaging effect on almost every aspect of American life. The federal regulatory sprawl, wrote Ford, was "stifling American productivity, promoting inefficiency, eliminating competition and even invading personal privacy. We as a nation were about to suffocate."[19] Regulations were issued that were unwieldy, costly, unnecessary, and contradictory. His administration's basic thrusts were in two directions: development of deregulation plans for railroads, airlines, and the trucking industry (not enacted by the Congress when Ford departed the White House) and introduction of regulatory reform through the use of executive orders.

By the mid-1970s, due to growing high inflation and the growth of regulatory activity in virtually all areas of the economy, both the President and Congress reacted to these economic and regulatory realities. In August 1974, Congress established the Council on Wage and Price Stability (COWPS) to "monitor activities of the private sector of the economy that might add to the rate of inflation. In addition, COWPS was directed to 'review the activities and programs of the federal government to discover whether they have any inflationary impact.' From the very beginning, the COWPS interpreted this mandate as requiring cost benefit analysis of important regulatory actions."[20] For the first time, a government-created agency would determine whether major regulatory actions were inflationary or anti-inflationary using a benefit-cost analysis.

The Ford Executive Orders

In November 1974 Ford issued executive order (EO) 11,821, which established the Inflation Impact Statement (IIS) program. On December 31, 1976, the program was extended and renamed the Economic Impact Statement (EIS) program. The EO complemented and supported the legislative creation of COWPS as it was an effort to make federal regulatory decisionmakers more sensitive to the hidden and excessive cost consequences of their proposed government regulations.[21]

In this attempt to sensitize mid-level bureaucrats to the importance of these benefit-cost considerations, the EO required that "major proposals for legislation, and for the promulgation of regulations and rules by any executive branch agency must be accompanied by a statement which certifies that the inflationary impact of the proposal has been evaluated."[22] The OMB was given the task of developing standards and criteria for this voluntary implementation by federal executive department agencies of this EO.[23]

The cost-benefit analytical criteria developed by OMB were to be used by those federal administrators whose agencies developed regulations that:

1. Increased costs of $100 million (for the national economy).
2. Affected productivity adversely (by reducing capacity of capital investment), increased required labor per unit of output, or caused reduction in adaption to new technologies.
3. Substantially lessened competition.
4. Would cause a 3 percent change in the levels of supplies of important materials.
5. Had an adverse effect on employment (specifically an industry loss of 10,000 or more jobs or a direct change of 0.2 percent of total national employment).
6. Had an adverse impact on energy (defined as an increase in demand or reduction of energy supplies of 0.1 percent).[24]

Under the EO, the OMB director could delegate functions to various units, including the COWPS. "COWPS was given a major role in administering the IIS program"; it would provide informal criticism of the agency's impact statements that were submitted to OMB and to COWPS.[25] The ultimate goal of the order was to curb inflation by lowering, where possible, government-mandated cost increases. This goal was to be achieved through the elimination of cost-ineffective regulations by the agencies themselves through this process.

Results of the Ford Executive Orders

"Virtually all regulatory agencies came under the purview of COWPS, where a small group of economists reviewed newly proposed regulations and their supporting documents."[26] Four products appeared: COWPS-written statements became part of the record in formal rulemaking processes; COWPS staff publicly testified at the agency hearing; detailed COWPS analyses were given to agency staff as part of the internal review; and COWPS staff developed studies of significant regulatory issues not related to any proposed rulemaking.[27] Since the federal regulatory agency did not have to accept the findings of COWPS, that agency's primary task was to "persuade agencies to avoid the tendency to serve special constituent interests, often at greater cost to the general public," according to James C. Miller III, an assistant director of COWPS during the Ford administration.[28]

The actual results of the EO, relative to increased agency sensitivity to the benefits and costs of their proposed regulations, varied according to the agency. According to Miller, some IISs were very detailed and analytically sophisticated, and others were grossly defective. There were "good estimates of costs but weak assessments of benefits and alternatives [to this regulation] were usually ignored."[29]

With two exceptions, the U.S. Department of Agriculture (USDA) and the Federal Energy Administration (FEA), Miller believed that most agency managers supported the EO. But there were a number of problems with the Ford order: the inflationary impact analysis came after the regulation had been developed by the agency, leading to ex post facto justifications of the cost-effectiveness of the proposed regulation; the agencies were not required to develop these IISs if, in their judgment, the proposed regulation was not a major one; and IRCs were not covered. Since COWPS reviews of these documents were advisory, agencies did not have to comply or delay or halt regulations that the agencies wanted to enforce. "Agency compliance with the Ford program depended to a large extent on the power of the President and his staff in OMB and COWPS to persuade through reasoned argument and/or through charm."[30]

Miller wrote a perceptive essay on the Ford IIS program in which he stated that a program of regulatory reform had to include more than the presidential EO as an instrument of change. Improving the quality of agency decisionmaking entails employment of EOs, as well as regulatory appointments, greater oversight by OMB, and changes in the civil service (the personnel dimension of reform). Many of his suggestions for improving the Ford IIS-EIS program became part of the Reagan administration's EO of February 1981. These suggestions included provisions that would: (1) ensure that the EIS was used as an input into the regulatory decisionmaking process, especially at the proposal formulation stage, by requiring agencies to submit their EISs to COWPS-OMB *prior to* publication in the *Federal Register*; (2) ensure that benefit-cost analysis was required of all agencies; (3) extend the EIS program to existing regulations and programs; and (4) extend EIS coverage to the IRCs.[31]

PRESIDENT JIMMY CARTER'S EFFORTS
TO CONFRONT REGULATORY SPRAWL, 1977-1981

Regulatory reform was an issue in the 1976 presidential campaign; both Ford and Carter discussed the value to the general community of streamlining the federal bureaucracy. President Carter came to Washington, D.C., with a primary goal: to reduce the complexity, duplication, wastefulness, and carelessness of federal regulatory practices. To accomplish this basic goal meant to develop strategies that would eliminate unneeded regulations and unnecessary burdens on consumers and businesses. The perennial challenge for any President concerned about the practical and normative consequences of regulatory sprawl is to overhaul the regulatory process without totally dismantling it and demoralizing those working in the agencies. Carter's administration was the first contemporary presidency to work on this challenge for the full term.

President Carter was also the first President to come into power with a fairly comprehensive understanding of the problem. The basic problem of most other Presidents—"our Presidents, more often than not, have been atrocious administrators, . . . they often come from an occupation (legislator) and a profession (law) that ill prepares them for management"—did not seem to be Carter's problem.[32] He prided himself on his ability to be a professional manager of the White House and of the federal regulatory process. He clearly understood the adverse consequences of overly rigid, costly regulations that are created without the "discipline and scrutiny of the regular budget process" and that "in addition to direct compliance costs, affect innovation and productivity by diverting capital, discouraging investment and delaying decisions."[33]

There were no fewer than five major plans—reorganizations efforts, personnel moves and development of the senior executive service, budgeting initiatives, economic deregulation, and regulatory management techniques in various executive orders—that Carter's administration tried to implement in order to reach their goal.

Reorganization, Personnel, and Budgeting Initiatives

During his administration, President Carter introduced a number of initiatives that, had they been accepted by the Congress or by his own executive department staff or had they worked in reality the way the idea theoretically should have worked, might have begun to turn the regulatory sprawl and democratic accountability tide. There were a number of executive branch reorganization efforts introduced by Carter during his presidency, including the successful call for a cabinet-level secretary of education in charge of the new Department of Education.

In his effort to coordinate better the actions of federal regulatory agencies in the areas of economic and community development, natural resources, food and nutrition, and trade, he proposed the formation of four new cabinet-level departments: Development Assistance, Natural Resources, Food and Nutrition, and Trade, Technology, and Industry. These reorganizations were never approved by Congress.

A major move in the area of personnel was the creation of the senior executive service (SES). This program was designed and implemented by the Office of Personnel Management (OPM) in the White House to give political appointees heading the federal regulatory agencies and the President greater control over career civil servants through selective transfers and monetary awards for exemplary service.[34] According to Alan K. Campbell, Carter's director of OPM, the SES program was designed to provide political appointees to executive departments with a tool to encourage greater cooperation between the political executive and the career bureaucrats. "Every new administration feels the negative aspects of the bureaucracy's pressure for continuity. New policymakers arrive with mandates for change and find that though they can change structures and appearances, it is very difficult to make dramatic changes in direction."[35]

As Norton Long and others have suggested, the intent of the SES was to "loosen the bureaucratic-legislative committee–constituency alliances which are seen to fragment the administration and to engender a feudal structure that resists presidential control."[36] While the logic of the SES, by providing for performance evaluations, personnel development, and personnel allocation, seems to emphasize increased individual and programmatic effectiveness, the reality is that it has been seen as an effort by the White House to force career bureaucrats into a more responsive and cooperative mode of operations with the political executives and with the President.

By either rewarding cooperative and loyal career bureaucrats or demoting, transferring, or firing uncooperative managers (on the basis of personnel evaluations), the SES strategy, it was hoped, "would make dramatic changes in direction. After 120 days, the political executive could take any number of actions to bring senior career executives into line with new policy directions of the White House."[37] The fact that the federal bureaucracy is extremely uncomfortable with the SES may indicate that, from the perspective of the White House and its political executives, it may be achieving its presidential management goals.[38]

Budgeting initiatives were introduced by Carter's staff. In particular, given Jimmy Carter's experience with ZBB while governor of Georgia, the White House encouraged the introduction of ZBB in an attempt to bring greater rationality to the budgetary process and also to gain greater control over the regulatory process. "ZBB demands a total rejustification of everything from scratch—from zero," stated then-governor Carter.[39] According to Thomas Lauth, noted scholar in the area of budgeting processes, ZBB procedures, while having only a slight impact on the budgeting process itself, work reasonably well "by requiring more extensive program information and greater justification for funding requests."[40] It was in the latter context that ZBB was to be developed into another instrument of presidential political control and coordination. The President and the OMB, by requiring rejustification of all line items in the agency budget, can exert control over the agency, except for the fact that so many items in an agency's budget are categorical and cannot be adjusted without congressional approval.

The two major thrusts in the Carter administration's efforts to reform regulatory activity in the federal government were economic deregulation and regulatory management in the form of greater centralizing review authority, EO 12,044.

Economic Deregulation

The Carter administration's perspective on regulatory reform stressed the elimination of unnecessary and unneeded regulations that hindered competition rather than fostering it. Federal regulatory agencies ought not to be in the business of protecting inefficiency and inflated pricing with unneeded rules. In a classic essay on the merits of deregulation of the airline industry, Alfred E. Kahn, formerly chairman of the CAB, pointed out that having CAB commissioners try to establish which carrier shall have exclusive rights to fly in and out of cities, whether an applicant is "fit, willing and able," and whether the "public convenience and necessity" require licensing were absurd responsibilities and inconsistent with the CAB's statutory instructions to "foster sound economic conditions."

The Board is not equipped to make a rational selection of carriers. It is not equipped to plan the optimum future structure and growth of this dynamic industry; to select for each market the ideal price, the ideal supplier, the ideal aircraft. No Board is. We are not equipped to run a single airline, let alone a nationwide air transportation system. . . . We *do* know that we are incapable of forecasting traffic, either for the system as a whole or for individual markets, and that our carrier selection decisions have often proved to be seriously mistaken.[41]

For Kahn, there was no way the CAB could develop regulations for the airline industry that would foster competitiveness. There are no decisional criteria "to be worked out" and employed, through the issuance of CAB regulations, that would make the airline regulatory situation rational.[42] Only economic deregulation of the airline industry would restore the competitive market and benefit the consumer, urged Kahn to the Carter administraton. (The Airline Deregulation Act was signed into law by President Carter in October 1978.)

In addition to airline deregulation, the Carter administration urged the following deregulations in order to foster greater competitiveness within the industries:

1. Energy deregulation—natural gas, crude oil (Natural Gas Policy Act 1978).

2. Trucking deregulation—Motor Carrier Act, 1980.

3. Banking deregulation—Depository Institutions Deregulation and Monetary

4. Railroad deregulations proposed through ICC modifications in its regulations dealing with antitrust immunity and price fixing.

5. Telecommunications deregulations proposed that would open telephone equipment and long-distance service to competition (approved by the Reagan administration and Congress in 1981).

EO 12,044 and Regulatory Management

The centerpiece of the Carter administration's efforts to get at the problem of controlling the federal agencies was his EO and two interagency panels designed to implement it. In his attempt to streamline and better coordinate the activities of the federal agencies, Jimmy Carter continued the Ford regulatory review idea, with three major changes.

In January 1978, the first of the additions appeared. Carter created the interagency Regulatory Analysis Review Group (RARG), which consisted of seventeen representatives from major executive branch agencies, including the Council of Economic Advisers. (The COWPS provided the economic staff support for the RARG activities.) Its primary task was that of selective oversight: to review and make recommendations on a small number (between 10 and 20) of proposed major rules and regulations of the executive branch agencies to determine if they had the potential to worsen inflation. It was an effort to improve top-level interaction between federal agencies and to shift rulemaking power within the executive branch.

This effort to gain greater control of the regulatory decisionmaking process was enhanced with the second of the Carter additions to the Ford strategy: the issuance of EO 12,044, entitled "Improving Government Regulations," on March 23, 1978. Among its major provisions were the following requirements:

1. Involve agency heads at the earliest stages in developing regulations for which they will be held accountable.
2. Prepare a regulatory analysis for each major rule, assessing its economic effects and the alternate means of achieving its objectives.
3. Select the least burdensome acceptable alternative.
4. Develop an evaluation plan to review the effectiveness of all new regulations.
5. Use simple, understandable English in writing rules.
6. Publish a semiannual agenda of regulations under development in each agency.
7. Involve the public in regulatory decisions.
8. Systematically review existing regulations to evaluate whether they are achieving their objectives and whether costs are being minimized.[43]

The regulatory analyses—both the preliminary and the final proposal—were to be published in the *Federal Register* for public review and had to include an economic analysis of the consequences of such regulations and a discussion of alternate ways of reaching the same goal. Although the economic analysis did not require a strict cost-benefit analysis, this analytical requirement did cause difficulties for many agency heads who were not economic analysts or whose agency did not have such experts on staff. Joan Bernstein, general counsel for the Environmental Protection Agency (EPA) during the Carter administration, recently stated that under the Carter EO, the EPA "found that we had to increase our economic analytical capacity. We had to hire people with new and different skills."[44]

Significant regulations were those proposals that would result in an annual economic impact of $100 million or more or major increases in the costs or prices for businesses, consumers, or governments. The key reviewers were the members of RARG, not the OMB, and the President himself.[45]

When necessary, President Carter intervenes personally in key regulatory decisions. Some have challenged his actions, arguing that when a statute assigns a decision to an agency, the President can participate only as a party and cannot direct the decision. The President and the Justice Department feel he has clear authority to direct his subordinates, and he will continue to use it when appropriate. The Constitution directs the President to see that the laws are faithfully executed. He is politically accountable for agency decisions and has the right to fire agency heads. It is senseless to say he can fire them but cannot tell them what he wants.[46]

Clearly, then, with the involvement of the major political executives in each agency at an early stage in the policymaking process and with the possibility of presidential intervention in the direction of agency rulemaking directions, the EO envisioned a strong centralization of regulatory authority and control in each department by the cabinet-level political executives and, ultimately, by presidential involvement in key policy issues. It was the president's counsel, Lloyd Cutler, who had said, prior to the EO, that "the power to make the final decision on rulemaking should rest with the President in those cases in which he finds that what an agency proposed to do, or was failing to do, has a critical impact on achieving other national goals."[47] Carter's EO gave the President the opportunity to provide the balance that Cutler and others claimed was lacking in regulatory practices to that point.

The third innovation was the creation, in October 1978, of the U.S. Regulatory Council. This council was composed of representatives from 35 executive branch and independent regulatory agencies (along with a staff of 20). Chaired by Douglas M. Costle, the administrator of EPA, the group tried to encourage interagency cooperation in specific regulatory areas such as regulation of cancer-causing chemicals and the automobile industry, and resolve conflicts in the federal regulatory process by publishing semiannual calendars of agency activities (to prevent duplication of effort).[48]

A number of problems confronted the political executives who tried to implement these regulatory reforms:

1. Legislative rejection of reorganization plans.
2. Career bureaucratic disenchantment with the 1978 civil service reforms, especially the creation of the SES, seen as an effort to "increase the career executive's dependence on the political executive."[49]
3. Agency disregarded or ignored the advisory recommendations of RARG, for that group did not have any legal sanctions at its disposal.[50]
4. Little time for careful analysis of many of the regulations, for the RARG analysis had to be accomplished during the public comment period (usually 60 to 90 days).
5. A horizontal political relationship developed; the political executives dealt with their peers who sat on RARG. If any agency head wanted to use the technical assistance provided the agency after it was reviewed by RARG, he or she could but was not under any major compulsion to do so unless the President took a personal interest in that major regulation and directly intervened to instruct the political manager as to what he wanted.

In addition to these Carter executive initiatives that tried to deal directly with regulatory reform, there were indirect efforts, working with the Congress, by the Carter administration to reduce regulatory inefficiency and burdensome regulations. In 1980, Congress passed two pieces of legislation Carter proposed: the Paperwork Reduction Act and the Regulatory Flexibility Act. The former statute gave the OMB the power to review all requests made by government agencies for information and reports from businesses and individuals in an effort to reduce the paperwork requirements. The latter legislation, written to protect small businesses from regulations that would be particularly burdensome, required all agency decisionmakers to analyze an agency's paperwork and economic impact on small businesses.[51]

SUMMARY

Of the chief executives of the three administrations examined in this chapter, only Jimmy Carter had a full term in office to begin to put into place his regulatory reform policies. Nixon really began to organize his presidency in this direction in 1972, two years before he resigned; Ford had only a little more than two years in office to try to put together a regulatory reform package. Nixon, Ford, and Carter shared certain presidential goals: use the administrative machinery to achieve changes in policy directions of the federal bureaucracy; streamline the federal regulatory program by trying to eliminate outmoded and unnecessary programs; try to coordinate and direct, through the use of political executives in the federal agencies, the activities of the federal executive branch regulatory agencies; in general, try to move the centralizing tendencies into the White House and have the President play a major balancing and advising role in the administrative process.

Political, White House, control of the federal administrative process was attempted through various structural, substantive, personnel, and procedural strategies. New executive agencies were created (OMB, Domestic Council, COWPS, OPM), deregulation occurred, personnel plans were developed by Nixon and by Carter (SES), and new procedures were introduced in the effort to move the bureaucracy in directions the President and his senior staff thought desirable.

What is revealed, in the end, is the frustration of each President in trying to move rapidly in this area. There is what Norton Long describes as the enduring tension between the "short termers" and the "long termers" in this effort to redirect and coordinate the activities of the federal administrative networks.[52] Sooner or later, because of Watergate, domestic politics, the seizure of Americans by the Cambodians or by the Iranians, inexpertness of the appointees, their high turnover, the short termers—the President and his political appointees in the White House and in the federal agencies—have to turn to other issues. In this turning away to react to other political issues of higher moment to the President, the President loses the contact and communications with the federal administrators.

The challenge that confronted the incoming administration of President Ronald Reagan in January 1981 was how to maintain a continuing dialogue with the federal agency careerists so that there would be continuing White House direction and coordination of federal regulatory activities. Carter, although he tried harder than any other President in our history to constrain and direct the federal bureaucracy, did not hit upon the answer to the question posed by political expediency. Reagan believed that he had the answer.

NOTES

1. Stephen Hess, *Organizing the Presidency*, Washington, D.C.: Brookings Institution, 1976, p. 131.

2. Richard M. Nixon, *RN: The Memoirs of Richard M. Nixon*, New York: Grosset and Dunlop, 1978, p. 414.

3. Nathan, *Plot*, p. vii.

4. Randall, "Presidential Power," p. 808.

5. Nathan, *Plot*, p. 7.

6. Ibid., p. 8.

7. Nixon, *RN*, p. 768.

8. Raymond Price, *With Nixon*, New York: Viking Press, 1977, p. 195.

9. Ibid., p. 194.

10. Nathan, *Plot*, p. 10.

11. Dianna Hoffman, "President May Regret Barely Qualified Appointees," *Legal Times*, June 29, 1981, p. 9.

12. *Congressional Quarterly, Nixon: The First Year of His Presidency*, Washington, D.C.: CQ Press, 1970, p. 81-A.

13. See Nixon, *RN*.

14. Hess, *Organizing*, p. 131.

15. Nixon, *RN*, p. 767.

16. Hess, *Organizing*, p. 129.

17. Rowland Evans, Jr., and Robert D. Novak, *Nixon in the white House: The Frustration of Power*, New York: Random House, 1971, p. 241.

18. Nixon's changes in the role and scope of OMB, his budget, and his impoundment actions led to a sharp congressional response. In 1974, Congress passed the Budget and Impoundment Control Act. The act established the Congressional Budget office and limited OMB's impoundment authority. The statute required Senate confirmation of the nominees for director and deputy director of OMB and enhanced the GAO's authority by providing the GAO with power to oversee the actions of federal administrative agencies. See Margaret J. Wyszomirski, "The De-Institutionalization of Presidential Staff Agencies," 42 *Public Administration Review*, No. 5, September-October 1982, p. 450, and Morton Rosenberg, "Beyond the Limits of Executive Power," 80 *Michigan Law Review*, No. 2, December 1981, pp. 223-224.

19. Gerald R. Ford, *A Time to Heal*, New York: Harper & Row, 1979, p. 271.

20. James C. Miller and Bruce Yandle, ed., *Benefit-Cost Analysis of Social Regulations*, Washington, D.C.: American Enterprise Institute, 1979, p. 5.

21. See, generally, James C. Miller, "Lessons of the EIS Program," *Regulation*, July-August 1977, and Charles W. Vernon, "The IIS Program: An Assessment of the First Two Years," 26 *American University Law Review*, 1138: 1977.

22. Executive Order 11,821, November 27, 1974, in *Presidential Documents, Gerald R. Ford, 1974*, Washington, D.C.: U.S. Government Printing Office, 1975.

23. Three OMB staff were given the task of implementing the executive order. Vernon, "IIS Program," p. 1139.

24. Ibid., p. 1150.

25. Miller and Yandle, *Benefit-Cost Analysis*, p. 6.

26. Ibid.

27. Ibid.

28. Miller, "Lessons," p. 26.

29. Ibid., p. 16.

30. Miller and Yandle, *Benefit-Cost Analysis*, p. 7.

31. Miller, "Lessons," p. 19.

32. Hess, *Organizing*, p. 146.

33. Richard Neustadt, *Regulatory Reform: President Carter's Program*, Washington, D.C.: U.S. Government Printing Office, 1980, pp. 1-2.

34. Benze, "Presidential Management," p. 472.

35. Alan K. Campbell, "Civil Service Reform: A New Commitment," 38 *Public Administration Review*, No. 2, March-April 1978, p. 102.

36. Norton E. Long, "The S.E.S. and the Public Interest," 41 *Public Administration Review*, No. 3, May-June 1981, p. 305.

37. Bernard Rosen, "Uncertainty in the S.E.S.," 41 *Public Administration Review*, No. 2, March-April 1981, p. 204.

38. See Long, "S.E.S.," and Lasko, "Executive Accountability."

39. Thomas P. Lauth, Jr., "ZBB in Georgia State Government: Myth and Reality," 38 *Public Administration Review*, No. 5, September-October 1978, pp. 420-421.

40. Ibid., p. 420.

41. Alfred E. Kahn and Michael Roach, "Commentary: A Paean to Legal Creativity," 31 *Administrative Law Review* 1979, pp. 105-106.

42. Ibid., p. 106.

43. Kathryn Newcomer and Glenn Kamber, "Changing the Rules," pp. 12-13.

44. *Role of OMB in Regulation*, Hearings before the Subcommittee on Oversight and Investigations of the Committee on Energy and Commerce, U.S. House of Representatives, 97th Congress, 1st Session, June 18, 1981, Serial No. 97-70, Washington, D.C.: U.S. Government Printing Office, 1982, p. 27.

45. See, generally, Patrick J. Hennigan, "Politics of Regulatory Analysis," paper presented at 1981 session of Annual American Political Science Association, New York City, September 1981.

46. Neustadt, *Regulatory Reform*, p. 12.

47. Cutler, quoted in MacAvoy, *Unsettled Questions*, p. 28.

48. Newcomer and Kamber, "Changing the Rules," p. 13.

49. Long, "S.E.S.," p. 308.

50. Eugene Bardach and Robert A. Kagen, *Going by the Book*, Philadelphia: Temple University Press, 1981, p. 309.

51. Laura Weiss, "Reagan and Congress Planning Regulatory Machine Repairs," *Congressional Quarterly*, March 7, 1981, p. 412.

52. Long, "S.E.S.," p. 305.

4

President Reagan's Strategy for Curbing Regulatory Sprawl

It is my intention to curb the size and influence of the federal establishment.
—Ronald Reagan

Not a single new regulatory law was enacted during the year, nor was a major new regulatory program promulgated by a federal agency. It was the first year in several decades that the federal dog did not bite.
—Murray L. Weidenbaum

It has taken us nearly 20 years to establish a central review office in OMB which has the authority to curtail the promulgation of onerous regulations.
—Jim J. Tozzi

Since the Nixon administration efforts, three Presidents have attempted to impose greater coordination of executive branch rulemaking by centralizing certain kinds of judgments in the White House. Each succeeded in improving and refining this presidential centralizing tendency, but until the ascent of the Reagan management team, "prior presidential efforts to influence and control have been essentially hortatory interagency advisory and review systems lacking centralized control and enforcement authority or ad hoc intercessions into particular rulemakings by the President or White House staff."[1]

President Reagan, a fierce opponent of governmental regulations that burdened the free enterprise system, business, and the general public, came into the White House confronting three different kinds of regulatory problems: a rapid flow of new regulations, a large stock of existing regulations, and the need to revise, with the Congress, existing statutes.[2] In an effort to deal immediately with the first problem, President Reagan, within hours of his assuming the powers of the

President, issued an EO that froze 172 midnight regulations of the Carter administration. (Since January 1981, 112 of those have gone through without change, 12 have been approved by the OMB with major revisions, 18 have been withdrawn, and 30 are still pending.)[3] Reagan's primary thrust has been to develop new strategies and improve old tactics of past administrations in a presidential effort to provide the nation, especially the business community (rocked by recession and inflationary spirals), with relief from the federal regulators. The language of regulatory reform has been replaced with the language of regulatory relief.

REAGAN STRATEGY

"Regulatory Ventilation": The Basic Goal of President Reagan

"Regulatory ventilation," a phrase coined by OMB director David Stockman, reflects the Reagan administration's "new mindset" about regulation.[4] Key Reagan administration staff in 1981—Stockman, Miller, Murray Weidenbaum (chairman, Council of Economic Advisers), and others—brought new thoughts to the White House about regulation of the federal bureaucracy that, when implemented, would "purify, cure, or refresh" the regulatory process.[5] In January 1981, President Reagan stated that a top priority of his administration was the establishment of a new regulatory oversight process "that will lead to less burdensome and more rational federal regulation."[6] His victory in November 1980 capped the ascendancy in national politics of conservative, pro-business political leaders. Reagan's response to the perceived excesses and irrationality of the regulatory process was to implement a wholesale reform of the federal executive agency regulatory process. ("For policy, not legal, reasons" the Reagan administration chose to forgo a confrontation between the Executive Office and the IRCs—and the Congress.)[7]

General Contours

One observer of the Reagan strategy stated that "the heart of the administration's developing strategy is to deregulate quickly and throw obstacles in the path of additional regulation."[8] A review of the Republican party platform statement on regulatory reform reveals the plan for the Reagan administration. The platform called for consolidation of agencies, deregulation, especially in energy, transportation, and communications, elimination of existing regulations that were outmoded, duplicative, or contradictory, support of congressional vetoes, sunset laws, and budgetary control of the bureaucracy, conduct of cost-benefit analysis of major proposed regulations to determine the impact on the economy, on public health and safety, on state and local government, and on competition, changes in APA, improved congressional oversight, and a reduction in the size of the federal work force.[9]

A review of Reagan's administrative regulatory activity since January 1981 indicates that there has been a fairly close parallel between the platform proposals of July 1980 and the decisions of the White House. Reagan Administration actions, in the form of budget cuts, EOs, and OMB benefit-cost analysis guidelines have had the practical effect of forcing federal executive agencies to review—with a view to eliminating—regulations already in existence, and halting or delaying new regulations until the OMB and the newly created Task Force on Regulatory Relief reviews them. In addition, he has appointed conservative, pro-business persons as heads of commissions and as administrators. "The President won't be naming zealots, people who view business as the enemy," said his then-executive director of the Task Force on Regulatory Relief, Robert C. Miller III.[10]

Another strategic move of the Reagan administration was to try to work with the Congress to change the organic statutes in order to reduce the potency of some independent regulatory agencies. "The President can't do a hell of a lot [with these agencies] unless the statutory standards are changed," said Miller.[11] There is also the need for congressional passage of an omnibus sunset bill.[12] "Absent this, undoing the past will most likely proceed at an agency-by-agency snail's pace."[13] As an attorney stated, "All the Republicans have to do is stop enforcement efforts and not initiate any new programs."[14] Through the use of management tools and through cooperative efforts with a Congress increasingly concerned about the negative impact of regulatory activities upon society, the Reagan administration has embarked on what the President himself labeled an "ambitious reform of regulations."[15]

Task Force on Regulatory Relief

One of the two primary foundation blocks of the Reagan administration's effort to control centrally the actions of the federal regulatory process was the creation, on January 22, 1981, of the presidential Task Force on Regulatory Relief. This task force, along with the other block (the President's EO of February 17, 1981), it was hoped, would "control the exercise of executive agency discretion under regulatory statutes."[16] Through "careful study and close coordination between agencies and bureaus in the federal structure," the task force would "cut away the thicket of irrational and senseless regulations," stated Reagan.[17] There were three essential duties of the task force: (1) to review major proposals by executive branch regulatory agencies, especially those proposals that have a major policy significance or where there is overlapping agency jurisdiction; (2) to assess executive branch regulations already on the books, especially those that are potentially burdensome to the national economy or to key industrial sectors; and (3) to oversee the development of legislative proposals in response to congressional timetables and, more importantly, to codify the President's views on the appropriate role and objectives of regulatory agencies.[18] The guiding principles of the task force reflected Reagan's plan:

1. Regulations are approved only when there is a compelling need.
2. The regulatory approach is taken that imposes the least possible burden on society.
3. Regulatory priorities should be governed by an assessment of the benefits and costs of the proposed regulations.[19]

The President created an agency that would review the actions of the federal executive branch agencies and determine which of the new and how many of the old regulations were truly needed, as well as cost-effective. It would, working in conjunction with the White House, the OMB, and with the agencies, determine the nature of new legislative proposals in the area of regulatory reform, and it would act as a brake on the actions of agencies in general.

The task force is led by Vice-President George Bush. In addition to chairman Bush, the members of the original task force were Donald Regan, Secretary of the Treasury; William French Smith, Attorney General; Malcolm Baldrige, Secretary of Commerce; Raymond Donovan, Secretary of Labor; David Stockman, Director, OMB; Martin Anderson, Assistant to the President for Policy Planning; and Murray Weidenbaum, Chairman, Council of Economic Advisers (CEA). Until he assumed the chairmanship of the FTC recently, James C. Miller III was executive director of the task force, as well as administrator of OIRA. The two other members of the task force group are C. Boyden Grey, who is also counsel for Vice-President Bush, and Rich Williamson, who is assistant to the President for intergovernmental affairs.

"Having the Vice President leading the task force makes a big difference," said Miller, who was on the COWPS staff during the Ford administration. "If it were just OMB [as was the case during the Ford administration when OMB and COWPS attempted to implement the IIS and EIS programs] versus the agencies it would be a loggerhead, it would be horizontal."[20] But with the vice-president, rather than the director of the OMB, as chairman of the task force, there is a vertical centralizing authority. The agency head, or bureau chief, in a dispute regarding a proposed regulation, for example, does not confront another department head; he or she has to confront the vice-president. There was, from the beginning of the task force's life, a basic political fact of life quite different from the regulatory control programs developed by Ford and Carter: buck the task force, and you are bucking the vice-president and the White House.

Another important characteristic of the task force is the linkage between the task force staff and the White House executive office. There is a fundamental interlocking between the two units: Miller was with OMB, Grey is counsel to the vice-president, and Williamson is a presidential assistant. The creation of the task force to coordinate efforts to curb regulations, in its makeup and in its scope of action, was quite different from Carter's RARG. The task force has political linkages with the White House and does not have the horizontal political characteristics of RARG.

EO 12,291: Federal Regulation

On February 17, 1981, President Reagan issued EO 12,291.[21] With its announcement, the Reagan administration officials hoped to complete the centralization of control process begun with the actions of the Nixon administration. The new EO established a centralized mechanism for presidential coordination and management of agency rulemaking activities "with substantial authority for intervention into and direction of the [regulatory] process at all stages."[22] With the new management tools in place, the thought was that federal agency rulemaking would be tamed dramatically. As one OMB senior official stated: "You're not getting any new 'turkey' regulations out anymore. The chances of burdensome or unjustified regulations coming out under Reagan's clock are nil."[23]

Parameters of EO 12,291

The order, written by Stockman, Miller, Weidenbaum, and Grey, key figures in the Reagan White House, is the centerpiece of the Reagan effort to centralize regulatory agency management control in the Executive Office of the President. The management tool established by the order, centralized review of agency activity by two agencies (OMB and the task force) politically loyal to the President, built on the Ford and Carter regulatory control EOs. However, by having Vice-President Bush, the chairman of the task force, as the resolver "of any issues raised under this order," the Reagan order advanced the role of centralized White House management to a much more sophisticated control level than appeared in the earlier programs.

The objectives of the order were, in the words of President Reagan, "to reduce the burdens of existing and future regulations, increase agency accountability for regulatory actions, provide for presidential oversight of the regulatory process, minimize duplication and conflict of regulations, and insure well-reasoned regulations."[24]

Section 2, General Requirements, declared that all regulatory decisions should be based on adequate information and that regulatory actions should not be taken "unless the potential benefits to society outweigh the potential costs to society." Agency policymakers were to "set priorities with the aim of maximizing net benefits to society." They had to take into account the condition of the particular industry being regulated, the national economy, and contemplated future regulatory actions in the regulated area.

Section 3, Regulatory Impact Analysis and Review, required every executive department agency to prepare a regulatory impact analysis (RIA) for every major rule it is considering.[25] These RIAs of all major rules must be submitted at two stages of the rulemaking process: with the notice of proposed rulemaking and with the final rule, to the director, OMB. Both submittals are prior to publication of information in the *Federal Register*. Preliminary RIAs must be submitted to OMB 60 days before the notice of the proposed rule is printed. Final RIAs must be submitted at least 30 days before publication. All other nonmajor rules must be submitted to the OMB at least ten days before publication.

In this preclearance procedure, much like the section 5 process developed by the DOJ to implement the 1965 Voting Rights Act,[26] the director of the OMB (delegating this to a deputy in OIRA) reviews the preliminary RIA and the final RIA to determine whether the agency has developed a cost-benefit analysis that describes potential benefits and identifies those likely to benefit; describes potential costs and identifies those likely to bear the costs; determines the net benefits of the rule; describes alternative approaches to the problem at lower costs with an explanation of the legal reasons why these are not acceptable to the agency, along with analysis of benefits and costs of each alternative approach; and explains, if appropriate, why the proposed rule cannot be reviewed in accordance with the EO. The OMB director, "subject to the direction of the Task Force, which *shall resolve any issues* raised under this order or ensure that they are presented to the President," is authorized to review these analyses and accompanying regulations. Unless he asks for additional information through consultation with the agency, the director must conclude the review of a proposed major rule within 60 days of submission, of a final rule within 30 days of submission, and of all other nonmajor regulations within ten days of submission.

If there are problems with a proposed rule, "upon the request of the director, an agency shall consult with the Director concerning the review . . . and shall refrain from publishing its RIA . . . until such review is concluded." The director, by requesting such a consultation, can delay the publication of rulemaking and the effective date of final regulations. As soon as the agency head receives word of the delay, the head "shall refrain from publishing . . . until the agency has responded to the Director's views, and incorporated these views and the agency's response in the rulemaking file."

Section 4, Regulatory Review, requires all executive branch agencies covered by the order to make a determination that the regulation they are proposing is "within the authority delegated by law and consistent with congressional intent." The agency must also state that the rule is based on the factual record and that full attention has been paid to public comments.

Section 5, Regulatory Agendas, requires the publication, by every agency, each October and April, of an agenda of proposed regulations that the agency has issued or is expected to issue, as well as currently effective rules that are under review by the agency. Agendas are required to contain a summary of each major rule being considered; the name and telephone number of an agency staff member working on the proposed rule; and a list of existing regulations to be reviewed by the agency and a brief discussion of each one. The director may request additional information from an agency about any of the rules listed in the agenda.

Section 6, The Task Force and the Office of Management and Budget, focuses on the relationship between the two executive branch units and on the powers of the director. The director, "subject to the direction of the Task Force," has the power to:

1. Designate any proposal or rule as a major one.
2. Prepare uniform standards for the identification of major rules.
3. Require an agency to obtain and evaluate additional information.
4. Waive sections involving RIAs.
5. Identify duplication, overlapping, and conflicting rules and require appropriate interagency consultation to minimize or eliminate them.
6. Develop procedures for estimating annual benefits and costs of agency regulations for the purpose of establishing a regulatory budget.
7. Prepare for the President recommendations for changes in organic statutes.
8. Monitor agency compliance with the order and advise the President accordingly.
9. Develop and implement procedures for the performance of all OMB functions vested in the director.

Section 7 sets guidelines for Pending Regulations. Agencies are required to suspend or postpone the effective dates of all major rules until the review has been completed. Exemptions are described in section 8. Any emergency rule mandated by statute or judicial decision is exempt from coverage; however, the agency head must explain the exceptional nature to the director, who can ask for consultation and additional information that could delay the effective date of the regulation. In addition, the director may, "under the direction of the Task Force," exempt any class or category of regulations from any or all of the requirements of the order.

Differences between the Reagan EO and Earlier Orders

There are a number of differences between the February 17 order and earlier presidential efforts to centralize control of federal regulatory activity.

1. Specific and detailed cost-benefit analyses of all major regulations are required "to the extent permitted by statute" (section 2). These can be waived by the OMB. (Indeed, of the 43 regulations classified as major by OMB to date, the Reagan administration waived the EO benefit-cost analysis requirement for 21.)[27]

2. Whereas earlier plans "depended wholly on hortatory means for achieving compliance,"[28] under the Reagan plan the OMB and the task force exert "unprecedented powers" over the development of agency regulations due to the preclearance tool found in section 3 of the February order.[29] James C. Miller III, who administered the IIS Ford program and is a key economic figure in the Reagan administration (he wrote and initially implemented the February order), said, noting the differences he experienced between the two programs, "I'd call up an agency [in 1976] and say, 'We just saw this morning in the *Federal Register* a regulation you published. We think it is a major rule which requires an IIS.' They'd say no and that was the end of the conversation. Today they say, 'Oh yes, we're very sorry, we weren't sure but if you think so, we'll prepare a RIA.' "[30]

3. Guidelines are developed by OMB to curb agency actions; consultations and the bargaining and negotiations that occur between OMB and the agency take place in the pre-public stage of the rulemaking process.

4. The order "places the onus on agencies to document the impact of their major regulations."[31]

The Reagan order is the most detailed, comprehensive, and mandatory regulatory agency activity review by White House personnel ever developed and put into place by a President. It is an effort to get agency policymakers in step with the goals and objectives of the chief executive and his economic advisers. It has had the effect, according to critics of the EO of turning these federal agency managers "from policy makers to policy pleaders in a tough, unsympathetic court."[32]

Supporters of the EO disagree. Weidenbaum stated that "the first line of defense against overregulation lies with the agencies themselves."

Miller has said that "the first line of offense in ferreting out ineffective and excessively burdensome regulations also lies in the agencies."[33] Said Miller, executive director of the task force until 1982:

Among the people whose behavior we're trying to influence are the GS-13s and -14s who draft the rules. The Executive Order says to them: even if you get a *nonconforming proposal* past your agency heads, even if you've captured them or just plain fooled them, that proposal is likely to be caught at OMB—and there's not a chance in Hades of your capturing these people. *So if you want to get ahead,* you're going to have to write new rules and review existing rules in conformance with the principles set forth by the President in the Executive Order. I believe that as internal agency procedures and the mechanism for centralized review settle into place, agency personnel will voluntarily comply.[34]

All agencies must now develop, unless they receive a waiver from the OMB director, systematic cost-benefit analyses of every major rule they would like to promulgate. As Miller suggests, OMB does exert control because it must review all regulations, major and minor. Thomas Hopkins, an economist at OMB, stated, "We provide the questions, and the agencies must get the answers."[35] And if the answers are not in conformance with administration objectives, then the regulation will not get by the OMB review, unless political pressures intervene and the OMB is overruled by the task force.[36]

Vice-President Bush in August 1981 said that the task force and the OMB are not "prejudging whether everything in these regulations is bad. We're trying to find a balance that has not been found in previous rules."[37] Finding the balance is the objective of the cost-benefit analysis. Cost-benefit "is used to improve agency decision-making, and this means getting the agencies to address the costs and benefits of their proposals . . . and avoid the tendency for agencies to serve special interests, often at greater cost to the public."[38]

All rules have to be justified in economic terms using the cost-benefit analysis. The Reagan OMB has argued that cost-benefit can be used to evaluate social regulations because "social problems and solutions take on an economic dimension, i.e., is it worth the cost? The old problems of scarcity and necessary trade-offs cannot be avoided."[39] It is somewhat more difficult to measure benefits and costs of clean air and clean water regulations, for example, "where benefits may be in terms of lives saved or pain and suffering avoided."[40] Such a benefit-cost analysis must take place, however, if the social rule is to be approved by OMB, unless the agency waives the requirement or is overturned by the task force.

Costs of social regulations have been calculated. One study concluded that EPA costs in fiscal year (FY) 1981 were $9 billion for air pollution controls, $4.7 billion for water purification standards, and $0.7 billion for solid waste treatment regulations.[41] Benefits of these kinds of regulations have also been calculated. For example, the MIT Center for Policy Alternatives concluded that $5 billion to $58 billion in health-medical benefits were not spent because of the control of air pollutants and that medical savings of $100 million to $1 billion due to water pollution control regulations (as well as recreational benefits of $9.5 billion) were realized by the environmental regulations. OSHA, the study calculated, prevented 350 work place deaths and about 60,000 work place accidents. The National Highway Traffic and Safety Administration (NHTSA), from 1966 to 1974, saved 28,000 lives with automobile safety regulations.[42]

To determine benefits in terms of lives saved, the agency must often take leaps of faith.[43] Roy Gamse, deputy associate EPA administrator for policy and resource management, described the process as applied to a water pollution effluent guideline:

If you want to quantify benefits, you must assign a dollar value to swimming or fishing. You must estimate the number of recreational visits there will be and how much they are worth. You must calculate the number of adverse health effects avoided and assign a dollar value to them. Each step is very uncertain. . . . The range of error is larger and larger. Is it really worth the large expense? . . . Why compound error by building sand castles?[44]

Although critics of the EO might argue the impossibility of assigning values to lives saved or injuries averted, OMB (and the February order) insists on quantification of benefits of all major regulations.[45] "Top administration officials seem to be *true believers* in applying strict economic tests to the government's regulatory endeavors."[46] For example, William A. Niskanen, Jr., on the Council of Economic Advisers, called himself "an advocate of more cost benefit analysis, most importantly in health and safety matters. Though people have backed off from using it here, no special conceptual problems stand in its way."[47]

The February 17 EO institutionalizes cost-benefit analysis for every major rule developed by an executive branch agency. The subsequent delay in rulemaking does not concern the Reagan administration. With this process settling into a routine pattern, it is made "almost impossible to issue an affirmative regulation, while at the same time making recision of regulations exceedingly easy."[48]

The Reagan administration has developed the politically astute practice of overlapping assignments in OMB and the task force for closer coordination in the effort to control the federal regulatory process from the White House. Absent large numbers of staff in OMB (there are only 70 persons to handle the RIAs), an effective war with the agencies is not probable.[49] Instead, a well-integrated and well-coordinated force, with agreed-on objectives and definitions, responds to agency initiatives.

There is an ideological linkage in that the line and staff personnel of the task force and OMB are philosophically committed to the notion of cost-benefit and the presidential view that there have been "irrational and senseless regulations" that must be rolled back and halted. "While previous efforts have failed to manage the proliferation of federal regulations," said Reagan when he issued the 2/17 EO, with the linkage of these two White House agencies, there will be the "establishment of central regulatory oversight at the highest level."[50]

This high-level linkage has the consequence of "stiffening the back of an agency head who's been pressured by a constituent," said Weidenbaum.[51] With the cost-benefit requirement and the presidential loyalty of OMB director Stockman and others implementing the EO, it is extremely difficult to imagine a regulation's getting approved that is not cost-efficient and in line with presidential objectives in that policy area, unless policy reasons dictate approval. Such is the character of White House clout after the announcement of the 2/17 order.

There is no doubt that the 2/17 order developed a centralized review mechanism in the White House with the power to "crack the whip" to bring agencies in line with Reagan objectives.[52] The 2/17 order has been characterized by William A. Butler, general counsel to the 430,000-member Audubon Society, as amounting to a "power play that shifts power from the regulatory agencies to the OMB."[53]

Agency heads must now decide how to conform to Reagan's goals and objectives. They will operate with a diminished expectation of influence over the direction of national policies."[54] EO 12,291 has made agency personnel uncomfortable; the mood in the agencies runs from "cautious pessimism to downright gloom."[55] Agency heads must continuously take cues from OMB and the task force, which will lead to delay and withdrawal of final regulations that have not been approved by the OMB. (See figure 2.) Commenting on the minimum time period for major regulations, 210 days if there are no consultations or requests for additional information by the director, Miller said: "We think the time is necessary—and well worth it—to make sure that new rules do more good than harm."[56]

Vice-President Bush pointed out in June 1981 that "the Reagan Administration has succeeded in *slowing the pace* of regulatory activity and its reviews of agency rules promises to save the private sector several billion dollars." Bush estimated that about 100 major regulations would be reviewed by OMB by the end of 1981.[57] As of January 1982 OMB had received over 2,700 rules for review; all but 5 percent were approved by the director. (The first federal agency to receive approval of a major rule by the OMB was the U.S. Postal Service. After consultations

Figure 2
EO 12,291: OMB and Agency Rulemaking

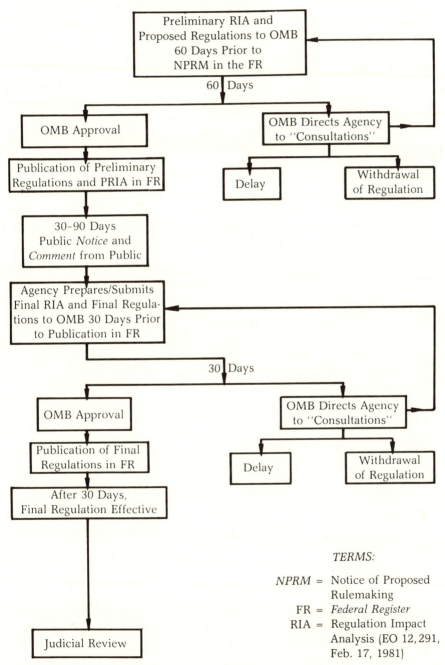

Preliminary RIA and Proposed Regulations to OMB 60 Days Prior to NPRM in the FR	

60 Days

OMB Approval

OMB Directs Agency to "Consultations"

Publication of Preliminary Regulations and PRIA in FR

Delay

Withdrawal of Regulation

30–90 Days Public *Notice* and *Comment* from Public

Agency Prepares/Submits Final RIA and Final Regulations to OMB 30 Days Prior to Publication in FR

30 Days

OMB Approval

OMB Directs Agency to "Consultations"

Publication of Final Regulations in FR

Delay

Withdrawal of Regulation

After 30 Days, Final Regulation Effective

Judicial Review

TERMS:

NPRM = Notice of Proposed Rulemaking
FR = *Federal Register*
RIA = Regulation Impact Analysis (EO 12,291, Feb. 17, 1981)

with OMB, its voluntary nine-digit zip code regulation was determined by the director to provide more benefits to the society than costs.)[58]

Also in June 1981 another form of OMB control over agencies appeared when the agency published its *Interim RIA Guidance* booklet. Some of the guidelines for developing the cost-benefit analysis follow:

- When costs and benefits cannot be measured in monetary terms, they must be "described in detail and quantified to the maximum extent possible."
- Agencies must state the "net benefits" of a major rule by subtracting the "monetary social cost estimate" from the monetary benefit estimate.
- A detailed statement must be prepared for each regulation, analyzing the need for each regulation, including alternative approaches—no action or solutions outside the reach of the agency, examining "market-oriented ways of regulation."[59]

Some agency heads voiced displeasure with the guidelines to OMB, claiming generality, increased paperwork, and economic jargon of the guidelines.[60] The language has not been modified; it serves to delay further and slow the pace of the rulemaking process.

OMB: Other Controls over Regulatory Agencies

In addition to the creation of the task force and the 2/17 order, both actions involving the use of the OMB to implement regulatory policy, the more traditional powers of the OMB have been used aggressively by David Stockman in his efforts to control regulatory actions. Some of the primary functions of the OMB, established in 1921 as the Bureau of the Budget, are preparation of the federal budget, including the budgets of all regulatory agencies (independent commissions and executive department agencies); improving efficiency of government services; expanding the coordinating mechanisms among agencies; promoting the development of improved plans of administrative management; program evaluations; and program performance data.[61]

The OMB's most important function, according to Stockman, is to control federal spending.[62] As a "full partner in the policy process," the OMB has been involved in the federal budgetary process.[63] More recently with the passage of the Paperwork Reduction Act and the Regulatory Flexibility Act, the OMB has gotten involved with federal agencies in other-than-budgetary matters. OIRA was created in 1980 to perform the additional monitoring responsibilities thrust on OMB. The office was given the authority to review federal regulations, including those developed by IRCs, that contain "a record keeping or recording requirement" in order to reduce the paperwork burden on the public by 15 percent.[64] This office is the unit in OMB responsible for implementing the 2/17 order. It assists the task force in conducting an omnibus review

Table 5
Change in Employment for Twenty-Eight Regulatory Agencies

Agency	Permanent Full-Time Positions			Percent Increase (Decrease)
	1981	1982	1983	1981–83
Consumer Product Safety Commission	812	631	577	(28.9)
Food and Drug Administration	7,521	7,142	7,169	(4.7)
Antitrust Division	939	829	789	(16.0)
Federal Railroad Administration	431	421	445	3.2
National Highway Traffic Safety Administration	797	686	686	(13.9)
Bureau of Alcohol, Tobacco, and Firearms	3,671	2,454	[2,450]*	(33.3)
TOTAL, *Consumer Safety & Health*	14,171	12,163	12,116	(14.5)
Mine Safety & Health Administration	3,808	3,471	2,996	(21.3)
Occupational Safety & Health Administration	3,009	2,354	2,354	(21.8)
Equal Employment Opportunity Commission	3,412	3,316	3,278	(3.9)
National Labor Relations Board	3,213	3,213	3,213	—
TOTAL, *Job Safety & Other Working Conditions*	13,442	12,354	11,841	(11.9)
Energy Programs, Department of Commerce	[429]ᵇ	159	135	(68.5)
Office of Surface Mining	1,036	737	638	(38.4)
Environmental Protection Agency	9,799	9,243	8,054	(17.8)
Nuclear Regulatory Commission	3,029	3,325	3,303	9.0
TOTAL, *Energy & the Environment*	14,293	13,464	12,130	(15.1)
Comptroller of the Currency	3,071	3,071	2,925	(4.8)
Federal Deposit Insurance Corporation	3,554	3,521	3,550	(0.1)
Federal Home Loan Bank Board	1,440	1,463	1,465	1.7
National Credit Union Administration	601	600	574	(4.5)
TOTAL, *Finance & Banking*	8,666	8,655	8,514	(1.8)
Civil Aeronautics Board	650	505	427	(34.3)
Commodity Futures Trading Commission	550	550	550	—
Federal Communications Commission	2,004	1,862	1,602	(20.1)
Federal Energy Regulatory Commission	1,607	1,648	1,789	11.3
Federal Maritime Commission	306	306	290	(5.2)
Interstate Commerce Commission	1,836	1,653	1,450	(21.0)
TOTAL, *Industry-Specific Regulation*	6,953	6,524	6,108	(12.2)

Table 5—*Continued*

Agency	Permanent Full-Time Positions			Percent Increase (Decrease) 1981–83
	1981	1982	1983	
Patent & Trademark Office	2,834	2,864	3,151	11.2
Federal Election Commission	235	202	212	(9.8)
Federal Trade Commission	1,587	1,380	1,235	(22.2)
Securities & Exchange Commission	1,928	1,860	1,765	(8.4)
TOTAL, *General Business*	6,584	6,306	6,363	(3.4)
TOTAL, TWENTY-EIGHT AGENCIES	64,109	59,466	57,072	(11.0)

Source: Center for the Study of American Business.

[a]Staffing distributed to Customs Service and Secret Service.
[b]Economic Regulatory Administration, Department of Energy.

of the organic statutes in order to make recommendations to the legislature for modifying these laws.

The budgetary process is being used as a way of controlling the regulatory agencies, particularly the IRCs. In all the Reagan budgets thus far (1984), "proposed cuts in funding for regulatory agencies were among the most controversial items. The budget and staff reductions for the Federal Trade Commission, Consumer Product Safety Commission, and similar agencies seemed designed not merely to save money, but to alter the fundamentals of policy."[65] Table 5 shows projected cuts in regulatory staffs totaling 11 percent.

During the early 1970's, most federal regulatory agencies nearly doubled the size of their staffs. In the Reagan administration's three fiscal year budgets, 1981-1983, staff size has shrunk at about the same rate, 16 percent, that it was growing in the previous decade.[66] Significant reductions in regulatory agency budgets were clearly "a key element of the administration's policies on regulation." In FY 1980, employment in 24 federal regulatory agencies totaled 72,835 and their budgets totaled $8.8 million; in FY 1983, the numbers, respectively, were 64,813 and $7.6 million.[67] These figures clearly illustrate this budgetary strategy of the Reagan administration: cutting back budgets and personnel will produce regulatory relief. Without sufficient personnel to handle the substantive mission of the regulatory agency and without economic analysts in the federal agencies to do the benefit-cost analyses required by the EO, there is some degree of agency inactivity in section 553 rule-making. The percentage change, between the last year of the Carter administration and the first year of the Reagan administration, in the number of proposed rules and final rules was a – 38 percent in proposed rules (from 446 to 276) and a −27 percent in the number of final rules (647 to 471).[68]

To the extent that the OMB has such control over the agency's budget, agencies generally try to establish good relations with the OMB.[69] Given the additional responsibilities of OMB under the Reagan administration (as well as the administration of the 1980 Carter legislaton on paperwork and regulatory flexibility), the OMB has assumed a major role in the Reagan strategy on centralizing control of federal regulatory agencies in the White House.

Reagan's Political Appointees

A fourth major strategy of the Reagan administration is the appointment of Reagan loyalists to key positions in the federal regulatory agencies, including the IRCs. Personnel change is an important factor in regulatory reform; it can hasten the policy shifts desired by a new President, especially when the election brings about partisan change in the White House.[70]

A President "cannot achieve management, policy, or program control unless [he has] established political control."[71] The Reagan appointees "are reverse images of their predecessors—they are persons who will make regulatory reform one of their primary missions."[72] Reagan appointed "people to these commissions who share his regulatory philosophy."[73] In Congress, the cry has been to upgrade the quality of the appointees. "No amount of improvements in organizations, procedure, or substantive mandate of the agencies can overcome regulatory problems if inadequate appointments are made in the first place," concluded a Senate study in 1977.[74]

Dianna Hoffman, writing in *Legal Times* about the poor quality of the Reagan appointees, suggested that the President's domestic staff intentionally selected persons who were purely political and had no knowledge or just slight familiarity with the agency's operations in order further to centralize control at the White House and at the OMB.[75] If welfare policy is established in the White House, for example, what is needed in the agency is a caretaker, not a policymaker. What is needed, in sum, is a good political appointee who will respond to the initiatives of OMB staff and other political staff in the White House by carrying them out quickly. This initiative could be a dismantling of an agency, deregulation proposals, or the modification, withdrawal, or ignoring of regulations.

Summary of Reagan Strategies to Curb Regulatory Sprawl

President Reagan introduced considerable change in regulatory reform presidential strategies. The creation of the task force, headed by the

Vice-President, "has lent the war on rules the patina of a top-priority project."[76] The EO gave the OMB staff, led by Chris DeMuth, administrator of OIRA (the office in OMB that actually implements the EO), extensive managerial power to coordinate agency activities. The benefit-cost analytical requirement has the potential for setting up a standardized analytical measurement for all major regulations.

In addition, the presidential policy of reducing the budgets and the staff of major regulatory agencies has had the effect of slowing down the regulatory process. Political appointees in major regulatory agencies have followed the presidential lead and have slowed down in the enforcement of certain regulations, such as the National Highway Traffic Safety Administration's efforts to kill the air bag rule (standard 208).[77] In the spring of 1983, however, the U.S. Court of Appeals, D.C. Circuit, ruled that the Reagan administration had illegally revoked the 1977 regulations that called for installation of passive restraints. In June, the U.S. Supreme Court unanimously upheld the U.S. Court of Appeals. In *Motor Vehicle Manufacturers Association of U.S. v. State Farm Mutual*, 51 *LW* 4953 (1983), the Supreme Court called the NHTSA's action "arbitrary and capricious" and ordered the agency to consider the issue further. There has not been any effort to change substantive laws in the Congress. (An effort to amend the Clean Air Act in the Congress was one of Reagan's failures in his first year in the White House.)

The basic signal from the Reagan White House was that it would do everything possible to regulate less by slowing down the pace of producing regulations through the section 553 rulemaking process. The goal: fewer regulations with a more limited reach—reviewed by an agency, OIRA (OMB) in the White House. Some critics have already expressed grave concern about the impact of these changes: "The new rules will likely alter the machinery of government. . . . Program managers in government will operate with a diminished expectation of influence over the direction of national policies regardless of the occupant of the White House."[78] One possible reaction, suggested by Antonin Scalia, is agency return to rulemaking through adjudication: "It seems inevitable that the recent encumberment of rulemaking will produce a renaissance of the previously favored mode of making law and policy—a movement back to basics, to adjudication."[79] This possible agency response to presidential efforts to curb regulatory rules is, however, being challenged in the federal courts at this time and may not be the answer to the agency manager's dilemma.

While there has been some success at slowing down the pace of regulatory activity, there are some practical problems the Reagan administration has not yet resolved: control of the IRCs, congressional plans for regulatory reform that may conflict with the actions of the Reagan administration, and judicial decisions and their impact on cost-benefit analysis and the informal consultations that take place between OMB and the agency (and between the OMB staff and other, unknown persons who have an interest in the regulation under examination).

SOME OBSTACLES IN REAGAN'S EFFORTS TO CONTROL THE REGULATORY PROCESS

The IRCs

"When an agency [IRC] is engaged in general policy making," stated Chris DeMuth, administrator of OMB's OIRA, "it has to be responsible to the President."[80] IRCs have existed since the creation of the Interstate Commerce Commission by Congress in 1887. IRCs are hybrid political actors, structurally isolated from most of the other operations of the executive branch of government. Created by Congress, each commission has from 5 to 11 commissioners selected by the President, with the advice and consent of the Senate. They serve a set term of office during which the commissioner cannot be removed by the President except for cause.

There are numerous controls on the activities of the IRCs, although the Reagan administration would like to provide more centralized control over them in the near future. Congress establishes their missions and, theoretically, has oversight responsibilities; it can review their actions to make sure the commission is performing the mission set out for it by Congress. The GAO is responsible for reviewing their information-gathering plans; the OMB examines and revises IRC budget requests, subject to adoption by Congress. The OMB also reviews recommendations for changes in the IRC statutes and, due to 1980 legislation, examines their paperwork requirements for the regulated audiences to ensure that there is a reduction in the paperwork load. The DOJ works with the IRC staff to coordinate and conduct litigation when adjudication is necessary. And the President, with the advice and consent of Congress, appoints the commissioners.[81]

The Reagan policy planners did not think that these controls were effectively constraining the IRCs from publishing regulations that did not conform to the economic and social policies of the Reagan administration. Independence of the IRCs leads to the protection of special interests by these units; the Reagan policy has been to break down this balkanization of the regulatory process. At one point, the administration came close to including the independents in the 2/17 order, but "it chose not to apply the Executive Order to the Independent Regulatory Commissions for policy—not legal—reasons," said former OMB administrator Miller recently.[82]

Larry Sims, acting head of the Office of Legal Counsel, DOJ, prepared a DOJ memorandum, dated February 12, 1981, that brought the Reagan administration "on the brink of asserting authority to require the IRCs to perform cost-benefit analyses of proposed regulations in accordance with (the soon-to-be-released 2/17 EO)."[83] He argued that such an attempt would probably be declared constitutional by the U.S. Supreme Court; however, "such an attempt to infringe the autonomy of the independent regulatory commission is very likely to produce a confrontation with Congress, which has historically been jealous of its prerogatives with regard to them."[84]

While the organic statutes, Sims concluded, did not imply broad presidential authority over the commissions, "we do believe that these statutes recognize the legitimacy of some presidential influence in the activities of the commissions, especially when it consists of a *coordinating* role with only an indirect effect on substantive policy making."[85] Since the 97th Congress debated this issue—review and control of IRC activity—the Reagan strategy was to wait and see about congressional actions and move cautiously in other areas to deal with the IRCs. It can "resurrect the Department of Justice reasoning if regulatory reform legislation does not allow the OMB to oversee independent regulatory commission compliance with cost-benefit analysis."[86] As Miller stated, it was a Reagan policy judgment not to include the IRCs in the 2/17 order.

The 97th Congress examined regulatory reform but did not act on the legislation. If passed, the Senate's Lexalt bill (S. 1080) would control IRC activity through legislative veto, cost-benefit analysis, and closer scrutiny by the judiciary. If legislation is not forthcoming, and if, for policy reasons, the Reagan administration does not extend the 2/17 EO to cover the independents, another internal White House memorandum, from OMB, suggested four alternative choices that the Reagan administration could take to assert control over the IRCs.[87]

Alternative 1 suggested using existing "IRC oversight mechanisms, however fuzzy, to assure OMB communication with the IRCs. The budget process can have a strong influence in shaping IRC policies, at least in general terms. To the extent OMB can minimize the distinctions between IRCs and other agencies in carrying out OMB oversight, OMB can gradually weaken IRC independence."[88]

Alternative 2 was OMB application of the 1980 Paperwork Reduction Act to control the substance of IRC regulatory policy. "Redirection of the OMB Paperwork Reduction Act . . . to control the substance of IRC regulatory policy related to information collection could involve, for example, disapproving a SEC ruling concerning company disclosure."[89] Alternative 3 was the use of a congressional veto. "Regardless of constitutionality, existing legislative veto proposals would delay issuance of regulations [and] increase congressional staff involvement in IRC management."[90] Alternative 4 was to have the President "seek alternatives to current legislative proposals [calling for legislative vetoes and judicial review] to give President authority to veto IRC regulations. . . . Until the issue of presidential oversight is raised directly, there will be little basis for any broader discussion of what forms of agency oversight are most appropriate for which branch."[91]

The OMB memo raised an important question for President Reagan: What is the best strategy for presidential oversight of the IRCs? Other than these alternatives to expansion of the 2/17 order, there is only one other approach and one political reality. Reagan can try to use his excellent persuasive powers, helped along by his appointees in the IRCs, to direct IRC behavior in his direction. If "Reagan will use a bit of moral suasion, . . . many of them [IRC commissioners] will get religion."[92] The political reality is that "the political system works; after the election of a new executive with a new thrust, the agencies tend to pull in their horns on their less popular proposals."[93]

The IRCs are a thorny problem for Reagan and his economic advisers. They want to redirect the regulatory process but feel constrained due to the policy implications of such a power move against the IRCs. For the time being, Reagan's strategy is to appoint supporters to key IRC positions, use the OMB to put pressure on the IRCs in numerous ways, and wait to see what regulatory reform legislation the Congress will produce. Reagan still has open options he can take to deal with the IRCs.

Congressional Efforts at Regulatory Reform

Since the Reagan administration entered the White House in January 1981, Congress has battled with the presidency over the question of who would be the basic controller of regulatory activity. The reason is power, for "both sides want to reserve the new powers for themselves."[94] Congressman John Dingell, the chair of the house subcommittee that has been examining OMB's role in regulatory control, has been very critical of the Reagan plan for reducing regulatory sprawl:

Unlike Reagan, I believe we can reduce regulatory burdens without totally displacing the discretionary authority of agency decision makers in violation of congressional delegations of rulemaking authority. . . . We can increase agency accountability without destroying safeguards against secret, undisclosed and unreviewable contacts by governmental and non-governmental interests seeking to influence the substance of agency action. . . . We can insure more reasoned regulations without the creation of substantively oriented procedures [cost-benefit analysis] designed to direct and control the rulemaking process.[95]

While Dingell and other legislators touch on interesting questions about the constitutionality of the EO, the fact is that the national legislature has not passed the regulatory reform measures discussed in the 97th Congress and will have to reexamine this theme in the next Congress.

Congress, like the President, "recognizes that the agencies have overstepped their bounds and that the American people are fed up with excessive regulations.[96] Although Reagan's economic and regulatory reform staff would like to see passage of an omnibus sunset bill, Congress is not about to go in that direction. Instead, during the 97th Congress (1981-1983), both in the Senate and in the House of Representatives less dramatic but very controversial substantive regulatory reform bills were introduced by Paul Lexalt (R-Nevada), S. 1080, and by Congressman George Danielson (D-California), H.R. 746. The Senate bill moved through committee fairly rapidly. It cleared the Senate Governmental Operations Committee on September 16, 1981, and passed the Senate in 1982. The House bill, however, was delayed, and the 97th Congress ended before final action was taken.

As it moved through committee mark-ups and modifications based on conversations with the White House staff, the Lexalt bill underwent a number of changes. In final committee form, its major features are stringent cost-benefit analysis of every major rule promulgated by all agencies, including the IRCs; more substantive judicial review of the substance of the regulatory policy; expanded public participation in the notice and comment stage of rulemaking; and a legislative veto.[97]

The Reagan administration cautiously backed the regulatory reform legislation in the Congress. The concern in the White House was that amendments would be added to the Lexalt bill that would interfere with Reagan's strategy for centralizing control of the agencies in the White House. "Right now, the Lexalt Bill is parallel to the Executive Order," said Miller in April 1981. "At the end [of the legislative process], it probably won't be quite so parallel."[98] What concerned Reagan administration advisers was the legislative handling of the questions of legislative veto, judicial review, and sunset legislation.

In March 1981, Attorney General William French Smith said that the DOJ "would argue before the U.S. Supreme Court that the legislative veto is unconstitutional if it intrudes on the power of the President to manage the Executive Branch."[99] Miller argued that the White House rejected only the legislative veto of executive agency actions; the legislative veto of the IRCs was not objectionable to the White House.

While Democrats and, surprisingly, some business interests want more judicial review and less executive oversight of the regulatory process, the Reagan administration is concerned with the emphasis the Lexalt bill places on more substantive judicial review of agency action. (The Danielson bill was held up because of this issue.) The administration wants as much White House oversight as possible "to allow it, with a minimum of interference, to erase rules it considers burdensome."[100]

Opponents of executive control want the courts to play a major role in the regulation of the federal agencies.

Without sunset legislation for all agencies, argues the White House, regulatory changes will have to come piecemeal, agency by agency. The White House urged, without success, the Congress to write into the regulatory reform legislation an omnibus sunset provision. The Lexalt bill does not contain this provision, and the Danielson bill was too bogged down on the question of judicial review to even raise the question of sunset legislation.

The basic question embedded in the legislative debate on regulatory reform is who should control the federal regulators: the courts, the Congress, or the White House? The question is difficult for the Congress to answer, given the constituencies that participate in such a discussion. Some legislators and interest groups are fearful of an all-powerful White House running the federal regulatory process; others are worried about the work load of the courts and the continued inability of the Congress to provide the proper oversight to ensure that the agencies do what Congress intended them to do.

The compromise bill reported out of committee and on to the floor of the Senate had the following general provisions: a one-house veto of IRC regulations; a two-house veto of executive department agency regulations with presidential authority to oppose the veto (this was changed in final markup to a two-house concurrent resolution without any formal presidential role in the veto process); the Bumpers amendment, which would give courts the power to set aside agency regulations by examining the record; cost-benefit analyses of all agency regulations classified as major unless the enabling statute "directs otherwise,"; and power to the President to delay final regulations he deems inefficient or costly.[101]

The House bill languished, in part because of a letter from the Judicial Conference of the United States to chairman Danielson on July 20, 1981. In a lengthy letter written by William E. Foley, director of the Administrative Office of the U.S. Courts, the conference objected to a number of provisions in both the Senate and the House regulatory reform bills. The basic concern for the Judicial Conference was that the bills would give to the federal courts substantive oversight responsibility that they are ill equipped to handle. "Judicial review should not become equated with complete oversight and redetermination of an administrative agency decision, including factual decision. . . . If Congress, as a matter of policy, wants this [type of] judicial review, then create a specialized Article I Court."[102]

Asking the courts to determine the scope of agency action, review the cost-benefit analysis, independently decide all relevant questions of fact and of law, and determine the meaning or applicability of the terms of an agency action (beside involving the courts in substantive agency oversight) would overwhelm the courts, the letter concluded: "It will generate new cases and will require more extensive judicial analyses than Congress intends or is practicable for federal courts to undertake. . . . Congress would impose an unmanageable burden upon the judiciary. . . . It is a difficult and time-consuming, if not impossible, task."[103] Congressman Danielson's response to the comments was that he would "drag his heels on moving the legislation through because the legislation would overwhelm the courts with litigation."[104]

If the Congress does not come up with legislation that deals with the problem of the IRCs or if it comes up with a solution unacceptable to the President, Reagan will strike on his own in his effort to deal with the IRCs, even if this means the veto of legislation created by Congress. The administration "would be compelled to oppose any congressional veto provision that applied to executive branch agencies," said Miller. "The responsibility for centralized oversight and the discretion to ensure compliance clearly rests with the President and his designees."[105]

JUDICIAL DECISIONS
AFFECTING THE REAGAN PROGRAM

The U.S. Supreme Court's
Benzene and Cotton Dust Decisions

The Benzene Standard Opinion

The Occupational Safety and Health Act of 1970 gives broad power to the secretary of labor to develop health and safety regulations for the workshops in our society. Until the 1980 Supreme Court opinion, *Industrial Union Department, AFL-CIO v. American Petroleum Institute*, federal courts, including the U.S. Supreme Court, have consistently shown deference to agency policymaking. However, in the *Industrial Union* case, a plurality of the Court invalidated the Occupational Safety and Health Administration (OSHA) health regulations limiting worker exposure to benzene, a chemical carcinogen. In a judgment of the U.S. Supreme Court, the plurality found that the OSHA benzene standard was not supported by an agency finding of fact that worker exposure posed a "significant risk" to their health. *"Industrial Union* may herald a trend toward narrower construction of congressional delegations of power to administrative agencies. . . . [This may have the salutary effect of forcing Congress to decide more explicitly how its statutes are administered."[106]

Industrial Union revolved around the meaning of two sections of the Occupational Safety and Health Act of 1970: section 3(8) and section 6(b)(5). Section 3(8) stated that a health standard is "one which requires conditions *reasonably necessary* or appropriate to provide safe and healthful employment and places of employment." Section 6(b)(5) states that the secretary of labor sets standards "which assures, *to the extent feasible*, on the basis of the best evidence, that no employee will suffer material impairment of health or functional capacity, even if such employee has regular exposure to the hazard dealt with by the standard."[107]

OSHA, finding linkages between benzene and leukemia, promulgated a standard reducing the amount of benzene in the workplace air from 10 parts per million (ppm) to 1 ppm. On pre-enforcement review of the standard in the federal courts, the affected industries argued that the statute required the OSHA to develop a cost-benefit analysis to justify the new regulation. The government argued that the statute gave OSHA the responsibility to develop standards that would reduce exposure to such toxic chemicals to a safe level without regard for costs and benefits balancing. The U.S. Court of Appeals invalidated the standard on two grounds: OSHA does not have unbridled discretion; it did not show that the standard was "reasonable necessary"; (2) the secretary of labor was under the duty to determine whether the unexpected benefits bore a reasonable relationship to the costs it imposed on the industry. On appeal to the U.S. Supreme Court, a divided court affirmed the judgment of the lower federal court.

Justice John P. Stevens, in a written judgment of the U.S. Supreme Court, joined by Chief Justice Warren Burger and Justice Potter Stewart, concluded that OSHA must show that the workplace is unsafe and that a significant risk is present to the workers. For a health standard, "reasonably necessary conditions" for that standard had to be present. It was determined by Justice Stevens that OSHA had to show a significant risk of harm to the employee in the workplace to satisfy section 3(8). That threshold finding of significant risk was the "reasonably necessary condition" before a health standard could be promulgated to deal with it. Furthermore, that health standard had to be shown on the basis of substantial evidence to reduce significantly the risk of harm.[108]

Findings of fact to support the health standard (the "significant risk" and the capacity of the regulation to deal with that unsafe situation) had to be part of the record. In the benzene case they were not; the 1 ppm standard was not supported by findings of fact but by a series of assumptions that some leukemia might occur at 10 ppm.[109] Stevens, however, did not state that there be a cost-benefit analysis developed by OSHA to justify the regulation. The secretary of labor did, however, have the burden of showing, on the basis of substantial evidence, that 10 ppm presented a significant risk. This was not shown; therefore, the regulation was invalid.

Justice Lewis F. Powell concurred in the judgment of the Court; he maintained, however, that the statute implied the necessity of some kind of cost-benefit analysis to accompany the regulation.[110] Justice William Rehnquist was the fifth, concurring, vote that settled the case. He argued that the section, 6(b)(5), was an unconstitutional delegation of legislative power to the executive branch.[111]

There were four dissenters: Justices Thurgood Marshall, William Brennan, Bryon White, and Harry Blackmun. The essential thrust of the dissenting opinion was that benzene standard was a valid OSHA regulation and that the Court was restricted by precedent from substituting its perception of substantive social policy in this area for that of an agency created by Congress to deal specifically with health and safety problems.

The plurality ignores the plain meaning of the OSHA of 1970 in order to bring the authority of the Secretary of Labor in line with the plurality's own views of proper regulatory policy. The unfortunate consequence is that the federal government's efforts to protect American workers from cancer and other crippling diseases may be substantially impaired. . . . The responsibility to scrutinize federal administrative action does not authorize this court to strike its own balance between the costs and benefits of occupational safety standards.[112]

The benzene opinion did have some impact on federal regulatory conduct. The plurality established that the threshold question of "significant risk of harm" in the workplace was one that had to be answered by the secretary of labor with sufficient findings of fact in order for a health measure to be valid. Absent that showing of significant risk, the health regulation would fail. The cost-benefit issue "was presented but not decided" in the 1980 case.[113] It became the question of law in the 1981 cotton dust case, *American Textile Manufacturing Institute v. Ray Donovan, Secretary of Labor*, however.

The Cotton Dust Standard Opinion

In 1978 the cotton dust standard was promulgated by OSHA to limit worker exposure to cotton dust, thereby cutting down the risk of contracting brown lung, a respiratory disease common to workers in the cotton industry. The standard set permissible exposure levels for different operations throughout the cotton industry. (The OSHA estimate of the costs for this one-time industrial change was $656.5 million to help the 35,000 workers currently in the industry, as well as thousands of workers who will enter this workforce in the future.) The petitioners were 12 individual cotton textile manufacturers and the 175-member American Textile Manufacturers Institute. They urged the federal court of appeals to invalidate the regulation because there was no significant risk to health present, and there was no cost-benefit analysis done by

OSHA to determine the cost-effectiveness of the health regulation. The court of appeals, addressing the cost-benefit argument, concluded that Congress had not required cost-benefit. Congress had written the "to the extent feasible" standard to guide OSHA in establishing health and safety standards for the workshop. On appeal to the U.S. Supreme Court, the court majority affirmed the lower federal court ruling.

In the 5 to 3 opinion, Justice Brennan for the Court majority found the lower court decision (that OSHA standards "must protect workers from health impairment subject only to the limits of technological and economic feasibility") to be an accurate assessment of the legislative intent.[114] Brennan acknowledged that the factual record reviewed by the secretary of labor indicated that cotton dust represented a "significant health hazard" to employees. With this threshold finding out of the way, the Court reviewed the OSHA interpretation of the 1970 statute. "OSHA interpreted the Act to protect against material health impairment, bounded only by technological and economic feasibility."[115]

"The principal question presented is whether OSHA requires the Secretary, in promulgating a standard, to determine that the costs of the standard bear a reasonable relationship to its benefits."[116] Looking at the intent of Congress when it passed the 1970 legislation creating OSHA, Brennan concluded that "Congress itself defined the basic relationship between costs and benefits by placing the 'benefit' of worker health above all other considerations save those making attainment of this 'benefit' unachievable. . . . Cost-benefit analysis by OSHA is not required by the statute *because feasibility analysis is.*"[117]

The plain meaning of feasibility is "capable of being done," stated Brennan. Any regulation that benefits the worker's health is placed above all other considerations unless it is not feasible. The Congress assumed, continued Brennan, that there would be substantial costs to the producers in the cotton industry: "Congress was fully aware that the Act would impose real and substantial costs of compliance on industry, and believed that such costs were part of the cost of doing business."[118] Congress, however, was primarily interested in having OSHA "create a safe and healthful working environment."[119] Turning aside the plaintiff's argument for cost-benefit analyses by OSHA, Brennan concluded by reiterating that "Congress chose to place pre-eminent value on assuring employees a safe and healthful environment, limited only by the feasibility of achieving such an environment."[120] Unless Congress and President revise the 1970 statute, OSHA is exempt from preparing cost-benefit analyses under EO 12,291.

The dissenters, Justices Stewart and Rehnquist, along with Chief Justice Burger rejected the majority argument. Stewart argued that there was no substantial evidence presented to indicate significant risk to cotton industry workers.[121] Rehnquist argued that since the Congress did not provide meaningful guidance, with respect to the meaning of "to the extent feasible" in section 6(b)(5), the Congress has exceeded its constitutional power to delegate legislative authority to nonelected officials.[122]

With the cotton dust opinion, the Reagan administration "takes it on the chin," wrote one commentator.[123] This is not necessarily the case, however, as suggested by the majority opinion. Congress can amend the 1970 OSHA to provide for cost-benefit analysis; the Reagan administration is working on that issue through the efforts of the Task Force on Regulatory Relief.

The Department of Labor's Solicitor's Office prepared an internal memorandum on options for OSHA based on the *Donovan* case in August 1981. After reviewing the principles that now govern OSHA policymaking, drawn from the Supreme Court opinion—significant risk, feasibility, and no cost-benefit analyses required—and conceding that the opinion "virtually precludes any utilization of cost benefit," the memo presented a number of options for consideration by the Reagan strategists:

(1) New rulemaking in the cotton dust area that "would minimize the impression that the Supreme Court decision seriously threatens the Administration's regulatory reform program." [These new rules would include the requirement for cost-benefit analysis.]

(2) A reconsideration of the existing standards that were affirmed by the federal courts "in a year or two, based on actual experience, will avoid the appearance of resistance to the Supreme Court's decisions."[124]

The Reagan strategists have already begun acting on option 2; in all likelihood, given the attitude of the President and the Congress, there will be a revision of the 1970 statute. For the time being, however, the Supreme Court has, for the first time, examined the issue of cost-benefit. All it has said, in effect, is that if the statute as written by the Congress does not explicitly call for cost-benefit analyses, then OSHA must do a feasibility analysis. If the statute is changed to include cost-benefit, OSHA must then follow the new congressional directions. As Robert V. Zener concluded, the cotton dust opinion "is a caution light more than a red light."[125]

Lower Federal Court Decisions

In a 1981 U.S. Court of Appeals decision, *Sierra Club v. Costle*, the federal court gave oblique judicial support for OMB preclearance oversight of executive department agencies under EO 12,291. In a case involving the EPA's procedures (conducting off-the-record conversations with President Jimmy Carter, White House staff, and Senate majority leader Harry Byrd of Virginia prior to and during the formulation of a rule), the federal court said that such conversations are not in violation of the Administrative Procedure Act (APA).[126] (The holding in this case, blanket approval of such EPA action, became the basis for a Stockman memorandum to the heads of all federal executive department agencies stating that OMB procedures "will be consistent with the holding and policies discussed in *Sierra Club.*")[127]

In another recent case, from the Ninth Circuit U.S. Court of Appeals, *Ford Motor Company v. FTC*, the federal circuit court ruled that the FTC had to use rulemaking procedures where a quasi-legal challenge could result "in a change or expansion of existing law." The FTC, the opinion concluded, exceeded its authority in following the adjudicatory policymaking route because the case was premised on a change in the existing law and would have had "general application" to other persons.[128]

An agency, in effect, is in a difficult dilemma.[129] If an agency head wishes to avoid the pitfalls, control, and delay provided in EO 12,291, there is the possibility of adjudicatory hearings, as suggested by Scalia, which are exempt from the 2/17 order. However, the *Ford* opinion, if upheld on appeal, severely limits that option. If upheld, the *Ford* judgment can close a loophole in the executive order that could have become an escape valve for nonconforming bureaucrats.

SOME CONSTITUTIONAL QUESTIONS RAISED BY THE REAGAN EXECUTIVE ORDER

Constitutional scholars,[130] legislative analysts,[131] and legislators[132] alike have criticized the Reagan EO as being an unconstitutional extension of presidential power in violation of the separation of powers inherent in the U.S. Constitution. Not only does the Constitution prohibit the centralizing of power that has developed through the OMB oversight and the requirement of cost-benefit economic analysis, these opponents claim, but also communications between OMB staff and interested pressure groups (concerned about the status of regulations that affect their activities) violate the strictures in the APA that call for public comment and notice of pending regulations on the record.

Arguments for Unconstitutionality

EO of February 17, 1981

Does the EO violate the concept of separation of powers? Does the President have the authority, either in the Constitution's grants of power or in statutes passed by Congress delegating powers to him, to enact an order that enables the White House to oversee and turn back proposed rules of federal regulatory agencies? For some, this is the question of the "facial legality" of the order.[133] There are no statutes that expressly authorize the President to displace agency discretion with cost-benefit analysis. Also, the Constitution does not "explicitly authorize the degree of presidential control of his subordinates' administrative discretion that order expressly contemplates."[134]

Although it is true that Supreme Court opinions have broadly defined Article II's oath of office—that the President "take care that the laws be faithfully executed"—these inherent powers of the President do not extend to oversee actions delegated to agencies by the Congress.[135] Congress created the statutes charging the federal regulatory agencies with acting to achieve certain policy goals. In many instances, the Congress, in creating the agency or the enabling legislation, has taken into account costs and benefits and has rejected that standard in order to have the agency deal with a substantive issue.[136]

More directly, Morton Rosenberg argues that Congress has clearly indicated in legislation that it did not want the President to have the power to review and nullify substantive regulatory policy. In the presence of legislation that clearly indicates that Congress was unwilling to allow the President to interpose in what is essentially a legislative oversight matter, an action of the White House that attempts such interposition is an unconstitutional abridgement of the separation of powers.

While there is a "zone of twilight"—a concurrent power shared by both the President and Congress in which each can act in the absence of initiative by the other branch—the Congress did not leave a congressional void in this area of regulatory agency controls.[137] In the 1970s, the Congress passed numerous pieces of legislation incorporating the idea of the legislative veto and in 1974 passed the Budget and Impoundment Act, a clear expression of congressional concern about executive efforts to intervene unilaterally in the regulatory reform arena.[138]

"Although the President is authorized to coordinate and supervise executive agencies," stated Rosenberg in reference to the *Meyers* opinion of the U.S. Supreme Court, "he has no authority to control executive agencies executing essentially legislative duties delegated to the agencies by the Congress."[139] In sum, the EO is an unconstitutional exercise of executive power in that it intervenes in areas in which the Congress has positively granted powers to agencies and has also, negatively, expressly legislated to negate such presidential excursions into essentially legislative matters.

Ex Parte Communications and Violation of the APA

A second basic condemnation of the review procedures established by the Reagan EO is the claim that private communications between White House senior staff in the Executive Office, OMB, and other White House offices would have a tendency to influence the OMB decision to approve or delay a proposed or final rule. Such a "hot-wiring of the regulatory proceedings at the agencies, . . . i.e., directing a result," in the words of Congressman Albert Gore, Jr. (D-Tennessee), is in direct violation of the concept of due process in agency rulemaking as embodied in section 553 of the APA (which involves public notice and comments about the proposed rules).[140] By denying to all the participants in the rulemaking process the information that passes between pressure group representatives and staff in the White House the EO is in violation of the guarantees in the APA. By acting as a central clearinghouse for all major regulations developed by agencies, the OMB becomes a critical access point for informal section 553 rulemaking, without providing the safeguards against ex parte communications.[141]

The following dialogue between a congressman and James Miller illustrates the concern that legislators have about this problem and the characteristic presidential response to this concern:

Mr. Synar (D-Oklahoma): Let me ask you one question: Are these *ex parte* communications ever going to be placed in the public record for all of us who are concerned about *why* and *how* decisions are made and the parameters of these decisions? Are they going to be made part of the record, such as the conversations you had . . . ?

Mr. Miller: If it is appropriate from a *policy standpoint* that they will be put in the record, if it is required by the law, they will be put in the record.

Mr. Synar: But now you are telling me you all will determine whether it is appropriate.

Mr. Miller: No, sir, I just said if it is consistent with the law. The APA is part of the law and we are going to act consistent with the requirements of the APA. If the communication is advice, or a privileged kind of communication that the President, the Vice President, or other members of the Task Force would not want shared with the public, then we will not share it. . . . However, if on the other hand, it has a factual basis—it is something relevant for the record itself—that will be transmitted.[142]

In a memorandum to heads of executive departments and agencies dated June 11, 1981, OMB director David Stockman reaffirmed the Miller position:

Regulatory relief is one of the cornerstones of President Reagan's program of economic recovery. As an important step in achieving regulatory relief, on

February 17, 1981, the President issued Executive Order 12291, "Federal Regulation." This memorandum explains how the Presidential Task Force on Regulatory Relief and the Office of Management and Budget (OMB) will communicate with the public and the agencies regarding proposed regulations covered by E.O. 12291. It also describes certain obligations of the public and agencies in this regard.

A major purpose of the Executive Order is to ensure that, to the extent permitted by law, regulatory decisions are based upon sound analysis of the potential consequences. Toward this end, a comprehensive factual basis is essential to assist agencies and other interested parties in assessing the economic and other ramifications of proposed regulations.

Under the Executive Order, both the Task Force and OMB will be reviewing factual materials related to regulatory proposals. Both the public and the agencies should understand that the primary forum for receiving factual communications regarding proposed rules is the agency issuing the proposal, not the Task Force or OMB. Factual materials that are sent to the Task Force or OMB regarding proposed regulations should indicate that they have also been sent to the relevant agency. Pursuant to this policy, the Task Force and OMB will regularly advise those members of the public with whom they communicate that relevant factual materials submitted to them should also be sent to the agency for inclusion in the rulemaking record. Accordingly, agencies receiving such materials from the public should take care to see that they are placed in the record.

Presidential Argument for Constitutionality of the EO

Defenders of the expanded role of the presidency in the effort to control regulatory sprawl focus on a broad reading of Article II powers, historical practice, and, more important, the practicalities of modern government. In the case of *Sierra Club v. Costle,* the U.S. Court of Appeals stated:

The authority of the president to control and supervise executive policymaking is derived from the Constitution; the desirability of such control is demonstrated from the *practical realities* of administrative rulemaking. Regulations such as those involved here involve a careful weighing of cost, environmental, and energy considerations. They also have broad implications for national economic policy. Our form of government simply could not function effectively or rationally if key executive policymakers were isolated from each other and from the Chief Executive. An overworked administrator exposed on a 24-hour basis to a dedicated but zealous staff needs to know the arguments and ideas of policymakers in other agencies as well as in the White House.[143]

Even the critic Rosenberg agrees that the "practical realities of administrative rulemaking . . . demand executive coordination and supervision." Given the single-mission character of agencies and the isolation the managers experience, "only the president with his overall view can provide the unified, coordinated direction necessary to integrate policy administration."[144]

A coordinator is needed to take care that the laws are faithfully executed. The Supreme Court, in the *Myers* opinion (1926), stated that the President "may properly supervise and guide their [executive officers'] construction of the statutes under which they act to secure that unitary and uniform execution of the laws which Article II of the Constitution evidently contemplated in vesting general executive power in the President alone." In a memorandum to David Stockman on February 12, 1981, a few days before issuance of the EO, the DOJ used the *Myers* opinion to maintain that the proposed EO was indeed constitutional.

In making the case for constitutionality of the proposed EO, the DOJ argued that the authority for the action flowed from Article II's admonition to the President that he take care that the laws be faithfully executed. "The 'take care' clause charges the president with the function of coordinating the execution of many statutes simultaneously. . . . Moreover, because the President is the only elected official who has a national constituency, he is uniquely situated to design and execute a uniform method for undertaking regulatory initiatives that responds to the will of the public as a whole."[145]

While subject to restraints in the form of legislation already passed by the Congress, "all of these requirements [in the proposed EO] must be followed 'to the extent permitted by law,' " concluded the DOJ.[146] But, commented the DOJ, Congress is aware that the federal agencies "perform their duties subject to presidential supervision on matters of both substance and procedure."[147] The DOJ concluded that the procedural innovation in the EO, the RIA assessing costs and benefits of major rules, was consistent with the general supervisory powers of the President. Substantively, requiring the agencies to use their "discretion in accordance with the principles of cost-benefit analysis," to the extent permitted by law, would not exceed the presidential supervisory powers under Article II.[148]

With respect to the question of private communications between members of the White House Staff (on the task force, OIRA, or OMB) or the President himself and private groups, and the possibility of bypassing the rulemaking process, the White House has tried to reassure Congress and the public that such an activity would not take place. In the June 11, 1981, letter to all heads of federal executive departments and agencies, OMB director Stockman directed that all "factual materials" received by the task force, OMB, or by agency heads must be made part of the rulemaking record. "Agencies receiving such materials from the public should take care to see that they are placed in the record," he concluded.

Chris DeMuth, the administrator for OIRA, the unit in OMB that does the actual screening of the RIAs, in recent testimony before the Manpower and Housing Subcommittee of the Committee on Government Operations, House of Representatives, addressed this question of ex parte information and the APA rulemaking process:

The basic principle is that any factual information given to OMB and the Task Force during rulemaking should also be transmitted to the agencies to be included in their rulemaking files. Because the rules issued by the agencies must be justified on the basis of the rulemaking record developed by the agency, it is crucial that such facts be submitted to the agencies concerned for inclusion in such records and consideration by the agencies.[149]

In addition, DeMuth created a public reading room in the New Executive Office Building, so that interested members of the public can read all outside information sent to OMB and the task force about regulations pending before the agencies and the OMB.[150]

Ultimately all discussion of the constitutionality of the President's actions rests on the question: If not the President, who can provide centralizing, coordinating authority in the effort to control regulatory sprawl? Certainly not a fragmented Congress. Certainly not the federal courts. Given the congressional void, whether for structural or personnel reasons, the President has had to act decisively in the matter of regulatory reform. Not to have acted would have been an abnegation of presidential responsibility.

SUMMARY

The Reagan regulatory relief effort is clearly the most difficult, most comprehensive procedural (RIA through OMB) and substantive (benefit-cost analysis) process developed by any President in the effort to "ameliorate three major deficiencies of our present regulatory scheme: singlemindedness, independence, and multiplicity of our regulatory agencies."[151] Using the OMB as the clearinghouse, the Reagan administration has created a dramatic centralization of federal regulatory agency oversight in OIRA, in OMB, in the task force, in the White House itself. These units, especially OIRA, "are the gate through which all important rules must pass—not once, but twice—on their way to becoming law."[152] This gatekeeping function is of fundamental importance.

Closing the gate drastically would lead to Congressman Gore's complaint: "This administration's real goal is to simply stop regulation."[153] Opening it up wide will lead to a return to the way regulatory agencies operated before the 1981 EO. How much or how little has the gatekeeping operation worked? A recent GAO study on the effectiveness of the EO, critical of OMB's efforts to subject all regulations to a rigorous cost-benefit analysis, concluded that "OMB has not consistently supported the integration of economic analysis into regulatory decisionmaking. Many of the regulatory analyses GAO reviewed, including several approved by OMB, do not provide adequate support for their inclusions. Cost benefit analysis was waived in 21 of 43 regulations classified as major and reviewed by OMB."[154]

The next chapter will examine one such interaction between a federal regulatory agency, OSHA, and the OMB, in an effort to understand the interactions between the two actors—and others—in this gatekeeping process. Suffice to say that the Reagan regulatory relief package is the most comprehensive one to date. It is the kind of effort that is needed in order to deal with the problem of regulatory sprawl.

NOTES

1. Morton Rosenberg, "Presidential Control of Agency Rulemaking," 23 *Arizona Law Review*, No. 4, 1981, p. 1200.

2. Antonin Scalia, ed., "Regulation: The First Year," *Regulation*, January–February 1982, p. 37.

3. Dick Kirschten, "President Reagan after Two Years," *National Journal*, January 1, 1983, p. 10.

4. Timothy Clark, "Do Benefits Justify Costs," *National Journal*, August 1, 1981, p. 1382.

5. *Webster's New Collegiate Dictionary*, Springfield, MA: Merriam, 1977.

6. Presidential memo, January 29, 1981, in *Weekly Compilation of Presidential Documents*, Washington, D.C.: U.S. Government Printing Office, 1981, pp. 73-74.

7. Scalia, "Deregulation HQ," p. 20.

8. Timothy Clark, "OMB to Keep Its Regulatory Powers," *National Journal*, March 14, 1981, p. 427.

9. *Congressional Quarterly*, July 19, 1980, pp. 2043-2044.

10. Emily Couric, "Altering the U.S. Regulatory Map," *Legal Times*, November 24, 1980, p. 1.

11. Ibid.

12. The Congress has not yet acted on these suggestions, but there have been agency-by-agency changes. For example, Energy Department officials have already rewritten "substantial changes in Carter administration Fuel Use rules. The new rules will be complete reversals of earlier ones." [*Legal Times*, May 4, 1981, pp. 1, 7] The Department of Justice is in the process of developing a more restrictive position on Freedom of Information.

13. Couric, "Altering," p. 9.

14. Ibid.

15. *Weekly Compilation*, p. 136.

16. Cass R. Sunstein, "Cost-Benefit Analysis and the Separation of Powers," 23 *Arizona Law Review*, No. 4, 1981, p. 1268.

17. *Weekly Compilation*, January 29, 1981, p. 34.

18. Ibid.

18. Ibid., February 18, 1981, p. 151.

19. Clark, "OMB," p. 427

20. Pierce and Hamilton, "Flypaper," p. 1637.

21. On January 29, 1981, President Reagan issued an EO freezing pending and proposed final rules from publication in the *Federal Register*. The freeze was for 60 days; 172 regulations were affected by the order. After March 30, 1981, 100 of the 172 were actually published; the remainder were either delayed or withdrawn. *Weekly Compilation*, February 2, 1981, pp. 73-74.

22. Rosenberg, "Presidential Control," p. 1199.

23. Michael Wines, "Reagan's Reforms Are Full of Sound and Fury, But What Do They Signify," *National Journal*, January 16, 1982, p. 92.

24. *Weekly Compilation*, February 17, 1981, pp. 124-130.

25. A major rule is defined in section 1 as any regulation that results in an annual effect on the economy of $100 million or more; a major increase in costs or prices for consumers; individual industries; federal, state, or local government agencies; geographic regions; or significant adverse effects on competition, employment, investment, productivity, innovation, or international economic competition. Section 6 empowers the director to designate any proposed or existing rule as a major rule. He also has the power to waive all requirements of the order with respect to other rules.

26. See Ball, Krane, and Lauth, *Compromised Compliance*.

27. Kirschten, "Reagan after Two Years," p. 10.

28. Scalia, "Deregulation HQ," p. 16.

29. See Ball, Krane, and Lauth, *Compromised Compliance*.

30. Pierce and Hamilton, "Flypaper," p. 1638.

31. Kosters and Eisenach, "Regulatory Relief," p. 22.

32. Newcomer and Kamber, "Changing the Rules," p. 17.

33. Scalia, "Deregulation HQ," p. 22.

34. Ibid.

35. Clark, "Benefits," p. 1383.

36. In a recent clash between OMB's OIRA and the California congressional delegation over the issue of navel orange production quotas (marketing orders filed annually with the U.S. Department of Agriculture), the shipping quotas were given preliminary approval by OMB. "Since the Reagan administration came to power, the orders have been a sore spot with OMB's deregulators, who contend that the quotas represent little more than an attempt to drive up food prices by artificially limiting the supply. . . . OMB officials began rejecting some marketing orders on the ground that they imposed more costs on the public than they repaid in benefits for the industry." However, the secretary of agriculture, John R. Block, in an October 8, 1982, letter to California growers, stated that the Reagan administration had a "renewed commitment" to the marketing orders. The approval by OMB came one month later. " 'OMB just got their wings clipped by the Department of Agriculture and others who wanted to do something for these guys before the election,' Lawrence (administration assistant to California Democrat George Miller) said. 'That's exactly what happened. It's a classic case of Administration rhetoric contrasting with reality.' " "OMB Free Marketers Lose a Regulatory Fight over Navel Orange Quotas," *National Journal*, December 11, 1982, pp. 2103, 2125.

37. Pierce and Hamilton, "Flypaper," p. 1637.

38. James C. Miller III, "Cost-Benefit," *Regulation*, July-August 1977, p. 26.

39. Miller and Yandle, *Benefit-Cost*, p. 4.

40. Ibid.

41. CQ, *Federal Regulatory*, pp. 40-41.

42. Fritschler, "Changing Face," p. 18.

43. Clark, "Benefits," p. 1385.

44. Ibid.

45. Ibid., p. 1383.

46. Ibid., p. 1382.

47. Ibid., p. 1383.

48. Clark, "OMB," p. 429.

49. Ibid., p. 425.

50. *Weekly Compilation*, p. 152.

51. Scalia, "Deregulation HQ," p. 23.

52. Clark, "OMB," p. 429.

53. Ibid., p. 429.

54. Newcomer and Kamber, "Changing the Rules," p. 17.

55. "Regulatory Watershed," *Legal Times*, November 10, 1981, p. 1.

56. Scalia, "Deregulation HQ," p. 18.

57. "Administration Boasts of Slowing Regulatory Pace," *National Journal*, June 20, 1981, pp. 1131-1132.

58. Clark, "Benefits," p. 1382.

59. "OMB Guidelines," *National Journal*, May 9, 1981, p. 845.

60. An example of the interim RIA guidance: "The monetary social cost should be subtracted from the monetary social benefit to obtain the monetary net benefit estimate (which could be negative). Any remaining non-monetary but quantifiable benefit and cost information also should be presented. Then, non-quantifiable benefits and costs should be listed, in a way that facilitates making an informed final decision. Where many benefits are not easily quantified, the results should show the cost-effectiveness of the several alternatives." Ibid.

61. A. Lee Fritschler and Bernard Ross, *Executive's Guide to Government*, Cambridge, MA: Winthrop, 1980, pp. 105-106.

62. Timothy Clark, "Reagan Gives OMB Sweeping Powers over Agency Rules," *National Journal*, March 25, 1981, p. 690.

63. Fritschler and Ross, *Guide*, p. 105.

64. *Weekly Compilation*, February 18, 1981, p. 153.

65. "Regulation and the 1982 Budget," *Regulation*, July-August 1981, p. 9.

66. Note, "Regulation and the 1983 Budget," *Regulation*, March-April 1982, p. 11.

67. See Kosters and Eisenach, "Regulatory Relief," p. 23.

68. Ibid., p. 22.

69. See Francis E. Rourke, *Bureaucracy, Politics, and Public Policy*. Boston: Little, Brown, 1976.

70. Scalia, "Deregulation HQ," p. 15.

71. Malek Report, in Thompson, *Classics*, p. 85.

72. Clark, "OMB," p. 426.

73. Scalia, "Deregulation HQ," p. 22.

74. CQ, *Federal*, p. 20.

75. Dianna Hoffman, "President May Regret," p. 9.

76. Wines, "Reagan's Reforms," p. 93.

77. Kirschten, "Reagan," pp. 8-9.

78. Newcomer and Kamber, "Changing the Rules," p. 17.

79. Antonin Scalia, "Back to Basics: Making Law without Making Rules," *Regulation*, July-August, 1981, p. 27.

80. Wines, "Reagan's Reforms," p. 95.

81. Congressional Quarterly, *Federal*, p. 18.

82. Scalia, "Deregulation HQ," p. 22.

83. Memorandum, Office of Legal Counsel, Department of Justice, February 12, 1981, reprinted in *Legal Times*, July 20, 1981, p. 9.

84. Ibid.

85. Ibid.

86. Ibid.

87. Memorandum, OMB, Oversight of Independent Regulatory Commissions, reprinted in *Legal Times*, June 1, 1981, p. 13.

88. Ibid.

89. Ibid.

90. Ibid.

91. Ibid.

92. Scalia, "Deregulation HQ," p. 23.

93. Couric, "Altering," p. 9.

94. Wines, "Reagan's Reforms," p. 95.

95. "Role of OMB in Regulation," Hearings, Subcommittee on Oversight and Investigations, Committee on Energy and Commerce, U.S. House of Representatives, 97th Congress, 1st Session, June 18, 1981, Washington, D.C.: U.S. Government Printing Office, 1982, p. 1.

96. Congressman Robert McClory (R-Illinois) quoted in Laura Weiss, "Markups Slated for Regulatory Reform Bill," *Congressional Quarterly*, June 20, 1981, p. 1100.

97. Laura Weiss, *Congressional Quarterly*, April 11, 1981, pp. 627-628, July 18, 1981, pp. 1291-1292.

98. Ibid., April 11, 1981, p. 628.

99. Ibid.

100. Ibid., p. 1292.

101. *National Journal*, September 19, 1981, p. 3. In *Chadha v. Immigration and Naturalization Service*, 634 F. 2d 408 (9th Cir., 1980), the Ninth Circuit decided that the one-house veto of INS judgments pertaining to suspension of deportation violated the separation-of-powers doctrine in that it usurped executive authority. This is the first major decision on the constitutionality of the legislative veto; the case is limited because the issue is a one-house veto of an adjudicatory hearing by the INS. Two recent circuit court decisions invalidated the legislative veto in agency rulemaking. The D.C. Circuit issued a ruling in *Consumer Energy Council of America v. FERC*, 673 F. 2d 425, 1982 and the Ninth Circuit Court struck down a legislative veto, on separation of powers, in *Consumers Union of the U.S. v. FTC*, 691 F. 2d 575, 1982. The Supreme Court examined *Chadha* during the 1982 term and upheld the Ninth Circuit's judgment that the legislative veto was unconstitutional.

102. William E. Foley, Director, Administrative Office of U.S. Courts to Congressman George Danielson (D-California), reprinted in *Legal Times*, July 27, 1981, pp. 20, 23.

103. Ibid.

104. Kim Masters, "Judicial Conference Report Slows Action on Regulatory Reform Bill," *Legal Times*, July 27, 1981, p. 1.

105. See *Legal Times*, May 18, 1981, p. 5, for interview with James C. Miller III.

106. "The Supreme Court, 1979 Term," 94 *Harvard Law Review*, No. 1, November 1981, pp. 242, 251.

107. Industrial Union Department, *AFL-CIO v. American Petroleum Institute*, 65 L.Ed. 2d 1010 (1980).

108. Ibid., at 1035.

109. Ibid., at 1042.

110. Ibid., at 1049.

111. Ibid., at 1054.

112. Ibid., at 1063, 1085.

113. *American Textile Manufacturing Institute v. Ray Donovan, Secretary of Labor*, 59 L.Ed. 2d 185 (1981), at 193.

114. Ibid., at 199.

115. Ibid., at 198.

116. Ibid., at 200.

117. Ibid., at 202.

118. Ibid., at 205.

119. Ibid., at 208.

120. Ibid., at 221.

121. Ibid., at 221-222.

122. Ibid., at 225.

123. *Legal Times*, June 29, 1981, p. 11.

124. Memorandum, Department of Labor, Solicitor's Office, Options for OSHA Based on the Donovan Case, August 1981, reprinted in *Legal Times*, August 3, 1981, pp. 18-20.

125. "The 'Cotton Dust' Standard," *Legal Times*, July 13, 1981, p. 13.

126. Michael Sohn and Robert Litan, "Regulatory Oversight Wins in Court," *Regulation*, July-August 1981, p. 17.

127. Ibid., p. 24.

128. Reprinted in *Legal Times*, September 7, 1981, p. 2.

129. Ibid.

130. See Kevin Whitney, "Capitalizing on a Constitutional Void: EO 12,291," 31 *American University Law Review*, No. 3, Spring 1982.

131. See Morton Rosenberg, "Beyond the Limits of Executive Power," 80 *Michigan Law Review*, No. 2, December 1981, his "Presidential Control of Agency Rulemaking," 23 *Arizona Law Review*, No. 4, 1981, and his "Report on Executive Order 12,291," *Congressional Research Service, Library of Congress*, reprinted in *Legal Times*, June 29, 1981, p. 16.

132. See Albert Gore, Jr.,'s comments, as well as those of John Dingell, in "Role of OMB in Regulation," *Hearings*, passim.

133. Peter M. Shane, "Presidential Regulatory Oversight and the Separation of Powers," 23 *Arizona Law Review*, No. 4, 1981, p. 1236.

134. Ibid.

135. *Myers v. US*, 272 U.S. (1926).

136. Rosenberg, "Beyond the Limits."

137. Ibid., pp. 199ff.

138. Ibid., pp. 223-224.

139. Ibid., p. 246.

140. *Hearings*, "OMB Role," p. 55.

141. Rosenberg, "Presidential Control," p. 1234.

142. *Hearings*, "OMB Role," pp. 56-57.

143. Ibid., p. 47.

144. Rosenberg, "Presidential Control," p. 1201.

145. Hearings, "OMB Role," pp. 153-54.

146. Ibid., p. 152.

147. Ibid., p. 154.

148. Ibid., pp. 154-156.

149. Statement before Manpower and Housing Subcommittee of the Committee on Government Operations of the U.S. House of Representatives, March 19, 1982, p. 6.

150. Ibid., p. 7.

151. Whitney, "Capitalizing," p. 649.

152. *Hearings*, "OMB Role," p. 10 (statement of George Eads, former member, Council of Economic Advisers, Carter administration, 1979-1981; also chair of RARG).

153. Ibid., p. 5 (statement of Congressman Albert Gore, Jr., D-Tenn.).

154. See GAO, "Improved Quality, Adequate Resources, and Consistent Oversight Needed If Regulatory Analysis Is to Help Control the Costs of Regulation," PAD-83-6, November 2, 1982.

5

Implementing EO 12,291:
The Politics of the Toxic
Chemical Labeling Standard

If we get good testimony, our hearings will probably be used as a basis for lawsuits challenging the President's authority to give such power over agency rulemaking to OMB.

> —Rick Graway, Staff Counsel
> Subcommittee on Manpower and
> Housing, House Government
> Operations Committee

There will be "significant political problems" if the toxic labeling proposal was sidetracked. "Labor has not yet been given a cudgel with which to beat this Administration. This [OMB refusal to preclear OSHA Chemical Labeling standard] would provide one."

> —U.S. Department of Labor official

A decision by Vice President Bush to override OMB objections to issuance of OSHA's proposed rule on chemical labeling . . . led to issuance of the controversial proposal. . . . Sources add that Bush received numerous letters from industry and labor groups requesting release of the rule.

> —*Inside O.M.B.*, March 26, 1982

With President Reagan's issuance of EO 12,291 in February 1981, the OMB was granted "unprecedented access to and control over the development of regulations by executive agencies."[1] This presidential action, and the creation of the Task Force on Regulatory Relief were the cornerstones of the administration's efforts to curb the outflow of federal regulations that were not necessary and cost-efficient. The bureaucracy within the OMB that is primarily responsible for administering the EO is a small 70-person staff in OIRA. The administrator of OIRA is Christopher DeMuth. Labeled a "principled deregulator" and a "free marketer"—that is, a person committed to the idea of the market's developing solutions to competition problems and who is deeply committed to the idea of cost-benefit analysis—DeMuth is also executive director of the presidential task force.[2] (The task force reviews the actions taken by the OIRA in OMB. A question posed by a House subcommittee majority staff attorney focused on this overlapping appointment: "Since DeMuth, who heads the OMB office which makes the final determination, is also the Executive Director of the Task Force, is the appeal to the Task Force a meaningful one?")[3]

In a recent essay, DeMuth validated the label given to him by scholars: "The greatest practical difficulties in applying economic reasoning to political decisions arise from its qualities of breadth, rigor, and disinterestedness."[4] At another point, he commented on another problem he has had to confront: "Imposing controls from within is politically thankless. . . . [OMB] disagrees with an agency's regulatory proposal: assuming OMB's view prevails, the administration has no good deed to advertise and OMB must enjoy its good deed in silence."[5] For DeMuth, the "overriding criterion" for OIRA reviewers "is that of economic efficiency or cost-benefit analysis."[6]

A key assumption made by DeMuth about the implementation of the EO's "economic assessment program" is that there is an essentially rational process inherent in cost-benefit analysis.[7] In addition "the presidency," stated DeMuth, "of all the offices in our system of government, is the one most suited to advancing a *consistent program* against narrow political pressures."[8] However, the White House is not immune from "narrow political pressures."[9] Can an OIRA economic analysis based on rational disinterestedness prevail over political pressures applied by the head of the executive agency who believes that the allegedly cost-inefficient rule the agency developed should be promulgated as a matter of sound public policy?

Another factor that may overwhelm the "rational disinterestedness" approach is, as DeMuth admits, the breadth of the cost-benefit analysis process itself and the fact that OMB-OIRA does not have the technical expertise to review the proposed regulation and its accompanying RIA. It is in this context that the cost-benefit analysis itself may "require discretionary judgment" by the OIRA staff, DeMuth, and others who ultimately review the OMB recommendation.[10] Finally, the staff views might not be unprejudiced and without bias. OMB-OIRA "may return the proposed regulations to promulgating agencies not because the social costs outweigh the social benefits, but because the proposals conflict with OMB's own organizational goals."[11]

In examining the OMB's efforts, through OIRA, to implement Reagan's EO 12,291, it is important to see how impartial and disinterested the OIRA economic analyses really are and to note the presence or absence of political pressures on the initial regulatory reviewers, OMB-OIRA, as well as the final reviewers (on appeals from OIRA judgments), the Task Force on Regulatory Relief, chaired by Vice-President George Bush.

CHEMICAL DANGERS IN THE WORKPLACE AND THE OSHA RESPONSE IN THE CARTER ADMINISTRATION

The hazard communication standard developed by OSHA in 1981, and revised by the Reagan OSHA administrator, Thorne G. Auchter, assistant secretary of labor for occupational safety and health (after the Reagan administration rescinded the earlier Carter administration proposal), will be the issue used to examine the character of Reagan's program to control regulatory sprawl. Not only is the issue an important one substantively, it is also the first major controversy between OMB-OIRA and an executive department agency, the Department of Labor, that moved to the Task Force on Regulatory Relief for arbitration by the vice-president and his task force members. (See Appendix B for documents mentioned throughout this chapter.)

The Need for a Hazard Information Standard in the Workplace

OSHA, created in 1971 after the Congress passed the 1970 Occupational Safety and Health Act (OSH Act), is charged with the promulgation and enforcement of mandatory health and safety standards "to assure so far as possible every working man and woman in the Nation safe and healthful working conditions."[12] Employers engaged in business affecting commerce are required to provide workers with a safe workplace and comply with safety and health standards developed by OSHA, promulgated by the secretary of labor, and administered by OSHA through workplace inspections and reviews of employer records.

During the first years of its existence, while developing and implementing safety standards, OSHA staff paid little attention to the health issue of consequences of toxic chemicals found in the workplace. These chemicals were an important source of chronic conditions such as heart ailments, kidney damage, sterility, and cancer. Although causality was not precisely determined, due to the long latency periods (20 to 30 years or longer) and the fact that workers are exposed to numerous toxic chemicals under varying degrees of exposure, it became clear to many in OSHA and in Congress in the mid-1970s that certain chemicals posed major health hazards that had to be corrected. Large numbers of laborers (OSHA estimated that 8.5 million to 9 million workers) were being exposed to chemical hazards produced by a large number of different products. According to the U.S. Public Health Service, every 20 minutes a new and potentially toxic chemical is introduced into industry.[13] There are over 600,000 different chemical products used by industry and the public. Thus this issue was an important one that greatly concerned the public. Each year 390,000 new cases of occupational disease occur; between 60 and 70 percent of all cancers are environmentally caused.[14] Furthermore, it is estimated by the National Institute for Occupational Safety and Health "that 100,000 Americans die each year from occupationally caused illness and disease."[15] Finally, many of these potential health hazards are unknown to the workers or to the employers. The manufacturers of these products are not supplying this hazard warning information because of unwillingness to reveal trade secrets and because of the costs of making this information available.

In 1976, the Congress held hearings on this issue. The Manpower and Housing Subcommittee of the House Committee on Government Operations, chaired by Congressman Floyd V. Hicks (D-Washington), held hearings on the issue in May 1976 and issued a report, *Chemical Dangers in the Workplace*. The core of the report was that the major cause of occupationally related illness, disease, and death was the consequence of exposure of workers over a period of years to toxic chemicals and that the presence of toxic chemicals in many industrial products was often hidden by the trade name of the product. The report's findings and conclusions pointed to the failure of self-regulation by industry and the failure by OSHA to focus on the development of health standards for the workplace: "OSHA has failed to implement [sections of the OSH Act] which requires that employees be apprised of and be protected from the hazards to which they are exposed and requiring employers to maintain accurate records of employee exposures to potentially toxic materials and to provide employees with access to these records."[16] The major recommendation of the subcommittee report was that OSHA should develop a regulation requiring mandatory labeling of toxic ingredients: "OSHA should develop a mandatory system of identifying toxic substances in the workplace. Knowledge of workplace dangers should not wait for the tortuous process of issuing standards on an agent-by-agent basis . . . and should issue standards . . . so that employees are aware of their exposure to potentially toxic materials."[17]

OSHA Response, 1976-1981

Toward the end of the Ford administration and throughout the Carter administration, OSHA began developing a comprehensive regulation requiring that toxic chemicals be identified by the manufacturer so that employers and workers would have knowledge of the hazards associated with such chemicals and take the necessary precautions when using them.

Consistent with the congressional recommendation that "the critical position of Assistant Secretary for OSHA should be occupied by a competent professional," President Carter appointed Eula Bingham, an industrial toxicologist, to the position of assistant secretary.[18] (The Reagan administration, consistent with the political partisans appointment strategy, appointed Auchter to this post. The Reagan appointee was a 35-year-old Florida construction executive who was Reagan's special events director in Florida during the 1980 campaign. He had no health and safety professional experience other than a brief appointment to the Florida Health and Safety Task Force Board in the early 1970s.)[19]

Due to "staff turnover and poor management of the standard-setting process, Bingham's OSHA waited until a few days before Reagan's inauguration to propose a hazard information rule in the *Federal Register*."[20] It was a complex standard that was proposed by the Carter OSHA on January 16, 1981: provide information to both workers and employers on the potential hazards of chemicals in their work environment through the following key mechanisms:

1. Coverage of all manufacturing industries and importers and repackagers of of chemical products and virtually all containers, including pipes and support systems such as pumps and valves.
2. Highly specific search and evaluation procedures required for hazard evaluation by all manufacturers.
3. Detailed labeling of chemical products with no adjustments for trade secrets.
4. Material safety data sheets (MSDSs) for hazardous chemicals filed in a central location if available or otherwise an information sheet with contents identical to the label.
5. Certification that a particular chemical does not pose a hazard, where applicable.
6. Extensive records on hazard search and evaluation procedures, to be kept for three years.
7. A phased-in compliance period of two years.[21]

Many concerns, both professional and political, were voiced about the Carter standard. Of particular concern to some, beyond the huge startup cost estimates ($2.6 billion) and the total present value cost of $22.8 billion, was the fact that the focus of the proposed standard was on the identification of chemicals rather than on communication of these hazards to workers and employers. The Carter proposal was printed in the *Federal Register* just days before the change in presidential administrations. Less than one month later, on February 13, 1981, President Ronald Reagan pulled this OSHA proposed rule back, along with dozens of other "midnight" Carter-proposed regulations.

REAGAN OSHA RESPONSE TO TOXIC CHEMICALS IN THE WORKPLACE

The withdrawal notice in the February 13, 1981, *Federal Register* stated that the action was taken "to permit the Department to consider regulatory alternatives that had not been fully considered and then, if appropriate, repropose the regulation." During the summer of 1981, another House subcommittee, Congressman Joseph M. Gaydos (D-Pa.)'s Subcommittee on Health and Safety, House Education and Labor Committee, held hearings on the efforts OSHA was making on the problem of toxic chemicals in the workplace. Although Auchter was not summoned to testify before the Committee, shortly after the hearings ended he instructed the OSHA Health Standards Office to draft the Reagan administration version of a toxic chemical hazard communication standard.

Auchter was concerned about the unmanageability of the Carter toxic chemical proposal. "Our purpose is to establish a system that will bring regulatory activities under appropriate management control, ensure successful adherence to existing legal, policy and administrative requirements and attain efficient and cost-effective control of workplace hazards."[22] For any health standard to be promulgated by OSHA, four standard-setting principles must be followed by Auchter's staff in the Health Standards office: (1) significant risk must be demonstrated; (2) the standard must actually reduce the risk; (3) along with scientific data to justify the proposed standard, OSHA must gather data to show that the standard is technologically and economically feasible for an entire industry; and (4) the Regulatory Flexibility Act of 1980 and EO 12,291 "require OSHA to carefully and systematically consider the economic and social consequences of proposed rulemaking, i.e., analysis of cost-effectiveness of various means of achieving [the] level of protection."[23]

In late 1981, the OSHA hazard communication proposed standard was sent to DeMuth's office in OIRA. In accordance with the 1980 legislation and the February 17, 1981, EO, noted in the *Federal Register* on December 21, 1981, the new toxic chemical draft standard and the preliminary RIA were received by OMB.

The December 1981 proposed hazard communication standard "is oriented towards providing hazard information to workers and employers, is largely performance-oriented, substantially reduces the paperwork burden of employers, and eliminates unnecessary regulatory requirements. As a result," concluded the OSHA report, "the costs of the current proposed hazard communication standard are substantially reduced over those estimated for the January [Carter administration] proposal."[24] (Table 6 presents a cost comparison, developed by OSHA, of the Carter and Reagan OSHA proposals. Table 7 presents a cost comparison of the two proposals, broken down into each proposal's basic components.)

The Reagan-OSHA proposal contained two types of requirements: chemical manufacturers had to assess the health and safety hazards of the chemicals they produced by reviewing the scientific literature on each chemical, and all manufacturers were required to inform employees in detail about chemical hazards.

DeMuth turned the proposed standard on toxic chemical warnings and the accompanying RIA over to John Morrall, a staff member of OIRA. He was the initial economic analyst in OMB to review the OSHA standard proposed by Auchter's staff.

Table 6
Cost Comparison of the January Proposal and the Current Proposal: Total Initial, Annual, and Present Value Costs

	January Proposal	Current Proposal
Total initial cost (startup cost)	$2.6 billion ($185.00 per employee)	$581.75 million ($41.00 per employee)
Total annual cost (ongoing cost)	$1.254 billion ($89.00 per employee)	$227.92 million ($16.00 per employee)
Total present value cost (40-year period; 10 percent discount rate)	$22.864 billion	$2.648 billion

Source: U.S. Department of Labor, Occupational Safety and Health Administration, Office of Regulatory Analysis.

Note: Cost estimates for the January proposal assume minimal procedures for hazard evaluation. Costs may exceed these estimates. For example, extensive testing may result from the certification requirement. The total initial cost could then rise as high as $3 billion, or $215 per employee. The total annual cost and present value cost would increase accordingly.

Table 7

Cost Comparison of Basic Components of the January and Current OSHA Proposals

January Proposal	Current Proposal
1. Cost of extensive hazard evaluation would include broad literature search and potentially some animal testing. The latter may occur in response to the requirement to certify that the chemical poses no hazard.	1. Cost of hazard evaluation would include literature search of a limited set of documents and files. No requirement for certification that the chemical poses no hazard.
Estimated cost may vary from $248 million to $1,000 million depending on testing conducted. (Initial, annual, and present value costs would increase accordingly.)	Estimated cost $230 million. Any testing costs would be voluntarily incurred by the chemical manufacturer.
2. Cost of extensive labeling would be incurred by most manufacturers since the existing systems would be required to change to comply. Labels with information this specific and extensive are not general industry practice.(a)	2. Cost of limited labeling would not be incurred by all manufacturers since many products already are appropriately labeled. For many establishments this is a general practice. Existing systems would not be distrupted.
Cost of labeling of containers of chemical products shipped and used in plant:	Cost of labeling of containers of chemical products shipped and used in plant:
Total initial cost $331.05 million	Total initial cost $66.21 million
Cost of modifying and reviewing label plates:	Cost of modifying and and reviewing label plates:
Total inital cost $242.65 million	Total initial cost $111.55 million
Total initial cost of labeling	Total initial cost of labeling
$573.70 million	$177.76 million
Total annual cost of labeling	Total annual cost of labeling
$350.87 million	$69.80 million

(a) Piping and piping systems not included in estimate.

110

Table 7—*Continued*

January Proposal	Current Proposal
3. Labeling of piping and piping systems would be required. The estimates provide the expected cost for the chemical and petroleum manufacturers only.	3. Labeling of piping and piping systems not required.
Total initial cost $1,727.06 million	Total initial cost $0
Total annual cost $889.44 million	Total annual cost $0
4. Cost of providing material safety data sheets or information sheets.	4. Cost of developing and providing material safety data sheets.
Total initial cost $16.05 million	Total initial cost $34.24 million
Total annual cost $1.81 million	Total annual cost $3.66 million
5. No education and training required.	5. Cost of education and training as basically time and materials:
Total initial cost $0	Total initial cost $124.87 million
Total annual cost $0	Total annual cost $133.61
6. Record keeping would include hazard evaluation documents and access.	6. Record keeping would include hazard evaluation documents, access, and compliance plan.
Total initial cost $31.35 million	Total initial cost $14.70 million
Total annual cost $4.69 million	Total annual cost $2.07 million

Source: U.S. Department of Labor, Occupational Safety and Health Administration, Office of Regulatory Analysis.

111

OMB-OIRA RESPONSE TO THE
OSHA HAZARD COMMUNICATION STANDARD

The Reagan EO, as implemented by OIRA staff, enables the reviewer to examine the qualities of four key elements in an RIA prepared by the agency:

1. The rationale for the government intervention—that is, identification of the need for such a regulation by a careful development of the problem that exists that will be addressed by the proposed regulation.

2. Identification of feasible alternatives, including no regulation at all, to the proposed regulation.

3. Identification and measurement of relevant benefits and costs of the proposed regulation, as well as the benefits and costs of alternative proposals.

4. Explanation of why one alternative was chosen over the alternatives, including the no-regulation option.[25]

The OIRA reviewers, in their efforts to determine the economic efficiency of proposed major regulations, must weigh the agency's identification, evaluation, and comparison segments in the RIA in the light of the purposes of EO 12,291.

Morrall's response to the OSHA reproposal was extremely negative. In a memorandum sent to Christopher DeMuth on December 28, 1981, Morrall concluded that the OSHA cost-benefit analysis was inadequate in part because it exaggerated the drop in cancer deaths; the benefits of the proposed standard were too high and too optimistic:

OSHA has not established to our satisfaction (a) that the rule is needed and (b) that the potential benefits to society outweigh the potential costs to society. . . . OSHA cannot show that unlabeled chemicals pose a significant risk, because OSHA lacks the information needed to make such a showing. . . . The regulations are costly. . . . We believe the key to the proposal is whether the benefits OSHA expects from it would actually materialize. We feel that OSHA has constructed a set of tenuous assumptions all of which must hold for OSHA's expectations to be fulfilled. . . . We believe that OSHA's benefit estimate of $5.2 billion is overstated by a factor of 80, i.e., a more reasonable benefit estimate would be $65 million, compared to costs of $2.6 billion.[26]

On the basis of this review, DeMuth, on January 7, 1982, in a document labeled "Administratively Confidential," issued a report critically reviewing "the proposed OSHA Hazard Communication Regulation."[27] Essentially an elaboration of the Morrall review, the confidential report maintained that OSHA did not show need and that the cost-benefit analysis results were "wildly optimistic."[28] Rejecting various arguments of OSHA—among them need, costs and benefits, estimate of current job-related illnesses and injuries, cancer projections, inflation of future benefits ("unwarranted"), support of industry and labor, and workers' right to know ("this knowledge should not be considered a 'right' in isolation from cost considerations")—OMB denied OSHA the opportunity to publish a notice of proposed rulemaking in the *Federal Register*.

In March 1982, DeMuth testified before a House subcommittee looking into the role of OMB in the rulemaking process. Questioned about the rejection of the OSHA hazard communication standard, DeMuth stated "that it was not clear from the evidence OSHA put together that the regulation was going to have the large benefits they suggested." The analysis, he continued, was based on a string of reasoning that disregarded certain facts, "but we had no hard evidence and OSHA went back and did some more analysis."[29]

The major impact of the Reagan EO was evident: OSHA was denied the right to publish the standard in the *Federal Register*—that is, the right to begin public rulemaking.

OSHA RESPONSE AND THE
TASK FORCE PROPOSAL, JANUARY-MARCH 1982

After the Morrall memorandum, DeMuth met with Auchter and T. Timothy Ryan, the Department of Labor's solicitor, to discuss the OMB judgment prior to the formal denial by the reviewing agency. Auchter and Ryan then went to Secretary of Labor Donovan in early January 1982. Auchter said, "Mr. Secretary, we have a difference of opinion here as to the data involved."[30] Donovan, a member of the task force, agreed to take the issue to the vice-president and the task force. The task force was thus presented with "the first dispute about an OMB attempt to kill a regulation generated by the Republican Administration."[31]

The task force heard arguments from OSHA and OMB in late January and, not surprisingly, supported the OMB position. The task force sent the standard back to OSHA for further justification in light of OSHA's critique. In addition, it requested that OMB and OSHA jointly provide support for an independent study commissioned by the two agencies to look at the rule's benefits.[32]

The author of the independent study commissioned to examine the cost-benefits of the proposed hazard communication standard was Professor W. Kip Viscusi, IBM Research Professor at Duke University's Fuqua School of Business' Center for the Study of Business Regulation. Viscusi, a member of COWPS during the Carter administration,[33] had been an economic adviser to Reagan's OSHA "on the economic merits of hazard communication."[34]

In a January 29, 1982, letter to Auchter, Viscusi wrote that "the original labeling proposal by Eula Bingham was fundamentally ill-conceived, as it would have imposed major burdens on firms and provided few benefits to workers since the information provided was in terms of a polysyllabic chemical description rather than a series of understandable warnings." The Auchter approach was, he wrote, "pursuing a much sounder policy." After noting the value of such a standard, Viscusi wrote that "the present debate between OSHA and OMB is not so much over the structure of the policy but over the benefits associated with it. . . . The difficulty is not that the analysis is methodologically unsound but that the numbers used in these calculations are questionable."

In writing his study of costs and benefits, Viscusi's aim was to focus "on the two greatest problems—(i) lack of precise evidence regarding the relationship between employment and cancer and, (ii) the uncertain link between hazard communication and worker behavior." He concluded his letter to Auchter with a ringing endorsement of a chemical labeling standard: the hazard communication proposal "would establish a new direction for OSHA policies. Instead of mandating standards for readily perceived safety risks, OSHA would be attempting to augment market forces to promote more efficient levels of health risks. If the Administration fails to pursue some form of chemical *labeling policy because the benefits are unclear, in effect it will be establishing a bias against all innovative efforts which, by their very nature, tend to have uncertain effects precisely because of their novelty."*

Viscusi, a supporter of this OSHA approach to health and safety in the marketplace, had been given the task of doing an independent study of the cost-effectiveness of the proposed standard. That his subsequent report to the task force, submitted in March 1982, supported the OSHA proposal should therefore come as no surprise to those who had seen his letter.

Indeed, in a letter written a few days later, on February 1, 1982, to Dr. Mary Ellen Weber, director of OSHA's Regulatory Analysis office, Viscusi suggested the substance of his March 16, 1982, report to the task force. In the letter he offered an unusual complaint about the chemical labeling analysis:

The lost income, lost production, and medical cost numbers that would be averted if worker accidents and illnesses were reduced . . . *do not represent the benefits* of the chemical labeling standard. These *entries comprise but a small portion of the total benefits* of risk reduction since they totally exclude the individual worker's willingness to pay for risk reduction that is not included in these statistics. My own research has indicated that the value of life and the value of injuries is several times higher than the results one would obtain using earnings and income statistics such as those used by OSHA. *Usually, the willingness-to-pay numbers are about ten times greater.* What seems to have happened is that rather than offend peoples' moral sensitivities by using a number for the value of life or the value of accidents, OSHA instead has used less controversial proxies for these values. . . . *By failing to place an appropriate value on life OSHA may have unwittingly made its chemical labeling proposal look much less attractive than it actually is.* [Emphasis added.]

On March 16, the Viscusi analysis arrived at the office of the Task Force on Regulatory Relief. It concluded that the benefits of the regulation would roughly total $2.85 billion, slightly higher than the estimated $2.6 billion costs imposed by the proposed hazard communication rule. His report indicated that OSHA made *"improper calculations by looking at only monetized benefits* [reduced medical costs, greater productivity from less illness] *and not measuring the more valid concern of how much each worker is willing to pay for risk reduction. . . .* Viscusi stressed that OSHA was looking in the wrong place and that measuring benefits by a worker's willingness to pay would yield benefits of $2.85 billion [emphasis added]."[35]

His conclusion was that the benefits outweighed the costs of the hazard communication standard. Viscusi wrote, "If OSHA were to rely on Hazard Communication as an alternative to more rigid regulatory controls, the attractiveness of the proposal would be enhanced considerably."[36]

TASK FORCE REASSESSMENT: MARCH 17, 1982

The review of Viscusi's report led task force officials, including Boyden Grey, counsel to Vice-President Bush, on the next day, March 17, 1982, to overturn the OMB ruling and to allow OSHA to publish the notice of proposed rulemaking in the *Federal Register* on March 19, 1982. The decision to publish was announced one day before the House Subcommittee on Manpower and Housing, chaired by Congresswoman Cardiss Collins (D-Ill), was to open hearings on this issue. Congressman Gore, who testified before the Collins' subcommittee, stated, "This is yet another example of what could be called fortuitous coincidence in the timing of congressional hearings and regulatory actions. . . . Unfortunately we cannot have congressional hearings on every single dereliction of duty by this [Reagan] wrecking crew."[37] It should also be noted that there were some ex parte contacts between Vice-President Bush and representatives from chemical manufacturers in February, relative to the question of the hazard communication standard. George H. R. Taylor, director of the AFL-CIO's Division of OSH, testified before a congressional committee that he too had ex parte meetings with Boyden Grey, OMB, and OSHA officials on this issue.[38]

In January 1982, the Chemical Manufacturers Association (CMA), in a letter to DeMuth, urged administration support for a chemical labeling standard. Prior to that industry communication, the American

Petroleum Institute had asked OMB to allow the chemical labeling standard to go through the rulemaking process.[39] Furthermore, a *New York Times* report noted that the Labor Department warned the White House staff of "significant political problems" if the chemical labeling proposal was sidetracked. "Labor has not yet been given a cudgel with which to beat this Administration. This [sidetracking] would provide one."[40] Finally, during testimony before the House Manpower and Housing Subcommittee hearings, March 18-19, 1982, it was disclosed that "executives of four major corporations and industrial trade associations that would be affected by the rules had held three closed meetings in January and February with staff people at the White House who opposed the regulations. The list of meetings also included one with representatives of organized labor, which has long favored the regulation."[41]

With preliminary notice of proposed rulemaking approval granted by OMB, public hearings relative to the merits of the proposed hazard communication standard, consistent with section 553 of the APA, were held in June 1982 in Washington, D.C. OSHA staff involved in the hazard communication rulemaking process expect that the final rule proposed by OSHA will not be brought before OMB-OIRA until June or July 1983.

THE OSHA-OMB CLASH IN PERSPECTIVE

A view of the chronology of events in the chemical labeling controversy between OSHA and OMB-OIRA (see Appendix A) is not a summary of disinterested decisionmaking by economic analysts applying the rational parameters of cost-benefit analysis. Neither is it a portrait of decisionmaking in the White House without narrow political interests involved in the final judgments. Rather, it is a reflection of the Reagan administration's broad efforts to control regulatory actions.

Chemical Labeling Controversy: Microview of OMB Review of Agency Actions

Impartiality of OMB

How impartial or disinterested were the OIRA-OMB reviewers? Were narrow political pressures at work in the decision to reject the hazard communication standard in December 1981 and then to let it be published in the *Federal Register* in March 1982? These are the two basic questions posed at the beginning of the chapter in response to the DeMuth view that the overriding objective of the OMB review process is to achieve economic efficiency in rulemaking through a disinterested economic analysis by OIRA. "OIRA's only function," DeMuth said before the March 1982 subcommittee, was to *"audit regulations* before they go to the *Federal Register*, to make an initial judgment as to whether they are consistent with the President's EO. The vast bulk of them," he concluded, "go to the *Federal Register* with dispatch, nearly 90% in 1981, for example."[42]

At another point in the hearing, however, DeMuth stated that the question before OIRA-OMB "is how [agency] discretion is to be exercised."[43] This raises a basic question about the role of OMB in the regulatory process. Is the OMB function merely an audit function, or is it one of determining how agency discretion is used (and rejecting proposed regulations that, in the estimate of OMB, go beyond certain lines developed by the White House policymakers)? If the OMB-OIRA function is substantive—the examination of major agency regulations with respect to the manner in which agency discretion was used—then how impartial and disinterested a role can OIRA analysts play?

In its review of OMB activities, the GAO concluded that the OMB role was substantive: "Given its location in the Executive Office of the White House, the OMB is likely to facilitate substantive oversight to make regulations conform to the President's general policy orientation, as well as to enforce purely procedural requirements."[44] Looking at OIRA-OMB activities in the hazard communication controversy with OSHA, there is a clear perception of substantive as well as procedural interposition by OMB in the rulemaking process.

Reading the Morrall and DeMuth comments on the need for a hazard communication standard, we find a clear, perceived substantive examination of the discretionary judgment of OSHA to develop a health warning process. The OIRA-OMB review essentially focused on the OSHA *"judgment* as interpreted by OIRA in its reading of the RIA."[45]

In concluding that there was no need for the regulation that would require employers to label toxic chemicals in the workplace, OMB-OIRA, Morrall, and DeMuth argued that no direct evidence had been presented by OSHA; it offered no significant proof that knowledge of chemical hazards will improve worker safety. "The record of mandatory labeling, i.e., smoking [alcoholism], and lack of seat-belt usage, in changing behavior is unimpressive," wrote Morrall in his report to DeMuth. The public does not follow label warnings; there has been no decline in smoking or nonseat belt usage, and there are no data that workers in the workplace will respond to warnings regarding toxic chemicals. Furthermore, manufacturers will take the initiative in placing warnings on toxic chemicals, and that should be sufficient.

OMB also rejected another need for the OSHA hazard communication standard: preemption in order to overcome at least 22 different state and city health hazard warning labels that created chaos for chemical manufacturers. OMB-OIRA maintained that "there was no need for this negation.'' Furthermore, the OMB assessment was that workers did not have a right to this knowledge about the consequences of exposure to toxic chemicals. Finally, Morrall rejected OSHA's position that, with the standard in place, worker illnesses, injuries, and toxic-chemical-induced deaths would be reduced by one-fifth (after 20 years).

Viewing the benefits and costs of the hazard communication standard, the OIRA report concluded that the benefits were overexaggerated and the costs underevaluated. Consequently, on the basis of the data provided by OSHA, Morrall concluded that the proposed toxic chemical labeling proposal was cost-inefficient.

Clearly these comments by OIRA-OMB were independent judgments about such facets as the nature of federal-state relations and the responsibility of manufacturers and employers (along with the additional costs involved) to warn handlers of the toxic chemicals. There was disagreement over policy directions between OSHA and OMB; the judgment of OSHA as well as the economic analysis was being examined by OIRA/OMB. Morrall, DeMuth, and others in the Executive Office were not impartial, disinterested reviewers of the OSHA regulation. For a number of substantive reasons, they rejected the preemption argument and OSHA's judgment that warnings, accompanied by education programs in the workplace, would reduce illnesses, injuries, and deaths caused by toxic chemicals.

The OSHA response to OIRA criticisms in February 1982 of the health agency's judgments was directed to both the substantive and the procedural facets of the Morrall and DeMuth reports. First, argued OSHA, recent Supreme Court decisions pointed out that the 1970 OSH Act ''does not permit the agency to make decisions on a narrow balancing of monetizable costs and benefits when human health is at stake, but allows the agency to choose the most cost-effective solution. . . . Although not required to do so, OSHA has demonstrated that even the monetizable benefits of its proposal outweigh the monetizable costs.''[46] ''Remaining areas of disagreement,'' stated OSHA, ''involve strictly judgment and policy-calls, responsibility for which is expressly retained by OSHA.'' (The secretary of an executive department may, at his or her discretion, publish a controversial regulation rejected by OMB if he or she believes that the publication of the proposal is consistent with the agency's mandate. ''He or she still has the legal authority to issue the regulation,'' noted James Miller, ''but that action could be risky—meaning that the President of the United States might decide to remove such a person from office.''[47] Technically, Secretary of Labor Donovan could have gone ahead and sent the hazard communication standard to the Federal Register, but probably he would have been fired and the regulation withdrawn by his successor.

Most of the 16-page OSHA response to the OIRA-OMB criticism of the toxic chemical standard was directed to these judgmental, policy calls of OMB. For example, OSHA maintained that OMB had presented a faulty argument when it compared pleasure-giving addictions such as drinking and smoking to injuries and deaths caused by toxic chemicals in the workplace; the latter situation was caused by "involuntary exposure to potentially hazardous workplace chemicals . . . whereas smoking and alcoholism are essentially 'voluntary exposures.' "[48]

Narrow Political Pressures

The economic analysis process, based on EO 12,291, is not only subject to judgment by OMB-OIRA staff; it is also open to political pressures by various interest groups concerned about the fate of a proposed standard. Between December 1981 and March 1982, various contacts were made by chemical manufacturers and labor organizations with Vice-President Bush, Secretary of Labor Donovan, officials in OMB, and Boyden Grey, counsel to the vice-president and general consel to the Task Force on Regulatory Relief.

The decision to let OSHA publish its notice of proposed rulemaking in the *Federal Register* one day before a critical hearing on that controversy was an equally political decision by the White House. Finally, the decision to free the hazard communication standard came about because of Donovan's warning of political repercussions if the proposed standard was not released.

Macroview of OMB Review of Agency Actions: The November 2, 1982, GAO Report

"We are not gutting or spoiling some statute," maintained DeMuth in March 1982 before the House subcommittee investigating the toxic chemical issue.[49] In November 1982, the GAO issued its report on the OMB's implementation of EO 12,291 that suggested the opposite conclusion. Entitled *Improved Quality, Adequate Resources, and Consistent Oversight Needed If Regulatory Analysis Is to Help Control Costs of Regulations,* the GAO report focused on the quality of the RIAs prepared by executive agencies, costs, effect on deregulation, conflict with regulatory regulations, IRCs, and the effect of the OMB centralizing regulatory oversight role.

After an examination of the activities of OIRA-OMB during 1981 (in which 2,679 regulations were reviewed by OIRA but only 22 regulations reviewed had prepared RIAs), it concluded that many RIAs were poorly prepared, that the costs averaged $212,000 for the RIAs, that deregulation was not affected by the order, and that some conflict could arise between

OMB actions and Congress because of the "sufficient ambiguity in existing regulatory legislation about the applicability of cost-benefit standards."[50]

Regarding the centralized oversight role of the OMB and the DeMuth contention that OMB was not scuttling regulations, the GAO report was critical of OMB activity. First, OMB had done little to encourage the use of other regulatory techniques by the agencies involved nor had it done much to identify conflicts in regulations between different agencies. With the exception of the few major regulations reviewed carefully, OMB had no impact on regulatory review because so many regulations were passed without substantive examination.[51]

Continued the GAO report: "For those few rules in which OMB takes a more active interest, however, it *appears to affect the substance and the timing of the rule significantly.*"[52] Why OMB singles out some rules for major review of RIAs and waives other major rules is a question GAO could not answer. Of the 43 major rules reviewed in 1981, 21 had the RIA requirement waived by OMB. "We are concerned that so many major rules were allowed to be issued without benefit of a RIA. *We do not believe that agencies are likely to take the value of RIA seriously if the analysis requirement is frequently waived.*"[53] Indeed, the major recommendations of the GAO were addressed to the problem of RIAs and waivers: broaden RIA oversight, develop guidelines to standardize and reduce the number of waivers, OMB comments on RIAs should be made public, and improvement of quality of RIAs prepared by the agencies.[54]

SUMMARY

This chapter has focused on one incident involving OMB and OSHA, not yet concluded, and on a preliminary assessment of the OMB by the GAO. On the basis of these incomplete assessments, certain tentative conclusions can be drawn.

First, when OMB-OIRA wants to act as gatekeeper by substantively reviewing agency RIAs, it can effectively delay the rulemaking process. Although James Miller's admonition that the EO's requirements "for thorough deliberation are all to the good," the approximately thousand-day delay in the toxic chemical standard's promulgation (if indeed it will be adopted as a final rule) takes deliberation too far.[55]

Second, OMB evidently acts as gatekeeper with respect to issues that seem to stand in opposition to the Reagan administration's philosophy of letting the private sector resolve economic problems rather than having the government develop regulatory standards. DeMuth, the free marketer, clearly believed that the chemical manufacturers could voluntarily and on their own initiative deal with worker exposure to toxic chemicals. In his *Regulation* interview, he stated that the market, not agencies such as OSHA, should be the agency to develop solutions to commercial and economic problems.[56]

Third, in the OMB-OIRA effort to delay, redirect, or kill proposals that seem to conflict with White House economic policy and philosophy, there is a clear, substantive attempt to nullify agency perceptions and judgments and replace these with OMB-OIRA assessments and judgments. Both the GAO report and the documents prepared by Morrall and DeMuth point to this substantive intervention in agency rulemaking. This is not inconsistent with the presidential commitment to regulatory reform—to control and redirect public policy developed by federal regulatory agencies through centralized oversight by the OMB.

Fourth, the notion of rational disinterestedness is, on its face, nothing but a fiction insofar as the EO of February 17, 1981, has been implemented by the OIRA staff. There have been substantive interventions in the rulemaking process by the OMB since 1981; the hazard communication standard controversy between Reagan administrators in the Department of Labor and OSHA and the OIRA-OMB staff is a reflection of this interest in the substance of policymaking by federal regulatory agencies.

Finally, there is the play of narrow political forces in the EO 12,291 regulatory review process. Ex parte communications are present in the review activities of the OMB. Indeed, DeMuth, discussing this issue at the March 1982 hearings, stated emphatically that "there are no legal restrictions on ex parte communications in informal rulemaking."[57] And, as in the toxic chemical controversy, decisions may be made by White House political actors above the free marketers in OIRA that set aside, for the time being, OMB judgments for political purposes.

These developments do, however, separate the Reagan effort from earlier White House attempts to control and redirect federal regulatory activity. There has been interposition by OMB in agency rulemaking; judgments made by administrative agencies have been set aside, temporarily on occasion, by OMB and the task force. The next chapter assesses these developments in light of the need that something must be done to control the federal regulatory process.

NOTES

1. Glen D. Nager, "Bureaucrats and the Cost-Benefit Chameleon," 6 *Regulation* September-October 1982, p. 40.

2. Scalia, "Regulation," p. 38; see also "OMB Free Marketers Lose a Regulatory Fight over Navel Orange Quotas," *National Journal*, December 11, 1982, p. 2103.

3. Rick Grawey, staff counsel (Maj), to Chairwoman Collins, Hearing Memorandum, March 17, 1982, p. 4.

4. Christopher DeMuth, "A Strong Beginning on Reform," 6 *Regulation*, January-February 1982, p. 16.

5. Ibid.

6. Ibid., p. 17.

7. Ibid., p. 18.

8. Ibid.

9. See "Free Marketers," p. 2103.

10. Nager, "Bureaucrats," p. 41.

11. Ibid.

12. OSH Act of 1970, sec. 2(b), 84 Stat. 1590 (1970).

13. *Chemical Dangers in the Workplace*, Report by House Committee on Government Operations, House of Representatives, 94th Congress, 2d session, Washington, D.C.: U.S. Government Printing Office, 1976, p. 2.

14. Ibid., p. 3.

15. Ibid.

16. Ibid., pp. 4-5.

17. Ibid., p. 5.

18. Ibid.

19. Michael Wines, "They're Still Telling OSHA Horror Stories, But the 'Victims' Are New," *National Journal*, December 7, 1981, p. 1985.

20. Grawey memo, p. 5.

21. OSHA, Hazard Communication, Report to OMB, SF 83, December 1981, p. I-4.

22. House, Government Opinions Committee, Subcommittee on Manpower and Housing, Statement of Thorne G. Auchter, Assistant Secretary of Labor for Occupational Safety and Health, *Hearings, Role of OMB in OSHA Rulemaking*, 97th Cong., 2d Sess., March 18, 1982, p. 14.

23. Ibid., p. 15.

24. OSHA, *Hazard Communication*, p. I-7.

25. U.S. Comptroller General, *Improved Quality, Adequate Resources, and Consistent Oversight Needed If Regulatory Analysis Is to Help Control Costs of Regulations*, GAO, DAD-8-6, November 2, 1982, Washington, D.C.: U.S. Government Printing Office, 1982, p. 8.

26. John Morrall, Memo, "OSHA Hazard Communication Standard," December 29, 1981, appendix A, pp. 1, 2, 4.

27. OMB, memo on OSHA Hazard Communication Standard, January 7, 1982, appendix A, p. 1.

28. Ibid., p. 10.

29. *House, Hearings*, Vol. II, p. 73.

30. House, *Hearings*, March 11-18, 1982, Vol. I, p. 58.

31. Kim Masters, "Agencies to Take Label Rule to Regulatory Task Force," *Legal Times*, January 11, 1982, pp. 1, 4.

32. *Inside OMB*, Volume 1, No. 7, March 26, 1982, p. 5.

33. Ben A. Franklin, "Novel Pressures in Toxic Label Case," *New York Times*, March 23, 1982, p. 18.

34. Viscusi letter, January 29, 1982. See Appendix B.

35. *Inside OMB*, p. 6.

36. Ibid.

37. House, *Hearings*, March 11, 18-19, 1982 (Stenographic Minutes), vol. III, p. 4.

33. Ibid., vol. I, p. 15.

39. Masters, "Agencies," p. 4.

40. Franklin, "Novel Pressures."

41. Ibid.

42. House, *Hearings*, vol. III, p. 74.

43. Ibid., p. 79.

44. GAO, *Improved Quality*, p. 55.

45. OSHA Hazard Communication Standard, OIRA-OMB Concerns, February 1982, p. 4.

46. Ibid., pp. 2, 4.

47. Miller, "Deregulation Hq," p. 16.

48. OSHA, *loc. cit.*, p. 9.

49. House, *Hearings*, Vol. III, p. 80.

50. GAO, *Improved Quality*, p. 5.

51. Ibid., pp. 3-4 passim.

52. Ibid., p. 4.

53. Ibid.

54. Ibid., pp. 5-6.

55. Miller, "Deregulation Hq," p. 17.

56. See DeMuth, "Strong Beginning."

57. House, *Hearings*, Vol. III, p. 95.

6

Conclusion: On the Need for Continuous Presidential Oversight

Congress is eager to establish for each special interest its own executive bureau or independent board. . . . The molecular politics of Washington, with power, and often authority and responsibility, fragmented among increasingly narrow, what's-in-it-for-me groups and their responsive counterparts in the executive and legislative branches, has the centrifugal force to tear the national interest to shreds.

—Joseph A. Califano, Jr.

I want each of you to assess your subordinates, their loyalty to us, whether they are team players, whether they will speak with one voice, whether they are good staff. . . . Get rid of all of those who are incompetent.

—Jimmy Carter

The concern of former Secretary of Health, Education and Welfare Califano, that the single-mission regulatory agencies were largely uncontrollable and working at odds with the national purpose has been shared by chief executives since Richard Nixon. "Regulatory oversight is a problem that has faced the last four presidents. Considering their differences in personality, all four of the presidents have seen the problem in remarkably similar terms," commented George Eads before hearings in 1981 on the role of OMB. The basic problem is "to walk the fine line *between continual oversight and arbitrary intervention* and try to figure out how to make the oversight process a reasonable and open one."[1]

All four presidents—Nixon, Ford, Carter, and Reagan—concluded that it is the responsibility of the chief executive and his White House staff to deal with the "molecular politics" of congressional staff-executive agency mid-level managers–interest group representative interactions that led to the promulgation of thousands of rules and regulations that were costly, duplicative, and carelessly drawn up. All four made the effort to create centripedal forces in the White House in order to direct and control and coordinate the activities of what Richard Neustadt called the "faceless glob of semipermanent and semisovereign Washingtonians."

In this continuous effort by the executive branch to develop strategies to cope with bureaucratic sprawl, the line between oversight and intervention (much like the line between coercion and inducement that confronted the U.S. Supreme Court in the 1930s) is a difficult one to draw with precision.[2] It is, however, a presidential effort that must be engaged in continuously.

RESTATEMENT OF THE REGULATORY SPRAWL DILEMMA

In the past decades, especially the decade of the 1970s, there has developed in Washington, D.C., a huge army of single-mission regulatory agencies located in the executive branch and as independent boards and commissions. Thousands of regulations, developed and promulgated in accordance with the informal rulemaking powers of these agencies (as described in the organic statute and in the APA, 1946), have flooded the society.

These many public policies have been written and implemented by unelected actors in the federal political system: the career bureaucrats who staff these federal agencies, the congressional staff members who interact with their bureaucratic counterparts, and the interest groups that interact with both the bureaucrats and the congressional staff members. There has been a noticeable shift in public policymaking from the political actors to unelected, anonymous bureaucrats. The shift has not gone unnoticed; politicians, scholars, and others are deeply concerned about this drift from elected to nonelected policymakers and policymaking.

There has developed a basic pattern in this nonelected decision making process: singlemindedness of purpose, independence, and a multiplicity of regulations. Regulatory agencies have developed regulations that have a narrow "one dimensional view of the world, too narrow for the formulation of broad policies in the national interest."[3] Their relative independence, until recently, from consistent and substantive oversight—by Congress or the President—has enabled the regulatory agencies to use the rulemaking process (section 553 of the APA) with freedom. The Congress, through the passage of scores of bills creating new agencies and giving broad mandates to existing agencies, has succeeded in creating a dynamic process that is "incapable of adjudicating in the national interest."[4] Finally, and as a consequence of these developments, there has been produced in America a large number of duplicative and cost-inefficient regulations.

With the growth of this administrative policymaking system, there has come the growth of concern about their impact on the politics and the theory of democracy. If public policymaking is in the hands of these unknown, unelected bureaucrats and other semisovereign Washingtonians, how are these people to be held accountable for their actions? Congress, an accomplice in their decisionmaking processes (and the creator of their authority to make rules and regulations), cannot effectively oversee the bureaucracy's activities. Neither can the federal courts hold the agency accountable on a day-to-day practical basis. It falls to the chief executive and his political staff to check and hold accountable and, ultimately, to manage and direct the federal regulatory agencies.

PRESIDENTIAL CONTROL
OF THE FEDERAL BUREAUCRACY

Accountability has been defined as the federal manager's answerability and willingness to take responsibility for the broad principles and initiatives set forth by the President."[5] Bernard Rosen has written that "career executives understand and believe in our democratic system; they know that political appointees are the vital link between the decisions of the citizens in choosing a president and the overall direction and management of agencies."[6] The President and his political appointees are the primary agents in the necessary effort to reduce the federal regulatory sprawl.

A coherent national policy calls for the President to monitor and oversee the actions of the federal executive agencies. The President must act as coordinator and balancer; he must make the final judgments (with the assistance of political subordinates in the White House, OMB/OIRA, or the cabinet) on major administrative activities that will affect national policy. Only the President has the broad perspective on matters of national concern; only the President has the capability to deal with this dilemma of holding the federal bureaucracy accountable.

The White House must continuously oversee major activities of the federal regulatory agencies. Control by the President and his staff cannot be episodic and still be successful; strategies must be developed by the White House that will enable presidential staff to monitor and review agency activities in an orderly and manageable manner. In addition, there must be positive leadership by the President in this area.

Continuous oversight by the President means the beginning of bureaucratic accountability. It also means an enduring constructive tension between the President and his staff and all those associated with the political world of the federal agency manager. The career bureaucracy, while subscribing to presidential loyalty, will continue to do mischief to the President's political appointees who head these federal agencies. For this reason the President must place into positions of power, in the agencies, men and women who are loyal to the President and to his policy goals. As a practical matter, it is the political appointee heading the agency "who interprets the will of the President [and] in the day-to-day world [of the federal manager] our accountability runs to our immediate bosses—and it will be they who determine whether we as executives are accountable."[7]

In developing strategies to cope with the problem of regulatory sprawl, every President since Nixon has been aware of the importance of qualified personnel to head the bureaus, departments, commissions, and boards that make up the federal bureaucracy. There has been the continuing search for men and women who were loyal supporters of the party and of the programs of the President. Nixon, Ford, Carter, and Reagan all were critically aware of the value of getting political appointees into the federal agencies who would clearly interpret the will of the President.

Beyond the personnel strategy, which emphasizes control of federal agencies through team efforts, loyalty to presidential initiatives, continual tension between the political appointee and the career bureaucrat, the White House has directed its efforts to structural, procedural, and substantive strategies in the struggle to control the federal regulatory agencies.

In the structural effort to control regulatory sprawl that goes against national policy, the OMB has figured prominently. As the President's arm for the exercise of managerial functions, the OMB is centrally involved with agency activities—within the executive departments and with the independent agencies and commissions. Every President since Nixon has attempted to use the OMB to check and direct agency activity, reduce agency activity through budget cuts, and control for excess paperwork burdens on industry. The Reagan effort is the most dramatic usage of OMB-OIRA: preclearance by that agency of all rules and regulations deemed to be major by the White House.

Substantively, there has been deregulation of a number of industries, especially during the Carter administration. There have been presidential efforts to persuade Congress to reexamine existing substantive law in order to deal with the problem of agency accountability. Nixon and Carter tried to reorganize the federal executive branch but were met with strong opposition in the Congress.

Executive orders written by Presidents Ford, Carter, and Reagan were directed to the problem of regulatory sprawl and were directed to the managers of federal executive department agencies. (As a matter of policy, the orders did not extend to the IRCs.) They were all, in varying degrees, efforts by the White House to try to get agency managers to think of broad issues when developing regulations: cost and benefits of the proposed rules, possible duplication with other rules, necessity of the rule itself.

BASIC OBJECTIVE OF PRESIDENTIAL INITIATIVES IN REGULATORY REFORM

The ultimate purpose of these presidential strategies is to come up with a formula that will control the major activities of the federal regulators. No longer is it possible for an incumbent in the White House to turn away from bureaucratic accountability. The promulgation of major regulations that have a forceful impact on the economy, without a political agent overseeing the potential rule and determining whether it is justifiable and consistent with the national interest, can lead to a serious democratic dilemma. The White House must take the lead in this oversight and approval of major legislation in order to administer for the national interest.

Forceful action by the White House (OMB-OIRA) will certainly be met by forceful reaction by the Congress. The separation-of-powers argument has been made by opponents of presidential initiatives; the White House must respond in a controlled yet equally forceful argument.

The major criticism has been directed at the Reagan executive order, the operations of the task force, and the oversight functions of the OMB-OIRA. Critics of the Reagan executive order argue that it takes away administrative discretion, the heart of the regulatory process; that cost-benefit analysis is a substantive interference with agency action; and that there is extra-agency control of the rulemaking process (by OMB)[8] If, however, administrative discretion means that "given a range of reasonable alternatives, the agency has the *task of selecting the one which best satisfies the public interest*,"[9] and if most statutes require agencies to consider a number of statutory public interest factors,[10] then having the agency develop a cost-benefit analysis for each major rule does not take away its discretion. Instead, it forces the agency decisionmaker to consider carefully the public interest and to develop a rule that is the most cost-effective.

The mission of each agency has not been changed by EO 12,291; executive department agencies such as OSHA and EPA still are obliged to follow the mission responsibility set forth in the enabling legislation. They must "act to establish or vindicate these mission goals" but must do so by following the requirements of the executive order and the cost-benefit guidelines developed by the OMB.[11] Given the proliferation and regulatory excess of the regulatory process in the past, the OIRA-OMB preclearance process in the Reagan EO is a unique remedy to a problem that had not been alleviated by less stringent advisory administrative responses developed by the Ford and Carter administrations.[12]

In sum, the executive order does not take away agency discretion, cost-benefit analysis is not a substantive interference in the regulatory process, and OMB oversight, which is accompanied by the other facets of informal rulemaking described in section 553, is not an unconstitutional extra-agency control of the policymaking process. Governmental leaders, especially the President of the United States, have a responsibility to ensure that public policies are administered and implemented in a fashion that is in the public interest. Whether Republican or Democrat, chief executives in the past decade have grown increasingly concerned about the uncontrolled growth of the federal regulatory process with its accompanying maze of rules and regulations. Reagan's "regulatory ventilation" is the latest effort to ensure that the federal regulators, when using their discretion, consider the costs and benefits of the proposed rules.

SUMMARY

The President is the only agency capable of holding the bureaucrats accountable to the will of the electorate. On matters of broad public policy, the President and his senior political appointees must act to ensure that the national interest is served. In order to carry out this primary domestic responsibility, President and staff must develop strategies that enable the White House to oversee the actions of the federal regulatory agencies.

When they act in this manner, there will always be cries c unreasonableness and closed decision making. When agency rules must pass muster before the OMB-OIRA staff in the White House, there is considerable tension. If the OMB rejects a proposal as being cost-ineffective or unnecessary, there is the accusation, by the offended agency and its clientele in Congress and in the private sector, that the White House has intervened in an arbitrary, unconstitutional manner.

Whether OMB activity is called arbitrary intervention or continual oversight, it is imperative that it continue. The process is inherently tension producing but is a necessary responsibility of the White House. There will always be "extremely difficult political judgments that must be made [between various public policy goals]," argued Lloyd Cutler, counsel to President Carter. "The power to make the *final decision* on rulemaking should rest with the President in those cases in which he finds that what an agency proposed to do, or was failing to do, has a critical impact on achieving other national goals."[13]

To turn away from this continuing activity, fraught with political danger and accompanied by accusations of unconstitutionality, means that the federal agencies win in this struggle for leadership and accountability. "The outcome [would be] a . . . stunning loss of governmental accountability."[14] The President cannot turn away from the enduring struggle with the federal bureaucracy. Since the 1970s, controlling the federal bureaucracy has become a central task for occupants of the White House. It must continue to remain a major task of the President.

NOTES

1. Hearings, *Role of OMB*, p. 38.

2. See *U.S. v. Butler*, 297 US1 (1936); and *Stewart Machine Company v. Davis*, 301 US 548 (1937).

3. Joseph Califano, Jr., *Governing America: An Insider's Report from the White House and the Cabinet*, New York: Simon and Schuster, 1981, p. 450.

4. Ibid., p. 451.

5. Lasko, "Executive Accountability," p. 4.

6. Rosen, "Uncertainty," p. 204.

7. Lasko, "Executive Accountability," p. 4.

8. Congressional Research Service, Library of Congress, "Report on Executive Order 12291," reprinted in *Legal Times*, June 29, 1981, p. 16.

9. Gary J. Edles and Jerome Nelson, *Federal Regulatory Processes: Agency Practices and Procedures*, New York: Harcourt Brace Jovanovich, 1981, p. 157.

10. Ibid., pp. 157-158.

11. Ibid., p. 158.

12. See Ball, Krane, and Lauth, *Compromised Compliance*, for a description of the implementation of another unique remedy to alleviate a problem, section 5 of the Voting Rights Act of 1965.

13. MacAvoy, *Regulatory Reform*, p. 28.

14. Gilmour, "Congressional Oversight," p. 20.

The Chemical Labeling Controversy: A Chronology of Events, 1971-1982

1971

Creation of OSHA.

1971-1976

Growing awareness of adverse health impact of toxic chemicals in workplace.

1976 (FORD ADMINISTRATION)

May, Congressional Hearings on chemical dangers in the workplace conducted by House, Manpower and Energy Subcommittee of the House Committee on Government Operations.

Summer, Ford OSHA begins to focus on health standards.

1977-1981 (CARTER ADMINISTRATION)

Spring, 1978, OSHA begins to develop *Hazards Identification Rule*—Eula Bingham.

January 16, 1981, NPRM, 46 *Federal Register*, 4412. *Hazards Identification*.

1981- (REAGAN ADMINISTRATION)

February 13, 1981, Hazards Identification Rule Withdrawn, 46 *Federal Register*, 12,214.

Auchter appointed Assistant Secretary, OSHA, DOL.

Summer, Gaydos Subcommittee on Health and Safety, House Education and Labor Committee, examines OSHA efforts to develop a new toxic chemicals rule.

Summer, Dingell Subcommittee on Oversight and Investigations of House Committee on Energy and Commerce holds hearings on the Role of OMB in Regulation.

Summer, Auchter instructs OSHA Health Standards Office to develop a new toxic chemical rule.

December 21, OBM/OIRA receives revised *Hazard Communication* rule from OSHA, 46 *Federal Register*, 61,947.

December 28, John Morrall memo on OSHA toxic chemical standard sent to DeMuth.

1982

January 7, OMB denies OSHA permission to publish NPRM in *Federal Register*.

January, Chemical Manufacturers Association and American Petroleum Institute communications with OMB in support of OSHA rule (with modifications).

January, informal contacts by industry and labor representatives with White House staff on the issue of Hazard Communication rule.

January, discussion between Auchter, Ryan and Secretary of Labor Donovan about OSHA appeal to Task Force on Regulatory Relief. Decision made to appeal OMB denial of PRM by OSHA.

January, Task Force on Regulatory Relief reviews conflict. Upholds OMB decision: (1) Rule sent back to OSHA, (2) OSHA and OMB jointly sponsor an independent analysis of the Hazard Communication rule's benefits.

January, Professor Kip Viscusi, Duke University, selected to conduct independent study.

January, DOL warns of political setback for Reagan Administration if the Hazard Communication rule is sidetracked from the 553 rulemaking process.

January 29, Viscusi letter to Auchter (OSHA).

February 1, Viscusi letter to Weber (OSHA).

February, Vice-President Bush receives messages from industrial trade groups.

March 16, Viscusi analysis to Task Force and OMB; benefits slightly outweigh costs of proposed OSHA Hazard Communication standard.

March 17, Task Force on Regulatory Relief allows NPRM of OSHA Hazard Communication proposal.

March 18-19, Hearings, House Subcommittee on Manpower and Housing, Committee on Government Operations, begin on OMB's role in agency rulemaking, especially OSHA.

March 19, NPRM, Hazard Communication, 47 *Federal Register* 12,092.

OMB-OSHA Toxic Chemical Controversy: Documents, 1976-1982

1. Committee on Government Operations Report: *Chemical Dangers in the Workplace*, Part III, Findings and Conclusions; Part IV, Recommendations, September 26, 1976

III. FINDINGS AND CONCLUSIONS

1. Identifying and controlling toxic substances in the workplace is becoming progressively more difficult as more chemicals, chemical processes, and chemical products are used in industry. Tens of thousands of trade-name products, whose chemical contents are not disclosed, are used daily. Lack of knowledge about exposure hampers the identification of occupationally caused diseases, illnesses, and deaths and is a major impediment to preventing them.

2. Both employers and employees are often unaware of the toxic chemicals in the trade-name products that they buy and use. An extensive NIOSH survey shows that toxic chemicals are found in almost half of the trade-name products and that 90 percent of the time the chemical composition of trade-name products is not known to the buyer or user.

3. Manufacturers and formulators of trade-name products often do not disclose the contents of their products on the grounds that such information is a trade secret or proprietary information. These claims are made for products that contain toxic chemicals, including known carcinogens.

Thirty-Fourth Report by the Committee on Government Operations, Union Calendar No. 848, House Report No. 94-1688, 94th Cong., 2d Sess, Washington, D.C.: U.S. Government Printing Office, 1976, pp. 4-5.

4. Attempts at self-regulation by the chemical industry have not generated adequate information for buyers and users about toxic chemicals in industrial products. Voluntary labeling guidelines developed by the chemical manufacturing industry are directed primarily to the avoidance of injury from single, accidental exposures and do not address the health hazards caused by chronic low-level exposure to toxic chemical substances.

5. For the first five years of its existence, the Occupational Safety and Health Administration emphasized safety issues while paying little attention to occupational health. OSHA's neglect of occupational health is reflected in the minuscule number of health standards promulgated by OSHA, and the inadequate number of health inspections and qualified inspectors. The present OSHA administration is now giving greater attention to occupational health. But it has yet to devise a strategy adequate to deal with the occupational health crisis facing the nation today.

6. The development of an occupational health standard is a very complex task, involving consideration of scientific, medical, legal, and economic factors. Data used to develop a standard is often susceptible to varying interpretations. Officials responsible for weighing these data and making judgments on them, particularly the Assistant Secretary of OSHA, must be exceptionally competent and unbiased. Too frequent replacement of OSHA executives has deprived the agency of accumulated experience in the complex process of setting standards and thus damaged its ability to perform this crucial function.

7. The Occupational Safety and Health Administration has failed to implement Section 6(b)(7) of the Occupational Safety and Health Act, which requires that employees be apprised of and be protected from the hazards to which they are exposed. OSHA has also failed to implement Section 8(c)(3) of the Act requiring employers to maintain accurate records of employee exposures to potentially toxic materials, and to provide employees with access to these records. Although the Threshold Limit Value list was adopted as a standard, this is only the first of several steps required to protect workers. Necessary reinforcement of the exposure limits through regulations requiring labeling, monitoring, and training has not occurred. In failing to propose any standards for hazardous materials labeling based on the advisory committee's recommendations, OSHA has failed to comply with the statutory mandate that it act on such recommendations in 60 days.

8. The General Services Administration and the Department of Defense have failed to enforce a mandatory Federal standard, requiring the submission of material safety data sheets when hazardous chemical products are procured by Federal agencies. Some suppliers of chemical products refuse to submit material safety data sheets to the procuring agency as required by the Federal standard. Consequently, workers and safety health officials often have no knowledge of toxic chemicals used in Federal workplaces.

IV. RECOMMENDATIONS

1. The Occupational Safety and Health Administration should continue its initiatives in the occupational health field. It should give the highest priority to development of a regulatory system adequate to meet the occupational health challenge in this country.

2. OSHA should develop a mandatory system of identifying toxic substances in the workplace. Knowledge of workplace dangers should not wait for the tortuous process of issuing standards on an agent-by-agent basis.

3. OSHA should issue standards called for in Section 6(b)(7) of the Act and follow these with regulations prescribed under Section 8(c)(3) so that employees are aware of their exposure to potentially toxic materials.

4. The critical position of Assistant Secretary for OSHA should be occupied by a competent professional, as it is now. The importance of continuity in this position should be recognized by any newly-appointed Secretary of Labor in developing his recommendations for filling Assistant Secretaryships.

5. The General Services Administration and the Department of Defense should protect Federal workers by enforcing the requirements of Federal Standard 313A. Both should determine how many data sheets are needed under this standard. Contractors should be notified that goods not accompanied by the required material safety data sheets will not be accepted by Federal agencies. These data sheets should be periodically checked for accuracy and completeness by qualified personnel and promptly disseminated to field installations.

2. Carter Administration: NPRM, *Hazards Communication*, 46 *Federal Register*, 4412, January 16, 1981

DEPARTMENT OF LABOR

Occupational Safety and Health Administration

29 CFR Part 1910

Hazards Identification; Notice of Public Rulemaking and Public Hearings

AGENCY: Occupational Safety and Health Administration, Labor.

ACTION: Notice of proposed rulemaking; notice of public hearings.

SUMMARY: The proposed standard requires employers to identify the hazardous chemicals in their workplaces, and to inform their employees of the identity and nature of the employees' hazardous exposures. OSHA has determined that this standard is necessary because most employees are not aware of the presence of hazardous chemicals in their workplaces, or of the health effects exposure to these hazards may produce. Furthermore, many employers are also unaware of the complete chemical identities and hazards of the chemicals in their workplaces. The proposed standard would alleviate these problems through specific hazard identification and evaluation procedures, labeling requirements, and records preservation. Public hearings are being scheduled to permit interested parties the opportunity to orally present information and data related to the issues raised by this proposed rule.

DATES: Comments must be received on or before April 18, 1981.

Notices of intention to appear at the public hearings must be received on or before May 1, 1981.

The hearings are scheduled as follows:

Date Hearing Will Begin and City

1. May 26, 1981, Washington, D.C.
2. July 7, 1981, Houston, Texas
3. July 21, 1981, Chicago, Illinois
4. August 11, 1981. Philadelphia, Pennsylvania
5. September 1, 1981, San Francisco, California.

ADDRESS: Comments should be submitted, in quadruplicate, to the Docket Officer, Docket H–022, U.S. Department of Labor, Occupational Safety and Health Administration, 200 Constitution Avenue, N.W., Room S–6212, Washington, D.C. 20210; (202) 523–7894.

Notices of intention to appear should be submitted to Mr. Tom Hall, Division of Consumer Affairs, Room N3635, U.S. Department of Labor, Occupational Safety and Health Administration, 200 Constitution Avenue, N.W., Washington, D.C. 20210, (202) 523–8024.

Addresses for the hearing locations will be published in the **Federal Register** at a later date.

Written comments received and notices of intention to appear will be available for inspection and copying in the Docket Office, Room S6212 at the above address.

FOR FURTHER INFORMATION CONTACT:

Proposal

Mr. James Foster, Room N3641, Office of Public Affairs, Occupational Safety and Health Administration, U.S. Department of Labor, 200 Constitution Avenue, N.W., Washington, D.C., 20210; (202) 523–8151.

Hearings

Mr. Tom Hall, Division of Consumer Affairs, Room N–3635, U.S. Department of Labor, Occupational Safety and Health Administration, 200 Constitution Avenue, N.W., Washington, D.C. 20210. (202) 523–8024.

SUPPLEMENTARY INFORMATION: The following is a table of contents for this section of the preamble:

I. Need for a Hazards Identification Standard

II. Background to the Hazards Identification Standard

A. Introduction

B. Survey Estimates of Potential Workplace Hazardous Exposures

C. Previous Recognition of the Need for Labeling
  1. Occupational Safety and Health Administration Standards.
  2. National Institute for Occupational Safety and Health (NIOSH) Criteria Document.
  3. Report of the OSHA Standards Advisory Committee.
  4. American National Standards Institute (ANSI) Standard.

D. Selected Labeling Regulations Which are Currently in Effect
  1. Occupational Safety and Health Administration (OSHA).
  2. Fair Packaging and Labeling Act.
  3. Environmental Protection Agency (EPA).
  4. Food and Drug Administration (FDA).
  5. Department of Transportation (DOT).
  6. Consumer Product Safety Commission (CPSC).
  7. State Regulations.
  8. European Economic Community (EEC).

E. History of OSHA's Proposed Labeling Standard

III. Summary of the Proposed Standard

IV. Major Issues for the Rulemaking

A. Issues of Scope and Type of Standard
  1. The generic approach to a hazard identification standard.
  2. Employers covered by the standard.
  3. Duty to disclose specific chemical identity and impact on trade secrets.

B. Scientific Issues
  1. Hazards covered by the standard (general issues).
  a. Universal vs. hazard labeling.
  b. General or workplace-specific hazard determinations.
  c. Impurities, Intermediates, By-products.

2. Hazards covered by the standard (definitional issues).
  a. General.
  b. Physical Hazards.
  c. Health Hazards.
  d. Specific definitional issues.
  e. Regulation of physical hazards by other agencies.
  f. Regulation of health hazards by other agencies.
  3. Hazard Determination Process.
  a. Description.
  b. Performance vs. specification standard for the hazard determination process and evaluation scheme.
  c. Literature search.
  d. Use of TDB, standard reference works and NIOSH documents.
  e. Search files.
  f. Concentration of constituent substances and mixtures hazard determination.
  4. Evaluation procedure.
  a. In general.
  b. Adequate and well-controlled study.
  c. Case studies use.
  d. Statistical significance.
  e. Expert opinions.

C. Regulatory Issues
  1. "Performance" vs. "specification" requirements.
  2. Content and format of labels and placards.
  3. Disclosure of chemical identity in labels shipped in commerce.
  4. Exclusion of small containers.
  5. Access to records and documents required by the standard.
  6. Worker access to safety data sheets.
  7. Material safety data sheets.
  8. Substance-employee identification lists.
  9. The need for generic training requirements.
  10. Impact on small business.
  11. Miscellaneous issues.

D. References

3. Reagan Administration: Withdrawal of Proposed Hazards Communication Rule, 46 *Federal Register,* 12,214, February 13, 1981

29 CFR Part 1910

Hazards Identification

Note.—This document originally appeared in the Federal Register for Thursday, February 12, 1981. It is reprinted in this issue to meet requirements for publication on the Tuesday/Friday schedule assigned to the Department of Labor.

AGENCY: Occupational Safety and Health Administration, Department of Labor.

ACTION: Withdrawal of Proposed Rules.

SUMMARY: On January 16, 1981, (46 FR 4412–4453), the Assistant Secretary for Occupational Safety and Health issued a proposed standard that would require employers to identify the hazardous chemicals in their workplaces through specific hazard identification and evaluation procedures, labeling requirements, and record preservation. The proposed rule is withdrawn. This will permit the Department to consider regulatory alternatives that had not been fully considered and then, if appropriate, repropose the regulation. This process will eliminate the need for the public to comment on a proposal that the Department may change significantly.

EFFECTIVE DATE: February 12, 1981.

FOR FURTHER INFORMATION CONTACT: Mr. James Foster, Room N3641, Office of Public Affairs, Occupational Safety and Health Administration, U.S. Department of Labor, 200 Constitution Avenue, NW., Washington, D.C. 20210; Telephone: (202) 523–8151.

Signed at Washington, D.C. this 29th day of January 1981.

David C. Zeigler,

Acting Assistant Secretary of Labor for Occupational Safety and Health.

[FR Doc. 81–4944 Filed 2–10–81; 4:00 pm]

BILLING CODE 4510-26-M

4. OSHA Hazard Communication Standard, September 1981

s1910. HAZARD COMMUNICATION

(a) *Scope and application.* (1) This section requires chemical manufacturers to assess the hazards of chemicals which they produce, and all employers in SIC Codes 20 through 39 (Division D, Standard Industrial Classification Manual) to provide information to their employees about the hazardous chemicals which they use by means of a hazard communication program, labels, placards, material safety data sheets, and information and training.

(2) This section applies to any chemical which is know to be present in the workplace in such a manner that employees may be exposed under normal conditions of use or in a foreseeable emergency.

(3) Any mixture which is comprised of at least one (1) percent (by weight or volume) of any chemical determined to be hazardous shall also be considered hazardous for purposes of this section, unless the mixture has been evaluated as a whole and the data indicates it is not hazardous.

(4) If employee protection necessitates disclosure of hazardous chemicals comprising less than one (1) percent (by weight or volume) of a mixture, the Assistant Secretary may lower or eliminate this concentration exemption by a rulemaking notice in the Federal Register.

(5) This section does not apply to chemicals being developed and used only in research laboratories.

(6) This section does not apply to chemicals which are foods, drugs, cosmetics or tobacco products intended for personal consumption by employees while in the workplace.

(b) *Definitions.*

"Assistant Secretary" means the Assistant Secretary of Labor for Occupational Safety and Health, U.S. Department of Labor, or designee.

"CAS number" means the unique identification number assigned by the Chemical Abstracts Service to chemicals.

"Chemical" means any element, chemical compound or mixture of elements and/or compounds.

"Chemical manufacturer" is an establishment where chemicals are produced for use or distribution.

"Chemical name" is the scientific designation of a chemical in accordance with the nomenclature system developed by the International Union of Pure and Applied Chemistry (IUPAC) or the Chemical Abstracts Service (CAS) rules of nomenclature.

"Combustible" means any liquid having a flashpoint at or above 100°F (37.8°C). Combustible liquids shall be divided into two classes as follows:

(i) Class II liquids shall include those with flashpoints at or above 100°F (37.8°C) and below 140°F (60°C) except any mixture having components with flashpoints of 200°F (93.3°C) or higher, the volume of which make up 99 percent or more of the total volume of the mixture;

(ii) Class III liquids shall include those with flashpoints at or above 140 °F (60 °C). Class III liquids are subdivided into two subclasses:

(A) Class IIIA liquids shall include those with flashpoints at or above 140 °F (60 °C) and below 200 °F (93.3 °C), except any mixture having components with flashpoints of 200 °F (93.3 °C), or higher, the total volume of which make up 99 percent or more of the total volume of the mixture;

(B) Class IIIB liquids shall include those with flashpoints at or above 200 °F (93.3 °C). This section does not cover Class IIIB liquids. Where the term "Class III liquids" is used in this section, it shall mean only Class IIIA liquids;

(iii) When a combustible liquid is heated for use to within 30 °F (16.7 °C) of its flashpoint, it shall be handled in accordance with the requirements for the next lower class of liquids.

"Common name" means any designation or identification such as code name, code number, trade name, brand name or generic name used to identify a chemical other than by its chemical name.

"Compressed gas" means:

(i) A gas or mixture of gases having, in a container, an absolute pressure exceeding 40 psi at 70 °F (21.1 °C); or

(ii) A gas or mixture of gases having, in a container, an absolute pressure exceeding 104 psi at 130 °F (54.4 °C) regardless of the pressure at 70 °F (21.1 °C); or

(iii) A liquid having a vapor pressure exceeding 40 psi at 100 °F (37.8 °C) as determined by ASTM D-323-72.

"Container" means any bag, barrel, bottle, box, can, cylinder, drum, storage tank, reaction vessel, or the like that contains a hazardous chemical. For purposes of this section, pipes or piping systems are not considered to be containers.

"Designated representative" means any individual or organization to whom an employee or former employee gives written authorization to exercise such employee's rights under this section.

"Director" means the Director, National Institute for Occupational Safety and Health, U.S. Department of Health and Human Services, or designee.

"Emergency" means any occurrence such as, but not limited to, equipment failure, rupture of containers, or failure of control equipment which may or does result in an uncontrolled release of a hazardous chemical into the workplace.

"Employee" means a worker who may be exposed under normal operating conditions or foreseeable emergencies to hazardous chemicals in a covered workplace, including, but not limited to production workers, line supervisors, and repair or maintenance personnel. Office workers, grounds maintenance personnel, security personnel or non-resident management are generally not included, unless their job performance routinely involves potential exposure to hazardous chemicals.

"Employer" means an establishment in SIC Codes 20-39 that manufactures or uses hazardous chemicals.

"Explosive" means a chemical that causes a sudden, almost instantaneous release of pressure, gas, and heat when subjected to sudden shock, pressure, or high temperature.

"Flammable" means a chemical that falls into one of the following categories:

(i) "Aerosol, flammable" means an aerosol that, when tested by the method described in 16 CFR 1500.45, yields a flame projection exceeding 18 inches at full valve opening, or a flashback (a flame extending back to the valve) at any degree of valve opening;

(ii) "Gas, flammable" means:

(A) A gas that, at ambient temperature and pressure, forms a flammable mixture with air at a concentration of thirteen (13) percent by volume or less; or

(B) A gas that, at ambient temperature and pressure, forms a range of flammable mixtures with air wider than twelve (12) percent by volume, regardless of the lower limit; and,

(C) Gaseous ammonia;

(iii) "Liquid, flammable" means any liquid having a flashpoint below 100 °F (37.8 °C), except any mixture having components with flashpoints of 100 °F (37.8 °C) or higher, the total of which make up 99 percent or more of the total volume of the mixture. Flammable liquids shall be known as Class I liquids. Class I liquids are divided into three classes as follows:

(A) Class IA shall include liquids having flashpoints below 73 °F (22.8 °C) and having a boiling point below 100 °F (37.8 °C);

(B) Class IB shall include liquids having flashpoints below 73 °F (22.8 °C) and having a boiling point at or above 100 °F (37.8 °C); and

(C) Class IC shall include liquids having flashpoints at or above 73 °F (22.8 °C) and below 100 °F (37.8 °C);

(iv) "Solid, flammable" means a solid, other than a blasting agent or explosive as defined in s1910.109(a), that is liable to cause fire through friction, absorption of moisture, spontaneous chemical change, or retained heat from manufacturing or processing, or which can be ignited readily and when ignited burns so vigorously and persistently as to create a serious hazard. A chemical shall be considered to be a flammable solid if, when tested by the method described in 16 CFR 1500.44, it ignites and burns with a self-sustained flame at a rate greater than one-tenth of an inch per second along its major axis.

"Flashpoint" means the minimum temperature at which a liquid gives off a vapor in sufficient concentration to ignite when tested as follows:

(i) Tagliabue Closed Tester (See American National Standard Method of Test for Flash Point by Tag Closed Tester, Z11.24-1979 (ASTM D 56-79))—for liquids with a viscosity of less than 45 Saybolt Universal Seconds (SUS) at 100 °F (37.8 °C), that do not contain suspended solids and do not have a tendency to form a surface film under test; or

(ii) Pensky-Martens Closed Tester (see American National Standard Method of Test for Flash Point by Pensky-Martens Closed Tester, Z11.7-1979 (ASTM D 93-79))—for liquids with a viscosity equal to or greater than 45 SUS at 100 °F (37.8 °C), or that contain suspended solids, or that have a tendency to form a surface film under test; or

(iii) Setaflash Closed Tester (see American National Standard Method of Test for Flash Point by Setaflash Closed Tester (ASTM D 3278-78)).

NOTE: For mixtures, if the result of any test method described in paragraphs (i)-(iii) is above 100 °F (37.8 °C), evaporate a fresh sample to ninety (90) percent of the original volume and retest. The lower of the two values shall be taken as the flash point.

Organic peroxides, which undergo autoaccelerating thermal decomposition, are excluded from any of the flashpoint determination methods specified above.

"Hazardous chemical" means any chemical which is combustible, a compressed gas, explosive, flammable, a health hazard, an organic peroxide, an oxidizer, pyrophoric, unstable (reactive) or water-reactive.

"Hazard warning" means any words, pictures, symbols, or combination thereof which convey the hazards of the chemical(s) in the container.

"Health hazard" means a chemical which, upon exposure, may result in the occurrence of acute or chronic health effects in employees. For further explanation, see Appendix A, Health Hazards, of this section.

"Identity" means any chemical or common name which is indicated on the material safety data sheet (MSDS) for the chemical. The identity used shall permit cross-references to be made among the required list of hazardous chemicals, the label and the MSDS.

"Organic peroxide" means an organic compound that contains the bivalent -o-o structure and which may be considered to be a structural derivative of hydrogen peroxide where one or both of the hydrogen atoms has been replaced by an organic radical.

"Oxidizer" means a chemical other than a blasting agent or explosive as defined in s1910.109(a), that initiates or promotes combustion in other materials, thereby causing fire either of itself or through the release of oxygen or other gases.

"Pyrophoric" means a chemical that will ignite spontaneously in air at a temperature of 130 °F (54.4 °C) or below.

"Unstable (reactive)" means a chemical which in the pure state, or as produced or transported, will vigorously polymerize, decompose, condense, or will become self-reactive under conditions of shocks, pressure or temperature.

"Use" means handle, react, process, package or repackage, or transport.

"Water-reactive" means a chemical that reacts with water to release a gas that is either flammable or presents a health hazard.

"Work area" means a room or defined space in an establishment where hazardous chemicals are produced or used, and where employees are present.

"Workplace" means an establishment at one geographical location containing one or more work areas.

(c) *Hazard determination and communication program.*

(1) Each chemical manufacturer shall evaluate the chemicals produced in his/her workplace to determine if they are hazardous. See Appendix B for guidelines.

(2) Each employer shall develop and implement a hazard communication program for his/her workplace which at least meets the criteria specified in paragraphs (d), (e), and (f) of this section for labels and placards, material safety data sheets, and employee information and training, and which includes the following:

(i) The procedures the employer will use to determine the hazards of the chemicals which he/she produces;

(ii) A list of the hazardous chemicals known to be present in the workplace (using an identity that is referenced on the appropriate material safety data sheet); and

(iii) The methods the employer will use to inform employees of the hazards of non-routine tasks, for example, repair and maintenance of unlabeled pipes or the cleaning of reactor vessels.

(3) The employer may rely on an existing hazard communication program to comply with this section provided that it meets the criteria established in this paragraph.

(4) The required list of hazardous chemicals shall be made available to employees or their designated representatives, the Assistant Secretary and the Director.

(d) *Labels and placards.* (1) The employer shall ensure that each container of hazardous chemicals in the workplace is labeled, tagged or marked with the following information:

(i) Identity of the hazardous chemical(s) contained therein; and

(ii) Hazard warnings.

(2) When stationary containers in a work area have similar contents and hazards, the employer may post signs or placards to convey the required information rather than affixing labels to each individual container.

(3) The employer shall ensure that each container of hazardous chemicals leaving the workplace is labeled, tagged or marked with the following information:

(i) Identity of the hazardous chemical(s);

(ii) Hazard warnings; and

(iii) Name, address and telephone number of the manufacturer.

(4) The employer need not affix new labels to comply with this standard if existing labels already convey the necessary information.

(5) The employer is not required to label containers of ten gallons (37.8 liters) or less in volume, into which hazardous chemicals are transferred from labeled containers, and which are intended only for the immediate use of the employee who performs the transfer.

(e) *Material safety data sheets.* (1) Each employer shall obtain or develop a material safety data sheet for each hazardous chemical which he/she produces or uses.

(2) Each material safety data sheet shall reflect the information contained in the sources consulted by the chemical manufacturer in his/her hazard determination under paragraphs (c)(1) and (2) of this section, and shall contain at least the following information:

(i) The chemical and common name(s), CAS Number(s) and the identity used on the label for all hazardous ingredients which comprise greater than one (1) percent of the chemical (except as provided by paragraph (g) of this section on trade secrets);

(ii) Physical and chemical characteristics of the hazardous chemical (such as vapor pressure, flash point);

(iii) The physical hazards of the hazardous chemical, including the potential for fire, explosion, and reactivity;

(iv) Known acute and chronic health effects of exposure to the hazardous chemical, including signs and symptoms of exposure, and medical conditions which may be aggravated by exposure to the chemical;

(v) The primary route(s) of entry and permissible exposure limit (for those hazardous chemicals for which OSHA has promulgated a permissible exposure limit);

(vi) Precautions for safe handling and use, including appropriate hygienic practices, procedures for decontaminating equipment prior to performing repairs and maintenance, and procedures for clean-up of leaks or spills;

(vii) Engineering controls recommended;

(viii) Work practices recommended;

(ix) Personal protective equipment recommended;

(x) Emergency and first aid procedures;

(xi) The date of preparation of the material safety data sheet or the last change to it; and

(xii) The name, address and telephone number of the manufacturer preparing the sheet.

(3) If no information is found for any given category on the material safety data sheet, the employer shall mark it to indicate no information was found. Blank spaces on existing material safety data sheets will be considered to indicate that information was sought but not found. It is the chemical manufacturer's responsibility to ensure that this interpretation is accurate. As the MSDSs are updated, the blanks shall be marked as required.

(4) If the employer becomes aware of any information which is both new and significant regarding the health hazard of a chemical, this shall be added to the material safety data sheet within a reasonable period of time.

(5) Chemical manufacturers shall ensure that manufacturing purchasers of hazardous chemicals are provided an appropriate material safety data sheet with their initial shipment, and with the first shipment after a material safety data sheet is updated. If the material safety data sheet is not provided with the shipment, the purchasing manufacturing employer shall obtain one from the chemical manufacturer as soon as possible.

(6) The employer shall maintain copies of the required material safety data sheets for each hazardous chemical in the workplace, and shall ensure that they are readily accessible.

7. Material safety data sheets for the hazardous chemicals they are exposed to shall be made available to employees and their designated representative, and upon request, to the Assistant Secretary and the Director.

(f) *Employee information and training.* The employer shall provide employees with information and training on hazardous chemicals in the workplace at the time of their initial assignment, and whenever a new hazardous chemical is introduced into their work area.

(1) *Information.* Employees shall be informed of:

(i) The requirements of this regulation;

(ii) Any operation in the work area where hazardous chemicals are present; and

(iii) The location and availability of the list of hazardous chemicals and material safety data sheets required by this section.

(2) *Training.* Employee training shall include at least:

(i) Methods and observations the employee may use to detect the presence or release of a hazardous chemical in the workplace;

(ii) The hazards of the chemicals in the workplace;

(iii) The measures employees can take to protect themselves from the hazards; and

(iv) The details of the hazard communication program developed by the employer and how employees can obtain and use the appropriate hazard information.

(g) *Trade secrets.* (1) An employer may withhold the precise chemcial name of a chemical if:

(i) The employer can substantiate that it is a trade secret;

(ii) The chemical is not a carcinogen, mutagen, teratogen, or a cause of significant irreversible damage to human organs or body systems for which there is a need to know the precise chemical name;

(iii) The chemical is identified by a generic chemical classification which would provide useful information to a health professional;

(iv) All other information on the properties and effects of the chemical required by this section is contained in the material safety data sheet;

(v) The material safety data sheet indicates which category of information is being withheld on trade secret grounds; and

(vi) In any event, the withheld information is provided on a confidential basis to a treating physician who states in writing (except in an emergency situation) that a patient's health problems may be the result of occupational exposure. A statement to this effect with the name of the manufacturer and an emergency telephone number shall be included in the material safety data sheet.

(2) To the extent that names of trade secret chemicals are disclosed, the employer may condition employee, designated representative, and downstream employer access to such information upon acceptance of a reasonable confidentiality agreement. The agreement may restrict use of the information to health purposes, prohibit disclosure of the information to anyone other than a treating physician without the consent of the originating employer, and provide for compensation or other legally appropriate relief for any competitive harm which results from a breach of the agreement.

(h) *Effective dates.* Employers shall be in compliance with this section within the following time periods.

Employer/No. of Employees	Pure Substances	Mixtures
Chemical Manufacturers		
More than 250	1 year	2 years
25 -250	1 ½ years	2 ½ years
Fewer than 25	2 years	3 years
Other Employers	3 ½ years	3 ½ years

APPENDIX A, HEALTH HAZARDS

Although safety hazards related to the physical characteristics of a chemical can be objectively defined in terms of testing requirements (e.g. flammability), health hazard definitions are less precise and more subjective. Health hazards may cause measurable changes in the body—such as decreased pulmonary function. These changes are generally indicated by the occurrence of signs and symptoms in the exposed employees—such as shortness of breath, a non-measurable, subjective feeling. Employees exposed to such hazards should be apprised of both the change in body function and the signs and symptoms that may occur to signal that change.

The determination of occupational health hazards is complicated by the fact that many of the effects or signs and symptoms occur commonly in non-occupationally exposed populations, so that effects of exposure are difficult to separate from normally occurring illnesses. Occasionally, a substance causes an effect that is rarely seen in the population at large, such as angiosarcomas caused by vinyl chloride exposure, thus making it easier to ascertain that the occupational exposure was the primary causative factor. More often, however, the effects are common, such as lung cancer. The situation is further complicated by the fact that most chemicals have not been adequately tested to determine their health hazard potential, and data does not exist to substantiate these effects.

There have been many attempts to categorize effects and to define them in various ways. Generally, the terms "acute" and "chronic" are used to delineate between effects on the basis of severity or duration. "Acute" effects usually occur rapidly as a result of short-term exposures, are of short duration, and generally reversible. "Chronic" effects occur as a result of long-term exposure, are of long duration, and may be irreversible. Neither of these terms gives sufficient guidance to those attempting to define a health hazard.

The acute effects referred to most frequently are those defined by the American National Standards Institute (ANSI) standard for Precautionary Labeling of Hazardous Industrial Chemicals (Z129.1-1976)—irritation, corrosivity, sensitization and lethal dose. Although these are important health effects, they do not adequately cover the considerable range of acute effects which may occur as a result of occupational exposure, such as, for example, narcosis.

Similarly, the term chronic effect is often used to cover only carcinogenicity, teratogenicity, and mutagenicity. These effects are obviously a concern in the workplace, but again, do not adequately cover the area of chronic effects, excluding, for example blood dyscrasias (anemia).

Although the goal of defining precisely, in measurable terms, every possible health effect that may occur in the workplace as a result of chemical exposures cannot realistically be accomplished, this does not negate the need for employees to be protected from such effects when they are known, and to be informed of all types of health hazards. Consequently, in assessing the health hazard potential of a chemical for purposes of compliance with this standard, the employer shall consider the scientifically well-established evidence of any type of health effect which may occur in any body system of his/her employees. Some sources of information which the employer may wish to consult in conducting the hazard evaluation are listed in Appendix B.

The following is a target organ categorization of effects which may occur, including examples of signs and symptoms and chemicals which have been found to cause such effects. These examples are presented to illustrate the range and diversity of effects and hazards found in the workplace, and the broad scope employers must consider in this area, but are not intended to be all-inclusive.

1. Hepatotoxic agents: Chemicals which produce liver damage
   Signs & Symptoms: Jaundice; hepatitis
   Chemicals: Carbon tetrachloride; nitrosamines

2. Nephrotoxic agents: Chemicals which produce kidney damage
   Signs & Symptoms: Decreased elimination of wastes
   Chemicals: Halogenated hydrocarbons; uranium

3. Neurotoxic agents: Chemicals which produce their primary toxic effects on the nervous system

Signs & Symptoms   Narcosis; behavioral changes; decrease in motor functions

Chemicals: Mercury; carbon disulfide

4. Agents which act on the blood or hemato-poietic system: Lower blood pressure; deprive the body tissues of oxygen

Signs & Symptoms: Leukemia; anemia

Chemicals: Carbon monoxide; cyanides

5. Agents which damage the lung: Chemicals which irritate or damage the pulmonary tissue

Signs & Symptoms: Cough; tightness in chest; fibrosis

Chemicals: Silica; asbestos

6. Reproductive toxins: Chemicals which affect the reproductive capabilities including chromosomal damage (mutations) and effects on fetuses (teratogenesis)

Signs & Symptoms: Birth defects; sterility

Chemicals: Lead; DBCP

7. Cutaneous hazards: Chemicals which affect the dermal layer of the body

Signs & Symptoms: Defatting of the skin; rashes; irritation

Chemicals: Ketones; chlorinated compounds

8. Eye hazards: Chemicals which affect the eye or visual capacity

Signs & Symptoms: Conjunctivitis; corneal damage

Chemicals: Organic solvents; acids

APPENDIX B, HAZARD DETERMINATION GUIDELINES

The quality of a hazard communication program is largely dependent upon the adequacy and accuracy of the hazard determination. The hazard determination requirement is performance-oriented. Chemical manufacturers are not required to follow any specific methods for determining hazards, but it is incumbent upon them to demonstrate that they have adequately ascertained the scientifically well-established hazards of the chemicals produced. This Appendix is intended to provide employers, who may desire to use it, with a list of some basic sources of reference for the hazards of chemicals.

Sources

—Any information employers have in their own company files such as toxicity testing results or illness experience of company employees.

—Any information obtained from the supplier of the chemical, such as material safety data sheets or product safety bulletins.

—Any information obtained from the following source list (latest editions should be used):

Condensed Chemical Dictionary, by A. and E. Rose
    Reinhold Publishing Corporation
    450 West 33rd Street
    New York, NY 10001

The Merck Index: An Encyclopedia of Chemicals and Drugs
    Merck and Company, Inc.
    126 E. Lincoln Avenue
    Rahway, NJ 07065

IARC Monographs on the Evaluation of the Carcinogenic Risk of Chemicals to Man
    Geneva: World Health Organization
    International Agency for Research on Cancer, 1972-1977
    (Multivolume work)

American Industrial Hygiene Association Hygienic Guides
    American Industrial Hygiene Association
    66 South Miller Road
    Akron, OH 44313

Industrial Hygiene and Toxicology, by F.A. Patty
    John Wiley & Sons, Inc.
    New York, NY
    (Five volumes)

Toxicology: The Basic Science of Poisons, by Louis J. Casarett and John Doull
    Macmillan Publishing Co., Inc.
    New York, NY

Industrial Toxicology, by Alice Hamilton and Harriet L. Hardy
    Publishing Sciences Group, Inc.
    Acton, MA

Toxicology of the Eye, by W. Morton Grant
    Charles C. Thomas
    Springfield, MO

Handbook of Chemistry and Physics
    Chemical Rubber Company
    18901 Cranwood Parkway
    Cleveland, OH 44128

Threshold Limit Values for Chemical Substances and Physical Agents in the Workroom Environment with Intended Changes
    American Conference of Governmental Industrial Hygienists
    1014 Broadway
    Cincinnati, OH 45202

Dangerous Properties of Industrial Materials, by N. Irving Sax
    Reinhold Publishing Corporation
    450 West 33rd Street
    New York, NY 10001

NOTE: the following documents are on sale by the Superintendent of Documents, U.S. Government Printing Office, Washington, D.C. 20402

Occupational Health Guidelines
    NIOSH/OSHA

NIOSH/OSHA Pocket Guide to Chemical Hazards
    NIOSH Pub. No. 78-210

Registry of Toxic Effects of Chemical Substances
    U.S. Department of Health and Human Services
    Public Health Service
    Center for Disease Control
    National Institute for Occupational Safety and Health
The Industrial Environment—Its Evaluation and Control
    U.S. Department of Health and Human Services
    Public Health Service
    Center for Disease Control
    National Institute for Occupational Safety and Health
Miscellaneous Documents—National Institute for Occupational Safety and Health

1. Criteria for a recommended standard . . .
   Occupational Exposure to "_____"

2. Special Hazard Reviews

3. Occupational Hazard Assessment

4. Current Intelligence Bulletins

Bibliographic Data Bases

Service Provider	*File Name*
Bibliographic Retrieval Services (BRS)	AGRICOLA
Corporation Park, Bldg. 702	BIOSIS PREVIEWS
Scotia, New York 12302	CA CONDENSATES
	CA SEARCH
	DRUGINFO
	MEDLARS
	MEDOC
	NTIS
	POLLUTION ABSTRACTS
	SCIENCE CITATION INDEX
	SSIE
Lockheed - DIALOG	AGRICOLA
Lockheed Missiles & Space Company, Inc.	BIOSIS PREV. 1972-PRESENT
P.O. Box 44481	BIOSIS PREV. 1969-71
San Francisco, CA 94144	CA CONDENSATES 1970-71
	CA SEARCH 1972-76
	CA SEARCH 1977-PRESENT
	CHEMNAME
	CONFERENCE PAPERS INDEX
	FOOD SCIENCE & TECH. ABSTR.
	FOODS ADLIBRA
	INTL. PHARMACEUTICAL ABSTR.

Lockheed-DIALOG
(continued)

NTIS
POLLUTION ABSTRACTS
SCISEARCH 1978-PRESENT
SCISEARCH 1974-77
SSIE CURRENT RESEARCH

SDC - ORBIT
SDC Search Service
Department No. 2230
Pasadena, CA 91051

AGRICOLA
BIOCODES
BIOSIS/BI06973
CAS6771/CAS7276
CAS77
CHEMDEX
CONFERENCE
ENVIROLINE
LABORDOC
NTIS
POLLUTION
SSIE

Chemical Information System (CIS)
Chemical Information Systems, Inc.
7215 Yorke Road
Baltimore, MD 21212

Structure & Nomenclature
    Search System
Acute Toxicity (RTECS)
Consumer Products Chemicals
Oil and Hazardous Materials

National Library of Medicine
Department of Health and
    Human Services
Public Health Service
National Institutes of Health
Bethesda, MD 20209

Toxicology Data Bank (TDB)
MEDLINE
TOXLINE
CANCERLIT
RTECS

5. *Request for OMB Review*, SF 83 (OMB), Hazard Communication Rule, December, 1981

REQUEST FOR OMB REVIEW
(Under the Paperwork Reduction Act and Executive Order 12291)

Important — Read instructions (SF-83A) before completing this form. *Submit the required number of copies of SF-83*, together with the material for which review is requested to:

Office of Information and Regulatory Affairs
Office of Management and Budget
Washington, D.C. 20503

1. Department/Agency and Bureau/Office originating request
Department of Labor, Occupational Safety & Health Admin., Direct. of Health Stds. Progs.

3. Name(s) and telephone number(s) of person(s) who can best answer questions regarding request
Joanne Linhard/Jennifer Silk (202) 523-7076/7166

2. 6-digit Agency/Bureau number *(first part of 11-digit Treasury Account No.)*
1 6 0 4 0 0

4. 3-digit functional code *(last part of 11-digit Treasury Account No.)*
5 5 4

5. Title of Information Collection or Rulemaking

Hazard Communication

C. Is this a rulemaking submission under Section 3504(h) of P.L. 96-511? *(Check one)*
1 ☐ No (Section 3507 submission)
2 ☒ Yes, NPRM. Expected date of publication: __Fall 1981__
3 ☐ Yes, final rule. Expected date of publication: _____
Effective date: _____

6. A. Is any information collection (reporting or recordkeeping) involved? *(Check one)*
1 ☒ Yes and proposal is attached for review
2 ☐ Yes but proposal is not attached — skip to question D.
3 ☐ No — skip to question D.

B. Are the respondents primarily educational agencies or institutions or is the purpose related to Federal education programs?
☐ Yes   ☒ No

D. At what phase of rulemaking is this submission made? *(Check one)*
1 ☐ Not applicable
2 ☒ Major rule, at NPRM stage
3 ☐ Major Final rule for which no NPRM was published
4 ☐ Major Final rule, after publication of NPRM
5 ☐ Nonmajor rule, at NPRM stage
6 ☐ Nonmajor rule, at Final stage

COMPLETE SHADED PORTION IF INFORMATION COLLECTION PROPOSAL IS ATTACHED

7. Current (or former) OMB Number
None

Expiration Date
N/A

8. Requested Expiration Date
1984

12. Agency report form number(s)
None

13. Are respondents only Federal agencies?
☐ Yes   ☒ No

9. Is proposed information collection listed in the information collection budget?
☒ Yes   ☐ No

10. Will this proposed information collection cause the agency to exceed its information collection budget allowance? *(If yes, attach amendment request from agency head.)*
☐ Yes   ☒ No

11. Number of report forms submitted for approval
None

14. Type of request *(Check one)*
1 ☐ preliminary plan
2 ☒ new *(not previously approved or expired more than 6 months ago)*
3 ☐ revision
4 ☐ extension *(adjustment to burden only)*
5 ☐ extension *(no change)*
6 ☐ reinstatement *(expired within 6 months)*

15.

16. Classification of Change in Burden *(explain in supporting statement)*

			No. of Responses	No. of Reporting Hours	Cost to the Public
a. Approximate size of universe *(if sample)*	N/A	a. In inventory	0	0	$ 0
b. Size of sample	N/A	b. As proposed	328,000	656,000	$14,168,000 *
c. Estimated number of respondents or record keepers per year	328,000	c. Difference (b-a)	328,000	656,000	$14,168,000 *
d. Reports annually by each respondent *(item 25)*	1	Explanation of difference (indicate as many as apply)			*Over first 3 years
		Adjustments			
e. Total annual responses *(item 15c x 15d)*	328,000	d. Correction-error	±	±	± $
		e. Correction-reestimate	±	±	± $
f. Estimated average number of hours per response	2	f. Change in use	±	±	± $
		Program changes			
g. Estimated total hours of annual burden in Fiscal Year *(item 15e x 15f)*	656,000	g. Increase	+	+	+ $
		h. Decrease	−	−	− $

Standard Form 83 (Rev. 3-81)
For Use Beginning 4/1/81

151

1 Abstract—Needs and Uses *(50 words or less)*
This standard is necessary because many employers and employees are not aware of the presence of hazardous chemicals in their workplaces. Compliance with the standard should serve to alleviate this lack of awareness and provide an impetus for employees and employers to devise better means of protection from these hazards.

18. Related report form(s) *(give OMB number(s), IRCN(s), internal agency report form number(s) or symbol(s))*	20. Catalog of Federal Domestic Assistance Program Number
None	17.500
	21. Small business or organization ☒ Yes ☐ No

19. Type of affected public *(Check as many as apply)*
1 ☐ *individuals or households*
2 ☐ *state or local governments*
3 ☐ *farms*
4 ☒ *businesses or other institutions (except farms)*

22. Type of activity of affected public—indicate 3-digit Standard Industrial Classification (SIC) code(s) (up to 10) — if over 10, check   ☒ Multiple   or   ☐ All

___ ___ ___ ___ ___ ___ ___ ___ ___ ___

23. Brief description of affected public *(e.g.,"retail grocery stores," "State education agencies," "households in 50 largest SMSAs")*
Chemical manufacturers and all manufacturers having facilities in the manufacturing division (SIC Codes 20-39).

24. Purpose *(Check as many as apply. If more than one, indicate predominant by an asterisk)*
1 ☐ application for benefits
2 ☐ program evaluation
3 ☐ general purpose statistics
4 ☒ regulatory or compliance
5 ☐ program planning or management
6 ☐ research

26. Collection method *(Check as many as apply)*
1 ☐ mail self-administered
2 ☐ other self-administered
3 ☐ telephone interview
4 ☐ personal interview
5 ☒ recordkeeping requirement:
   Required retention period: ___*___ years
6 ☐ other—describe: *Varies--see support. stat.

25. Frequency of Use
1 ☐ Nonrecurring
   Recurring *(check as many as apply)*
2 ☒ on occasion   6 ☐ semiannually
3 ☐ weekly   7 ☐ annually
4 ☐ monthly   8 ☐ biennially
5 ☐ quarterly   9 ☒ other—describe: As necessary to keep current.

27. Collection agent *(Check one)*
1 ☐ requesting Department/Agency
2 ☐ other Federal Department/Agency
3 ☐ private contractor
4 ☒ recordkeeping requirement
5 ☐ other—describe:

28. Authority for agency for information collection or rulemaking—indicate statute, regulation, judicial decree, etc.
P.L. 91-596   29 U.S.C. 651, et. seq.

30. Do you promise confidentiality?
(If yes, explain basis for pledge in supporting statement.)   ☒ Yes   ☐ No

31. Will the proposed information collection create a new or become part of an existing Privacy Act system of records? *(If yes, attach Federal Register notice or proposed draft of notice.)*   ☐ Yes   ☒ No

29. Respondent's obligation to reply *(Check as many as apply)*
1 ☐ voluntary
2 ☐ required to obtain or retain benefit
3 ☒ mandatory—cite statute, not CFR (attach copy of statutory authority)   29 U.S.C. 655, 657

32. Cost to Federal Government of information collection or rulemaking $ 0

COMPLETE ITEMS 33 THRU 35 ONLY IF RULEMAKING SUBMISSION

33. Compliance costs to the public	34. Is there a regulatory impact analysis attached?	35. Is there a statutory or judicial deadline affecting issuance?
$_____	☐ Yes ☐ No	☐ Yes. Enter date _____ ☐ No

CERTIFICATION BY AUTHORIZED OFFICIALS SUBMITTING REQUEST—We certify that the information collection or rulemaking submitted for review is necessary for the proper performance of the agency's functions, that the proposal represents the minimum public burden and Federal cost consistent with need, and is consistent with applicable OMB and agency policy directives. Signature and title of:

APPROVING POLICY OFFICIAL FOR AGENCY	DATE	SUBMITTING OFFICIAL	DATE

6. Memorandum, OSHA's *Hazard Communication Rules*, December 28, 1981, John Morrall to Chris DeMuth (OMB)

DEC 28 1981

MEMORANDUM TO: CHRIS DeMUTH

FROM   : JOHN MORRALL

THROUGH   : TOM HOPKINS AND JIM TOZZI

SUBJECT   : OSHA'S HAZARD COMMUNICATION RULES

OSHA has submitted for OMB review under E.O. 12291 its proposed Hazard Communication rule (so-called "chemical labeling"). This proposal would require chemical manufacturers to assess the hazards of chemicals which they produce. Moreover, all employers in SIC Codes 20 through 39 would be required to provide information to their employees about the hazardous chemicals which they use by means of a hazard communication program, labels, placards, material safety data sheets, and information and training. By the sixty day clock for major proposals, OMB has until January 18 to make a determination about the consistency of this rule with the Executive Order. OSHA, however, would like that determination as soon as possible. LaVerne Collins and I have discussed this matter and are in agreement.

Findings

We do not believe that the proposed rule is consistent with sections 2(a) and (b) of E.O. 12291. OSHA has not established to our satisfaction (a) that the rule is needed and (b) that the potential benefits to society outweigh the potential costs to society. OSHA would disagree with this assessment. OSHA's extensive Regulatory Impact Analysis finds that the rule is needed and that the present value of the discounted benefits is $5.2 billion compared to $2.6 billion in compliance costs.

OSHA claims the rule is needed because the identity of the thousands of hazardous chemicals used in manufacturing is frequently not known by the workers that come into contact with them. Moreover, states and localities are promulgating their own labeling standards, causing a burden to companies involved in interstate commerce. OSHA argues that a federal standard is needed to preempt these state and local regulations. OSHA argues that benefits would exceed costs because of the potential for great savings in medical costs and lost production from the decrease in illnesses (including cancer) and injuries that a better informed workforce would bring about. Finally, OSHA points out that the present proposal is far more cost-effective than the previous one OSHA proposed in January 1981. We disagree with all of these statements except the last.

Need for Standard

The need for the standard depends on, first, how dangerous the chemicals are which now exist unlabeled in the workplace, and, secondly, even if not dangerous, whether a federal OSHA standard would reduce the burden of compliance with state and local standards. OSHA cannot show that unlabeled chemicals pose a significant risk, because OSHA lacks the information needed to make such a showing; indeed the provision of such information is what the proposed rule would mandate. Furthermore most chemicals that pose a "significant" risk are regulated under section 6 (b) (5) of the OSH Act and are required to have labels as well as exposure limits, specified work practices and respirators. Thus with this proposed generic regulation, OSHA is attempting to regulate chemicals that OSHA probably could not regulate through substance by substance rulemaking because the hazard might not pass the "significant risk" criterion established in the Supreme Court's benzene decision. Through this rule OSHA also is attempting to shift the burden of determining what is hazardous to the firms in the chemical industry.

To explain why present institutions do not provide the proper incentive for voluntary labeling, OSHA asserts that information is a "public good" and that therefore free markets will not provide enough. However, while the development of new information may be under-provided, because it is difficult to charge the development costs to all those that benefit, it is not generally thought that the dissemination of existing information is under-provided. The OSHA rule does not require the development of new information, only the transmittal of existing information. Furthermore since workers frequently bargain as a group, their demand for information on hazardous substances should be reflected in their bargaining agreements with employers. In fact, in the cost section of the Regulatory Impact Analysis, OSHA estimates that at present there is 60 percent compliance with the proposed labeling requirements. OSHA does not establish why the "efficient" outcome is 100 percent labeling.

OSHA also claims the rule is needed to preempt state and local labeling standards. However, the OSH Act allows states to promulgate more stringent standards than the federal standard. Thus OSHA can only preempt state standards by promulgating more stringent federal standards. Standardization will also not be promoted because the OSHA proposal allows considerable flexibility in meeting the specific requirements. Thus firms operating in interstate commerce could end up having to comply with many different state requirements as well as a more comprehensive federal standard. In any case, the preemption agreement runs counter to the federalist principle supported by the Administration that the lowest geographical level consistent with meeting public needs should administer regulations.

Potential Benefits and Costs

The regulations are costly: OSHA estimates $582 million in startup costs and $228 million in ongoing costs for a present value cost after forty years of $2.6 billion. Furthermore these costs are the first new cost to be imposed by the Administration in the OSHA area. Previous regulations proposed by OSHA reduced the costs of existing rules. Although the previous Administration proposed more costly chemical labeling rules, the present proposal is entirely new and contains additional requirements. Thus this proposal should receive a thorough and careful review.

We believe the key to the proposal is whether the benefits OSHA expects from it would actually materialize. We feel OSHA has constructed a set of tenuous assumptions all of which must hold for OSHA's expectations to be fulfilled. OSHA assumes that the information provided to workers will result in behavioral changes that lead to a 20 percent decline in illnesses and injuries caused by chemicals in manufacturing workplaces. OSHA also produces an extremely high estimate of the number of illnesses and injuries caused by chemical exposure. Finally, OSHA in effect discounts costs by 10 percent and benefits by 5 percent, a procedure that almost doubles benefit estimates relative to costs over the 40 year discount period. We believe, therefore, that OSHA's benefit estimate of $5.2 billion is overstated by a factor of 80, i.e., a more reasonable benefit estimate would be $65 million, compared to costs of $2.6 billion. The following examines OSHA's assumptions and the problems with them:

(1) As OSHA admits, its assumption is completely arbitrary that, as a result of this rule, 20 percent of all illnesses caused by workplace exposure to chemicals will be eliminated after twenty years. One should recall that 60 percent of hazardous chemicals already are labeled and that individual OSHA standards already require labeling as well as many other preventive measures for the most significantly hazardous chemicals. Furthermore, when labels and warnings were required on the two most significant health hazards, smoking and lack of seat belt use, no measurable decline in these activities resulted. Perhaps a more reasonable estimate, but one just as arbitrary, would be a 5 percent reduction in illnesses. This alone reduces the benefit estimate (medical costs and lost production saved) to $1.3 billion.

(2) OSHA double counts illnesses. OSHA uses BLS data on the number of illnesses and multiplies this estimate by 10 to correct for underreporting because it believes many chronic illnesses are not reported. OSHA then goes on to estimate chronic illnesses in two additional ways and then adds all three approaches together. Since the latter two methods should correct any underreporting problem, there is no reason for OSHA to multiply the BLS estimate by 10. The BLS estimate itself is supposed to include chronic illnesses, and there is no reason why it should not except for illnesses with long latency periods between exposure and onset of symptoms such as cancer. Not multiplying the BLS illness estimates by 10 reduces this benefit estimate from $156 million to $16 million.

(3) To pick up chronic hazards, Osha uses a social security survey of disabled adults. About 11 percent claimed that their disability was due to job-caused diseases. However less than 5 percent of the partially disabled (⅔ of the total disabled) were

receiving workers compensation indicating that self-reporting may overstate the extent of occupational causes of illnesses. In addition, this survey is a prevalence rather than an incidence survey. Assuming that workers already disabled will benefit from the labeling rule, as OSHA does, obviously overstates benefits. If one assumes an average 10 years of disability (the median age is about 55) so that turnover is 10 percent and discount by 10 percent, benefits are reduced by about 35 percent. Finally, OSHA estimates (based on a study that OSHA previously pointed out mainly picked up acute health hazards) that 25 percent of all chronic occupational illnesses are due to chemical exposure. Thirty percent of reported illnesses were skin diseases, according to this study, many presumably caused by chemical exposures. Using this 25 percent estimate for chronic illnesses is thus unsupported. Most of the health hazards that are thought to cause large numbers of chronic illnesses do not appear to be manufactured chemicals; instead they are dusts and by-products such as cotton, coal, silica, and asbestos dust, and coal tar, arsenic, and lead emissions. The identified hazardous chemicals such as vinyl chloride, benzene, and acrylontril probably cause an insignificant number of illnesses each year (less than 10 each). For these reasons, a more reasonable chronic illness estimate is probably about $270 million rather than $2.7 billion.

(4) OSHA also claims that the Social Security estimates of chronic illnesses do not include cancers. This is incorrect. In fact, 375,000 cases are included in the total of disabled adults but only about 1.5 percent attribute their cancers to their jobs. OSHA believes this is too small, pointing out that some estimates of the percentage of cancers caused by occupational exposure range up to 40 percent. OSHA then uses a 10 percent figure as its best estimate to calculate the cost of cancer to society. Since half of chemical exposures are in manufacturing and OSHA expects a 20 percent reduction in cancers from the labeling requirement, OSHA is estimating that this single rule will reduce 1 percent of all U.S. cancer deaths per year (about 4,000). This is a wildly optimistic estimate. The best estimate of the incidence of occupationally related cancer deaths is the 4 percent figure by Doll and Peto published June 1981 in the *Journal of the National Cancer Institute*. The higher numbers are from a completely discredited study thrown together in the previous Administration. Citing it is a disservice to scientific inquiry. Furthermore Doll and Peto attribute half of the 4 percent to asbestos. Another 25 percent can probably be attributed to substances already regulated by OSHA such as vinyl chloride, coke oven emissions, acrylonitrile, DBCP, arsenic, cadmium, and ionizing radiation. This leaves only 1 percent of cancers potentially reduced by the chemical labeling rule rather than OSHA's 10 percent estimate and reduces OSHA's cost savings estimate for cancer reduction to $230 million. Finally OSHA adjusts for a 15 year lag between exposure to a carcinogen and symptoms, yet states that the average lag is 20 years. Adjusting for a 20 year lag reduces the cost savings estimate to $150 million.

(5) OSHA also estimates benefits attributable to reduced turnover costs and chemical fires. A discussion of the latter estimate is not provided, and I believe they did not intend to include this chemical fires estimate. For the reason stated above, turnover costs decline because of the safer workplaces that result from the regulation. Since our calculations have reduced OSHA's above estimates by a factor of 10, turnover cost savings also should be reduced by a factor of 10, from $9 million to $900 thousand.

(6) OSHA also assumes that benefits will grow by 5 percent per year for the next 40 years because new chemicals are expected to be introduced at a 3 percent per year rate and real medical costs and private sector productivity are both expected to grow at a 2 percent rate. The effect of these assumptions is to almost double discounted benefits relative to costs. First it is risky to extrapolate compound rates into the future for 40 years. Second, note the asymmetry between the medical sector and the rest of the economy. The implicit assumption is that medical productivity is declining by 2 percent per year while productivity in the rest of the economy is growing by two percent. Note that if productivity is assumed to grow at the same rate in both sectors then no adjustments should be made since illnesses will be cured and medical costs reduced at the same rate as lost productivity (from illnesses and premature death) grows. Third, it seems highly unlikely that the stock of hazardous chemicals commonly used in the workplace will grow at 3 percent per year. Most new chemicals do not find themselves in common use and presumably some chemicals drop out of common use. Also both OSHA and EPA (TSCA) regulations as well as private institutions operate to screen out new hazardous chemicals while causing existing hazardous chemicals to drop out of use. A plausible case can be made that the risk posed by hazardous chemicals in the workplace has been declining over the past ten years rather than increasing. Assuming a constant benefits stream reduces the discounted benefit estimate by almost ½.

(7) The net effect of the adjustments discussed in (1) through (6) above is to reduce the benefit estimate from $5.2 billion to $65 million ($5.2 billion × ¼ × $\frac{1}{10}$ × ½).

cc: Official File
    Chron
    DeMuth
    Hopkins
    Collins
    Morrall
    Tozzi

OIRA/RA:JMorrall:mng 12-28-81

7. Memorandum, Chris DeMuth to Members of Presidential Task Force on Regulatory Relief; *Subject*: OSHA's Hazard Communication Proposal, January, 1982

MEMORANDUM FOR MEMBERS OF THE PRESIDENTIAL TASK FORCE
ON REGULATORY RELIEF

FROM: Christopher DeMuth

SUBJECT: OSHA's "Hazard Communication" Proposal

OSHA's proposed "hazard communication" (or "chemical labeling") regulation is before the Task Force at the suggestion of Secretary Donovan. This regulation obviously merits serious deliberation: it would cost over a billion dollars to implement over the next few years, and would be the first major new regulation to be imposed by the Reagan administration.

The chemical labeling proposal has been reviewed by OMB under the President's Executive Order 12291 (Federal Regulation). Our view is that the proposal is inconsistent with the Order's requirements that regulations be based on adequate information concerning need and on evidence that potential benefits outweigh potential costs. Because of the importance of this proposal, we prepared a detailed critique, which is attached for your review along with the briefing paper prepared by the Department of Labor. The OMB analysis is sharply critical of OSHA's proposal; it is offered in the spirit of lively internal debate and should, for this reason, be kept strictly confidential.

I believe the principal arguments against the chemical labeling proposal are as follows:

- *There is no direct evidence of a need for universal labeling of chemicals in workplaces—and much indirect evidence that it is not needed.* Known chemical hazards are already extensively regulated by OSHA and EPA, and employers have strong private incentives to take appropriate steps to minimize chemical hazards. Doubtless there are cases where more and better labeling would be worthwhile, but no one knows the extent of such cases, or whether they come close to justifying a national policy of universal labeling.

- *This is not an appropriate area for federal preemption of state and local regulation.* Federal preemption should be limited to cases where state policies impose substantial burdens on interstate commerce. In this regard, workplace labeling standards are no different from scores of other regulatory standards that vary from state to state. While eleven states and cities have enacted chemical labeling standards, nine of them did so just in the past year—the result of an effort by unions to encourage manufacturers to press for a uniform federal regulation. In any event, the possibilities for federal preemption are limited under the OSHA statute.

- *The potential costs of the regulation far exceed the potential benefits.* OSHA's Regulatory Impact Analysis suggests that the costs of the regulation would be $2.6 billion while the benefits would be $5.2 billion (both stated in present values). The benefit estimate, however, is based on a string of dubious assumptions—in particular, that a very large proportion of current illnesses and injuries are job related, and that better labeling of chemicals would dramatically reduce these illnesses and injuries. More balanced assumptions on these and other matters reduce potential benefits to less than $100 million, a small fraction of compliance costs.

Attachment

EXECUTIVE OFFICE OF THE PRESIDENT
OFFICE OF MANAGEMENT AND BUDGET
WASHINGTON, D.C. 20503

7 January 1982

A CRITICAL REVIEW OF OSHA'S PROPOSED
HAZARD COMMUNICATION REGULATION

A. Summary of the regulation

OSHA's proposed "hazard communication" or "chemical labeling" regulation contains two types of requirements. First, it requires chemical manufacturers to assess the health and safety hazards of the chemicals they produce by reviewing the scientific literature on each chemical. Second, it requires all manufacturers to inform employees in detail about chemical hazards.

Specifically, manufacturers are required to:

1. Provide lists of the hazardous chemicals known to be present in the workplace to employees or their representatives and to OSHA (under limited trade-secret protections);

2. Label every container of hazardous chemicals with the identities of the hazardous contents and appropriate warnings;

3. Label every container of hazardous chemicals leaving the workplace with the name, address, and telephone number of the manufacturer;

4. Make available to employees "material safety data sheets" for every hazardous chemical (which chemical manufacturers are required to prepare and send to customers in their initial shipments of such chemicals); and

5. Provide information and training to employees on the requirements of the OSHA regulation, the methods of detecting chemical hazards in the workplace, the hazards of the chemicals in use, and the measures employees can take to protect themselves.

While OSHA describes its proposal as "largely performance-oriented," the regulation is in fact highly prescriptive and detailed in the obligations it imposes on manufacturers. Literature searches, hazard warnings, and safety data sheets are required not only for every hazardous chemical but every hazardous ingredient of 1 percent or more; as a result, the information on labels and data sheets will often pertain to the hazards of minute constituents rather than the actual mixtures present. In most cases, labels must be attached to every container in the workplace containing 1 percent or more of a hazardous chemical, regardless of location or actual hazard. Each safety data sheet must include 12 categories of information—including physical and chemical characteristics; acute and chronic health hazards; and recommended handling procedures, engineering controls, work practices, and personal protective equipment.

B. Summary of the issues

The primary regulatory policies set forth in President Reagan's Executive Order 12291 are that new regulations (a) "shall be based upon adequate information concerning the need for and consequences of proposed government action," and (b) "shall not be undertaken unless the potential benefits to society outweigh the potential costs to society." OSHA has prepared an extensive Regulatory Impact Analysis which concludes that the chemical labeling regulation is needed and that its costs would be far less than its benefits—$2.6 billion in compliance costs versus $5.2 billion in benefits, both stated in present values. We believe, to the contrary, that OSHA's proposal fails to meet either of the primary policies of the Executive Order.

Specifically, OSHA states that:

1. The regulation is needed because the identities and risks of thousands of hazardous chemicals used in manufacturing are frequently unknown to workers who come into contact with them, leading to large numbers of accidents and illnesses that would be prevented by better labeling.

2. The regulation is also needed in order to preempt state and local regulation, since several states and localities are issuing their own (inevitably differing) labeling requirements.

3. Although the costs of the regulation would be very large, the benefits would be even larger because better informed employees would experience fewer injuries and illnesses—saving medical costs and boosting productivity.

4. The present proposal is far more cost-effective and reasonable than the Carter administration's "midnight regulation" on chemical labeling, which was proposed on January 16, 1981 and withdrawn early in the Reagan administration.

We disagree with all of these statements except the last. Below we discuss the first three statements in detail, and conclude with a brief discussion of two further arguments that have been offered in support of OSHA's proposal.

C. The need for regulation

The need for a chemical labeling regulation depends on the degree of unnecessary danger presented by lack of labeling (and other "hazard communication" activities) under current circumstances. OSHA estimates that there is already about 60 percent compliance in American industry with the requirements of its proposed regulation. In many cases, existing labeling practices are the natural and voluntary result of market incentives—in particular, the incentives of employers to maintain healthy and productive workforces, to avoid workers compensation and tort liability payments for illnesses and injuries, and to respond to job-safety pressures from employees and unions. In other cases, labeling is the result of the extensive panoply of federal chemical and health regulations that already exist. Those chemicals which present the most significant and well-understood hazards are already regulated in detail by OSHA under rules specifying not only labeling but exposure limits and work practices for individual chemicals. Labels are also required for certain substances under OSHA's "consensus" workplace standards, and employee access to information on exposure to hazardous substances is guaranteed by OSHA's "Access to Employee Exposure and Medical Records" regulation. In addition, EPA's toxic substances program (under the Toxic Substances Control Act of 1976) provides a comprehensive regulatory scheme for controlling toxic substances in and out of the workplace.

Given the numerous private and public mechanisms and taking appropriate account (through labeling and other means) of known chemical hazards, what is left to be accomplished by OSHA's proposed regulation? By definition, all that is left is for labels (and data sheets, etc.) to be added in those situations where OSHA, other regulatory authorities, and manufacturers themselves are not already providing them. Yet OSHA's analysis presents no direct evidence that unreasonable chemical hazards would be eliminated by requiring labeling in such circumstances. No doubt there are cases in American industry where more and better labeling would be worthwhile—but neither OSHA nor anyone else knows even approximately the number of such cases or whether they justify a national policy of universal labeling. This is the crux of the problem with OSHA's proposal under the Executive Order's requirement that regulations must be based on adequate information demonstrating need. Where OSHA has compiled specific information on the health or safety risks of particular chemicals, it has the authority and responsibility to issue reasonable standards for the protection of workers. Here, however, OSHA is proposing a very costly and comprehensive regulatory scheme to address a problem whose extent is a matter of speculation rather than concrete evidence.

Lacking specific evidence of the hazards it proposes to regulate, OSHA relies instead on general assertions about information being a "public good" that is undersupplied by private markets. It is true that there may be too little investment in research and development of new knowledge in private markets, because it is often more difficult for investors to capture the economic returns from new knowledge than from other, more tangible innovations. But the chemical labeling regulation would not require the development of new knowledge—only the "communication" of existing knowledge. And, as mentioned, those who possess specific knowledge about chemical hazards already face strong private incentives and public obligations to supply that information to those who might be harmed by the lack of it. Hence, OSHA's reliance on the economics of "public goods" is misplaced.

OSHA also asserts that its proposal is needed to preempt state and local regulation of workplace labeling. But this is an inappropriate area for the federal government to preclude states and localities from exercising their police powers, especially under the Reagan administration's policies of decentralization and renewed federalism. In general, federal preemption of state and local regulation is appropriate in only two circumstances, both involving clear burdens on interstate commerce. First, to prevent states from pursuing policies for the benefit of their own citizens at the expense of citizens of other states (as in the case of states setting uneconomically low rates for intrastate trucking services, forcing trucking firms to recoup intrastate losses through higher interstate fares). Second, to avoid inconsistent state standards that would introduce large inefficiencies in uniform national markets (as in the case of numerous different state automobile emission standards). Neither of these circumstances is present here—the preemption argument for federal workplace labeling standards could just as well be advanced for federal building and housing codes. In any event, the OSHA statute permits preemption only of state and local standards that are not "at least as effective in providing safe and healthful employment," and some states and municipalities have enacted chemical labeling rules that are more comprehensive than OSHA's proposal. So there appears to be little prospect of eliminating the costs of meeting multiple labeling rules under any federal regulation appropriate to this administration.

D. Potential costs and benefits

The chemical labeling regulations are costly: OSHA estimates $582 million in startup costs and $228 million in annually recurring costs for a present value of $2.6 billion. These costs would be the first substantial new regulatory costs to be imposed by the Reagan administration (to date our major regulations have reduced the costs of inherited regulations), and they are even greater than the costs of controversial Carter initiatives such as the cotton dust regulation.

The cost-effectiveness of the chemical labeling proposal depends on whether the large benefits OSHA predicts would actually materialize. OSHA has constructed a set of overly optimistic and tenuous assumptions about benefits, *all* of which must hold for its expectations to be fulfilled. First, OSHA assumes that compliance with its regulation would bring about changes in the behavior of workers that would lead to a substantial reduction in the current rate of job-related illnesses and injuries —a 20 percent decline over 20 years. Second, OSHA applies this reduction to an extremely high estimate of the current number of illnesses and injuries caused by hazardous chemicals in the workplace. Third, OSHA projects a 5 percent annual growth rate in benefits of chemical labeling throughout the regulation's assumed life span of 40 years, a procedure that nearly doubles its estimate of benefits relative to costs. Using more reasonable assumptions, we show below that OSHA's benefit estimate of $5.2 billion may be overstated by a factor of 80. A more reasonable benefit estimate is $65 million, compared to costs of $2.6 billion.

1. *OSHA's projection of reduced illnesses and injuries is too optimistic.* OSHA projects that better labeling (and other activities required by its regulation) would reduce the number of illness and injuries caused by workplace exposure to chemicals by 20 percent over the next 20 years (at a cumulative rate of 1 percent reduction per year). OSHA concedes that this figure is completely arbitrary—and obviously this is a projection that must depend largely on judgment. Yet the figure OSHA has chosen is implausibly high. As noted previously, OSHA estimates that 60 percent of hazardous chemicals are already labeled. For the most significant hazardous chemicals, individual OSHA standards already require labeling as well as many other preventive measures. OSHA's existing "Access to Employee Exposure and Medical Records" regulation also provides information important to employees exposed to chronic hazards.

The record of mandatory labeling in changing behavior is unimpressive. When labels and warnings were required on two of the most significant health hazards—smoking and lack of seat belt use—no measurable decline in these activities resulted. Recently, HHS withdrew the Carter administration's prescription drug "package patient insert" rules because it could not be demonstrated that perceptible benefits would result from the mandatory labels. OSHA, in fact, does not present any evidence that chemical labeling will cause workers to act any more safely than they do now. Perhaps a more reasonable estimate, but one just as arbitrary, would be to assume that the regulation would result in a 5 percent reduction in illnesses rather than 20 percent. This change alone reduces the benefit estimate (from saved medical costs and productivity) to $1.3 billion—about half of estimated compliance costs.

2. *OSHA's estimate of current job-related illnesses and injuries is greatly overstated.* OSHA uses data from the Bureau of Labor Statistics on the number of occupational illnesses and multiplies the data by 10 because it believes many chronic illnesses are not reported to BLS. OSHA next estimates chronic illness in two *additional* ways—using a Social Security survey of disabled adults and an estimate of occupationally caused cancer—then adds all three estimates together. Since the latter two methods should correct for any underreporting problem, there is no reason for OSHA to multiply the BLS estimate by 10. In any event, the BLS estimate itself is supposed to include chronic illnesses, and there is no reason why it should not except for illnesses (such as cancer) with long latency periods between exposure and onset of symptoms. Not multiplying the BLS illness estimates by 10 reduces this part of the benefit estimate from $156 million to about $16 million. OSHA's other two upward revisions of the BLS data are discussed in the following paragraphs.

The Social Security survey: OSHA's second adjustment of the BLS data to increase chronic illnesses is based on a Social Security survey of disabled adults. About 11 percent of those surveyed claimed that their disability was due to job-caused diseases. However, according to this same survey only about 5 percent of the partially disabled (2/3 of the totally disabled) were receiving workers compensation—indicating that self-reporting may greatly overstate the true extent of occupational causes of illnesses. (OSHA also believes, however, that workers compensation data understate the extent of occupational illness.)

A further problem here is that the Social Security survey is a survey of prevalence rather than incidence. Assuming that workers already disabled will benefit from the labeling rule, as OSHA does, obviously overstates benefits. If one assumes an average 10 years of disability (the median age of the disabled is about 55), so that turnover is 10 percent per year, the present value of benefits (at the 10 percent discount rate) is reduced by about 35 percent.

In addition, OSHA estimates that 25 percent of all chronic occupational illnesses are due to chemical exposure. This estimate, however, is based on a study OSHA previously pointed out mainly picked up *acute* health hazards. Using the 25 percent estimate for chronic illnesses is thus quite arbitrary. Most of the health hazards that are thought to cause large numbers of chronic illnesses do not appear to be manufactured chemicals; instead they are dusts and unwanted by-products of manufacturing processes such as cotton, coal, silica, and asbestos dusts, and coal tar, arsenic, and lead emissions. The identified hazardous chemicals such as vinyl chloride, benzene, and acrylonitrile probably cause an insignificant number of illnesses each year (less than 10 each). For these several reasons, a more plausible estimate of the cost savings in chronic illness reduction produced by the standard is probably about $270 million rather than $2.7 billion.

The cancer adjustment: As the basis for its third upward estimate of the BLS data, OSHA claims that the Social Security survey estimates of chronic illnesses do not include cancers. This is incorrect. In fact, 375,000 cases are included in the total of disabled adults, but only about 1.5 percent attribute their cancers to their jobs. OSHA believes this is too small, pointing out that some estimates of the percentage of cancers caused by occupational exposure range up to 40 percent. To calculate the cost of cancer to society, OSHA relies on a "best estimate" of 10 percent as the share of all cancer that is occupationally related. Since half of chemical exposures are in manufacturing, and OSHA estimates a 20 percent reduction in all illnesses from the labeling requirement, OSHA is estimating that this single rule will reduce U.S. cancer deaths by one percent ($\frac{1}{10} \times \frac{1}{2} \times \frac{1}{5}$), which comes to about 4,000 fewer cancer deaths per year.

This is a wildly optimistic estimate. The high estimates of job-related cancers (ranging up to 40 percent) cited by OSHA are from a thoroughly discredited study assembled in the previous administration to generate support for the "generic cancer policy" OSHA is now revising. Probably the best scientifically serious estimate of the incidence of occupationally related cancer deaths is provided by Doll and Peto in a study published in the June 1981 issue of the *Journal of the National Cancer Institute.* Doll and Peto's best estimate is that occupational factors explain about 4 percent of the U.S. cancer incidence, about half of which is attributable to asbestos which OSHA already regulates. Another 25 percent can probably be attributed to other regulated substances such as vinyl chloride, coke oven emissions, acrylonitrile, DBCP, arsenic, cadmium, and ionizing radiation. This leaves only 1 percent of cancers potentially reduced by the chemical labeling rule rather than OSHA's 10 percent estimate, and reduces OSHA's cost savings estimate for cancer reduction from $2.3 billion to $230 million. Moreover, OSHA adjusts for a 15 year lag between exposure to a carcinogen and symptoms, yet states that the average lag is 20 years. (Actually it is probably even longer than twenty years.) Adjusting for a 20 year lag further reduces the cost savings estimate to $150 million.

OSHA also estimates benefits attributable to reduced employee turnover. OSHA expects turnover costs to decline because of the safer workplaces that result from the regulation. Our revisions (explained above) reduce OSHA's estimates of safer workplaces by a factor of about 10, and hence turnover cost savings should be reduced by a similar amount —from $9 million to $900 thousand.

3. *OSHA's inflation of future benefits is unwarranted.* OSHA projects that the benefits of its regulation will grow by 5 percent each year for the next 40 years. This projection is based on the assumptions that (a) new chemicals, including hazardous ones, will be introduced at a net rate of 3 percent per year, and (b) real medical costs and private sector productivity will both grow at a rate of 2 percent per year. Extrapolating compound rates 40 years into the future in this way is very risky. But even accepting the procedure for purposes of argument, the effect of OSHA's assumptions is nearly to double discounted benefits relative to discounted costs.

Note first the asymmetry between the medical sector and the rest of the economy—OSHA's implicit assumption is that medical productivity will decline by 2 percent per year while productivity in the rest of the economy will grow by 2 percent per year. It is true that price indexes show medical costs growing at higher rates than other goods and services, but these do not account for the large productivity improvements in health care and medical science (that is, for the health benefits of costly medical innovations). If we take the more reasonable assumption that productivity is growing at the same rate in both the medical and non-medical sectors then no adjustments should be made, since illnesses will be cured and medical costs reduced at the same rate as lost productivity (from illnesses and premature death) grows.

Furthermore, it seems highly unlikely that the stock of hazardous chemicals commonly used in the workplace will grow at 3 percent per year. Most new chemicals are not produced in volume, while presumably some existing hazardous chemicals are replaced by the new chemicals. Also, OSHA and EPA regulations as well as private institutions (private liability law, voluntary industry standards) discourage the introduction of hazardous new chemicals and encourage the removal of existing ones from widespread use. Under the Toxic Substances Control Act, EPA reviews all new chemicals before they are manufactured commercially to determine whether they will present a health or environmental risk. If EPA finds that a new chemical is hazardous, it may ban, regulate, require labeling, or notify OSHA of the hazard. Thus, it seems plausible that the level of risk posed by hazardous chemicals in the workplace without an OSHA labeling standard will decline rather than increase over the next 40 years; it is certainly reasonable to assume hazards will remain constant. Assuming a constant rather than growing stream of future benefits reduces the benefit estimate by almost ½.

4. *Conclusion.* The net effect of combining the three types of adjustments suggested above is to reduce OSHA's benefit estimate from $5.2 billion to $65 million ($5.2 billion $\times$ ¼ $\times$ $\frac{1}{10}$ $\times$ ½). This is only 2.5 percent

of OSHA's estimate of $2.6 billion in (present value) compliance costs. Any one of the three types of suggested adjustments reduces the benefits of this regulation such that benefits approximately equal, or are considerably less than, costs.

E. Other considerations

OSHA points out that several trade associations, including the Chemical Manufacturers Association and the American Petroleum Institute, have submitted statements favoring some (though by no means all) aspects of the chemical labeling proposal. Several reasons are worth mentioning why regulated firms might demand, or at least acquiesce in, a new regulation of this kind.

First, firms may believe that a nationwide standard would halt the growth of state and local regulation; this aspect of OSHA's proposal has already been discussed. Second, some large firms and industry groups have already established hazard communication programs that they hope would qualify under the OSHA standard. For example, the American Petroleum Institute argues that a labeling standard is needed because, although larger petroleum companies already have labeling programs, many smaller ones do not. A uniform OSHA program, by increasing the smaller companies' overhead costs, would put them at a competitive disadvantage relative to companies that already have such programs.

Finally, companies that already have such programs and that purchase chemicals from others may believe they can shift to chemical manufacturers the costs and potential liabilities of identifying hazardous chemicals and preparing the required safety data sheets. The Motor Vehicle Manufacturers Association argues this point explicitly. On the other hand, the Chemical Manufacturers Association favors a program that does not place any special requirements on manufacturers to originate hazard identification and material safety data sheets or require that this information be shipped to purchasers. Furthermore, CMA's proposal would not require firms to identify chronic chemical health hazards, but only to label those that OSHA regulates. In summary, industry's demand for federal regulation is based on strategic considerations and is neither unanimous nor argued with one voice.

A final argument for the regulation, offered by labor and "public interest" groups, is simply that workers have a "right to know" what it is they are working with even if this knowledge would not affect their behavior. OSHA points out in the preamble that this regulation, combined with its medical records access regulation, would "carry out OSHA's intention to fully address the worker 'right to know' issue." However, although some value should be ascribed to knowledge even if it does not improve safety, this knowledge should not be considered a "right" in isolation from cost considerations.

8. *Letter,* Chemical Manufacturers Association to OMB, January 7, 1982

CHEMICAL MANUFACTURERS ASSOCIATION

ROBERT A. ROLAND
President

January 7, 1982

Laverne V. Collins
Office of Management and Budget
New Executive Office Building
Room 3208
Washington, D.C. 20503

Reference: *Agency Forms Under Review* (OSHA 239),
46 Fed. Reg. 61947, 61966 (Dec. 21, 1981).

Dear Ms. Collins:

The list of agency forms under review published by OMB in the December 21, 1981 Federal Register (46 F.R. 61947) includes a record-keeping requirement that would be imposed under a proposed OSHA standard on chemical hazard communication that is currently under review by OMB. The supporting documentation for this proposed record-keeping requirement—obtained by the Chemical Manufacturers Association (CMA) from the Department of Labor in response to the Federal Register notice—consists of a "Supporting Statement" as well as the actual text of the proposed standard.

The Chemical Manufacturers Association represents 195 member companies who represent over 90 percent of the production capacity for basic industrial chemicals in this country. CMA has consistently and publicly favored a reasonable and effective federal standard on hazard communications. We believe that the proposed OSHA standard on hazards communication now under review represents a substantial improvement over the published proposal that was withdrawn last year. It is a performance-oriented standard to an encouraging extent. Nonetheless, the proposed standard contains a number of requirements that will be unduly burdensome, costly or confusing, and which are not necessary for an effective standard. While we recognize that this opportunity to comment to OMB on the proposed recordkeeping requirements is not the appropriate setting for full blown comments on the proposed standard, we do think it would be useful to both OSHA and OMB for us to identify briefly what we see as positive elements along with several major deficiencies in the proposed standard.

OSHA's proposal contains the essential elements of a meaningful hazard communications program. We believe the deficiencies—outlined below—can be readily remedied and we urge that this be done before the Proposed Standard is published.

1. *Disclosing ingredients of hazardous mixtures.* The OSHA proposal would require a material safety data sheet ("MSDS") for a hazardous mixture to disclose every hazardous ingredient that comprises one percent or more of the mixture. This is a perfect example of an unnecessarily burdensome requirement. Protection of the worker requires that he be informed about the hazards of materials. In the case of a mixture, those interests are completely satisfied by informing the worker of the hazards of the mixture and of the identity of all ingredients (whether above or below one percent) that contribute substantially to the hazard of the mixture. As OSHA itself recognizes, the hazards of a mixture may not be identical to the hazards of individual ingredients. To require disclosure of ingredients that might be hazardous when used alone but which do not contribute to the hazard presented by the mixture to which the worker is exposed is both misleading and unnecessary. Moreover, this would impose enormous burdens on manufacturers to undertake precise analyses of mixtures. It would also require revision of many existing MSDS's. There is no justification for imposing these burdens and costs.

2. *Labeling.* While the labeling requirements of the OSHA proposal are a substantial improvement over the January 1981 proposal, they are too rigid because they still place employers in a costly and unnecessary straitjacket. There simply is no justification for a requirement that every container in the workplace be labeled, tagged or marked with hazard information. What is important is that the employer—through labels, placards, markings *or other means*—effectively communicate essential hazard information to workers at the work site. In many cases, a simple placard or warning code that workers have been instructed to understand will be sufficient, and labeling each container is unnecessary.

3. *Treatment of "acute and chronic health hazards".* The proposed standard treats what it calls "physical" hazards of chemicals in a sensible fashion—using well-recognized, objective definitions for flammability and other physical hazards. The standard's treatment of what it calls "health hazards" or "acute and chronic health effects," however, is confusing and unsatisfactory. Employers are required to communicate information about "known" acute and chronic health effects, and are given

guidance as to the types of effects they must consider and the types of sources they may wish to consult.

We believe that in the absence of objective definitions or tests for these hazards, it is impractical and unreasonable to impose upon employers a flat, unqualified obligation to communicate hazard information.

CMA's Alternative. The alternative approach CMA proposed was (1) to define *acute* health hazards where possible—and this is possible, for example, in the case of toxic or highly toxic materials as well as the "physical hazards" defined in the OSHA proposal—and to require employers to include information on those hazards in their hazard communication program; and (2) to require employers to communicate information on *chronic* health hazards of substances (such as acrylonitrile or benzene) covered by specific OSHA standards. CMA believes that until there is a scientific consensus as to the definition of chronic health effects, OSHA must proceed on a substance-by-substance basis. In a generic standard, OSHA should adopt our suggestion that each employer should communicate to his employees "information about any substance or mixture which the employer concludes may cause significant adverse acute or chronic health effects".

There are a number of other issues—relating to trade secrets, hazard evaluations, and the list of hazardous chemicals—where we believe the proposed standard presents some problems. We believe that those problems are also amenable to solution, and that with appropriate changes, the OSHA proposal can form the basis for a cost-effective, reasonable standard.

If it would be useful in connection with OMB's review of this proposal, we would be happy to meet with representatives of OMB and OSHA to discuss our views further.

Sincerely,

Robert A. Roland
President

cc: Christopher DeMuth, OMB
    Boyden Gray, Esq., OMB
    James Tozzi, OMB
    Honorable Raymond Donovan, DOL
    Thorne Auchter, DOL
    Mark Cowan, DOL

9. OSHA (Revised) Hazard Communication Justification, to OMB/OIRA, February, 1982

HISTORY AND NEED

Issue

- Should the Department of Labor issue a proposed hazard communication standard.
- The exposure of America's workers to hazardous chemicals in industrial use today results in lost production and medical costs to industry and society of over one and a half billion dollars annually. There is unanimity of opinion that significant cost-effective reduction of these hazards is desirable. This memorandum discusses an OSHA proposal to achieve this goal.

History

- The Occupational Safety and Health Act requires the Secretary of Labor to develop, promulgate and enforce safety and health standards. The Act further states that any standard promulgated shall:

  prescribe the use of labels or other appropriate forms of warning as are necessary to insure that employees are apprised of all hazards to which they are exposed.

- In its waning days, the Carter Administration issued a proposed hazard communication regulation requiring extensive labeling of all chemical substances that might arguably be dangerous. This rule would have cost employers nearly $23 billion, discounted over 40 years.

- In the interests of regulatory reform, the new Administration withdrew the Carter proposal. Thereafter, individual companies and trade associations representing 2000 employers, unions representing 18 million employees, and numerous Senators and Congressmen have urged the Department to develop a new more reasonable labeling rule. The Department reviewed the evidence and testimony. On that basis, it determined that a standard was in fact necessary, but that such a rule could be much more tightly fashioned than the prior one had been. Thus, the Department developed a proposed rule that emphasized communication of the hazards rather than of meaningless technical data and trade secrets. This proposal would cost one-tenth as much as the Carter rule.

Need for the Regulation

There is a widespread concern among business, labor and the general public about the risk of illness and injury from workplace exposure to chemicals. This is because:

172

- There are over 500,000 potentially hazardous chemicals in use in the workplace today.
- Nearly 14 million workers are exposed, and there are at least 360 million potential exposures per year. (This figure is probably low, because it assumes only one exposure every two weeks.)
- Because of this exposure, over 260,000 production days are lost each year.
- The resultant cost to our economy, just in lost production and medical expenses, reached $1.5 billion in 1980.
- There is a growing consensus among business, labor, and industrial health specialists that greater dissemination of information about chemical hazards will enable individual workers and employers to take suitable steps to reduce injuries and illnesses.
- Trade associations and employers acknowledge that the marketplace is not providing enough information because of the fear of competitive disadvantage.
- The adoption of widely differing labeling and hazard communication rules by several states and municipalities has created a demand by both the states and regulated employers for uniform federal requirements to prevent the resulting cumulative regulatory burden on multistate employers. Currently, there are 11 such state or local rules, and several more are likely to be enacted in the near future in the absence of Federal action. OSHA has estimated the initial cost of compliance with state and local standards to be at least $2.4 billion and present value of costs of $18.7 billion over a 40-year period.

Summary of Proposed Regulation

The Labor Department has developed a narrowly drawn, performance-oriented proposed rule. It stresses communication of hazards and avoids command-and-control methods that alienate industry. Comments received as a result of the proposal will be thoroughly reviewed, and modifications will be made where appropriate.

Our proposal has the following significant features:

Hazard Determination by Chemical Producers Only

- The proposal requires that chemical producers determine which of their chemicals are hazardous and furnish their own employees and industrial users of their products with appropriate information about the chemicals and their hazards.

Emphasizes Hazard Communication

- The proposal provides employers with the means to protect their workers from chemical hazards through a combination of labels, back-up data sheets, and education and training.

Labeling is Simple and Performance-Oriented

- The label only need provide the basic information about the chemical and its hazards.

- Each employer is permitted to use whatever labeling method he considers most appropriate, including existing methods.

Trade Secret Protection

- Protection of trade secrets is provided to the maximum extent possible.

Public Support

OMB has taken the position that there is no need for an OSHA hazard communication standard. Since copies of the draft proposal were made available to the public by OMB's Paperwork Reduction Act staff, it has received wide circulation, and OSHA has been besieged with letters and telephone calls from all segments of the economy demanding that OSHA publish a federal proposal.

- Labor unions representing 18 million employers have assigned the highest priority to the promulgation of a federal standard.
- Trade associations representing more than 2 thousand companies, many of which are small businesses, have endorsed the need for a federal chemical hazards standard.

Excerpts from some of the written submissions follow.

Aerospace Industries Association of America, Inc.

Under the OSHA Act our aircraft and aerospace member companies are responsible for ensuring that their workplaces are "free from recognized hazards" that may cause illness or injury. The promulgation of an OSHA "Hazards Communication" standard is a key step towards assuring that this responsibility is fulfilled. We therefore support the aggressive development and promulgation of such a standard. Since the agency considered viewpoints from a number of interested parties in preparing the draft, we believe the proposal to be a balanced reflection of these interests.

Chemical Manufacturers Association (200 Companies)

We believe that the proposed standard on hazards communication now under review represents a substantial improvement over the published proposal that was withdrawn last year. It is a performance-oriented standard to an encouraging extent. CMA has consistently and publicly favored a reasonable and effective federal standard on hazards communication.

The Boeing Company

In our opinion, the development of a hazard identification and communication standard is the single most important rulemaking that OSHA has undertaken to facilitate employer efforts to protect the safety and health of our employees. We urge the prompt publication of the proposed standard, without modification, in the Federal Register.

We have recently reviewed OSHA's supporting statement and the draft standard. We find that, generally, the concept and scope of the proposal are appropriate and reasonable.

A standard is needed which assures that suppliers will provide downstream industrial users with the necessary and sufficient information for the control of short-term as well as long-term hazards in the workplace.

National Paint and Coatings Association (750 Companies)

. . . the performance orientation of the proposal will demonstrate the commitment to effective regulation at reasonable cost that proponents of regulatory reform have sought for years.

OSHA's proposal should issue (sic) so that regulatory reform, cost/benefit and cost-effective are no longer terms of abstraction, but have real meaning in the context of needed federal action.

Motor Vehicle Manufacturers Association (10 Companies)

MVMA believes that the current OSHA draft proposal reflects the input of a wide spectrum of interests and that the appropriate setting for additional comments on the draft proposal is a public hearing. More importantly, the time for such a hearing is now.

Monsanto

A Federal OSHA Hazards Communications Regulation is vitally needed and should be approved by OMB and Vice President Bush. . . .

CMA, labor and the public in general seem to agree that a Hazardous Communications Regulatory proposal is needed. . . .

Economically, a federal regulation would be more cost-effective than leaving the issue up to each individual state and local government.

Atlantic Richfield Company

Differing laws and regulations already in existence in the area of identification and labeling of hazardous materials demonstrate the need for a consistent policy. . . . A single Federal performance-type rule, rather than a variety of conflicting rules, would enhance industry's ability to effectively communicate hazards information to employees.

Dr. W. Kip Viscusi, Director, Center for the Study of Business Regulation
Fuqua School of Business, Duke University

My enthusiasm for a chemical labeling standard derives from the strong economic basis for such a regulation. . . . This policy works through existing market forces. . . . The original labeling proposal by Eula Bingham was fundamentally ill-conceived. . . . More recently, I gave a speech on health and safety regulation at the AEI Public Policy Week. . . . I advocated a chemical labeling system, which I viewed as possibly the best OSHA policy ever. . . . A sound labeling system should have the general character of that proposed by OSHA. . . . The approach would establish a new direction for OSHA policies.

I am writing to express a major complaint about the chemical labeling analysis. . . . The chemical labeling analysis . . . included many of the monetary benefits. . . . Both OMB and OSHA seem to be talking about these numbers as if they represent the benefits of the chemical labeling standard. They do not. These entries comprise but a small portion of the total benefits of risk reduction since they totally exclude the individual worker's willingness to pay for risk reduction that is not included in these statistics. Usually, the willingness-to-pay numbers are about ten times greater.

Need for Resolution

- *November 1981.* OSHA submitted a draft proposed standard and regulatory impact analysis (RIA) to OMB for review. (Preliminary copies of the draft RIA had been sent to OMB as early as July 1981.)

- *December 1981.* Christopher DeMuth, Administrator, Office of Information and Regulatory Affairs, OMB, met with Assistant Secretary Auchter, Deputy Assistant Secretary Cowan and the Solicitor of Labor, Timothy Ryan and staff. During this meeting, OMB informally transmitted their comments on the draft RIA for hazard communication, and expressed the opinion that there is no demonstrated need for an OSHA standard in this area. OMB's comments dealt exclusively with the benefits of the proposed standard—they acknowledged the cost-effectiveness of the regulation drafted by OSHA.

- *January 21, 1982.* OMB's sixty day review period expired without a formal response to OSHA's submission. Assistant Secretary Auchter and Deputy Assistant Secretary Cowan met with the Regulatory Relief Task Force to discuss the situation and the Task Force established an additional thirty day review period for OMB and OSHA to resolve their technical differences.

- *February 3, 1982.* Representatives from OSHA's Office of Regulatory Analysis (Mary Ellen Weber, Director, and Nancy Wentzler), DOL's Solicitor's Office (Diane Burkeley, Nathaniel Spiller), and from the office of the Assistant Secretary for Policy, Evaluation, and Research staff (Peggy Connerton), met with John Morrall (OMB). OSHA sought to define potential areas of compromise. However, the differences were fundamental and were not resolved.

We have an excellent opportunity to demonstrate a pragmatic approach to government regulation. There is an established need for a hazard communication standard at this time; the record supports that need as well as the cost-effectiveness of a market-oriented, information approach to regulation. We are offering a proposal that emphasizes cooperative measures instead of mandatory limits and policing, performance instead of specification, and communication rather than just identification. It is a proposal that fulfills our statutory obligations, is cost-effective, has the general support of labor, industry and influential segments of Congress, and supports the President's goals.

We also wish to emphasize that this is only a proposal, not a final rule. Changes suggested by affected parties can be made before the rule becomes final.

Impact of the Proposed Rule

While all interested parties will not necessarily endorse the specifics of our proposal, we are confident that it will be generally well-received and will achieve its intended goal in a cost-effective fashion.

The Proposal Will Have Broad-Based Support

- The proposal responds to the combined requests of employers, trade associations, labor unions, the Congress, and state officials that the Department issue a hazard communication standard.

The Benefits of the Proposal Will Outweigh Its Costs

- The discounted present value of benefits will be a $5.2 billion savings in lost production time and medical costs alone; employers will also face lower workers' compensation and litigation costs.
- Over that same time period (40 years), the total cost of the standard will be $2.6 billion.

The Rule Will Be Cost-Effective Relative to Carter Proposal

- The rule will provide the same benefits as the Carter proposal, but at approximately one-tenth the costs.
- The cost of the Carter proposal was expected to be at least $22.9 billion over a 40-year period.

The Rule Will Be Cost-Effective Relative to State and Local Regulation

- The rule will provide at least the same benefits as the state and local regulation. It is expected that the benefits will actually be greater due to uniformity of treatment. The potential for confusion is lessened considerably with a federal standard.
- A preliminary estimate of the expected cost of compliance with state and local regulation is at least $18.7 billion over a 40 year period. Preliminary industry estimates of the cost of compliance with state and local regulation based on the recently issued reference list from the State of California indicate that this Department estimate may be too low. Using the information provided by industry, the cost of compliance with state and local regulation may be $21 billion for the 40-year period.

STATEMENT IN SUPPORT

Executive Summary

The Administration has met with many successes to date in its regulatory reform program. For example, revised enforcement policies have been issued by the Occupational Safety and Health Administration (OSHA) which have met with the approval of most parties with an interest in worker safety and health; more positive changes are contemplated.

While OSHA has effected a number of improvements in the policy area, it is critical that they be accompanied by some "regulatory successes" that demonstrate the Administration's commitment to reasonable and responsible regulation. The business community in the past has been confronted with excessive and, in many cases, unnecessary regulation. But it has not called for abandonment of all regulations.

In this regard, OSHA has developed a proposed rule on the labeling of hazardous materials, otherwise known as "hazards communication."

Status. Pending resolution of this matter, *i.e.,* OSHA complying with OMB directions, there will be no Federal rule. At the same time there is a great deal of activity at the state and local level in the form of "worker right-to-know" laws—in effect, labeling laws; such laws presently exist in about 9 states and 2 cities (Philadelphia, PA and Santa Monica, CA). Many other states and cities have such laws pending and the potential effects on interstate commerce are not insignificant. Organized labor has been pushing for this regulation and, in the absence of action at the Federal level, has been active at the state and local level.

Forecast. Labor and other groups have criticized the administration for "gutting" environmental and safety and health laws. Superimposing OMB over the regulatory process in a manner where they become the de facto regulator will lend credence to those criticisms. This, in turn, portends significant political problems. The pendulum in the future will return to extreme positions and we will have lost any real opportunities for responsible regulations and reforms. Further, it is likely that legal action may be taken to force the release of rules undergoing OMB action on the grounds of unconstitutional delegation of authority.

Recommendation. Labeling is a controversial issue and, as a consequence, it is unlikely that any rule will meet with total approval. The process of developing a proposal has generated a wide divergence of opinion within the business community on what a rule should look like. But participants support the concept of a Federal rule. We have attempted to reconcile these concerns with this proposal. As a proposed regulation, it would be now subjected to public scrutiny and comment prior to the issuance of a final rule. The process should be given the opportunity to work.

With regard to the Administration's position on the "new Federalism," we believe that this is an instance where regulation is best suited at the Federal level so that uniform rules apply nationwide.

We would hope that the differences which exist regarding the labeling proposal may be submitted for resolution through the rulemaking process. This would begin to provide the "regulatory successes" that are needed and would undercut criticisms that the Administration is retreating from its commitments.

Introduction

There is widespread concern among business, labor and the general public about the risk of illness and injury from workplace exposure to chemicals.

Mandatory Controls Versus Flexibility. OSHA's usual course of action has been to set exposure limits and prescribe work practices and administrative procedures, including financial penalties, to control potential hazards from specific substances. But that is a lengthy procedure not feasible for potential hazards from 575,000 products and one that is neither in keeping with this administration's philosophy nor cost-effective to business, labor or government.

OSHA Statute. The statute that established and empowered OSHA mandates a more innovative solution. The Occupational Safety and Health Act of 1970 requires the Secretary of Labor to develop and promulgate Occupational Safety and Health Standards and to enforce these standards effectively. This act further states that any standard promulgated

Shall prescribe the use of labels or other appropriate forms of warning as are necessary to insure that employees are apprised of all hazards to which they are exposed. . . .

OSHA Proposal. Accordingly, we have designed a standard that assures that employers and employees in manufacturing industries have enough information about the chemical products they are working with so they can handle these materials in an economically efficient and effective way without damage to their health. Our standard only requires that producers of chemicals furnish the downstream industrial users of their products with appropriate information as to content and hazard—not including trade secrets—through information sheets and labeling. It would also oblige all manufacturing employers to train employees in the hazards associated with, and the safe use of, these substances. The proper training of employees is a key to production efficiencies and reduced costs, in both the short and long term.

Need for the Standard

Data from both the Department of Health and Human Services' National Occupational Hazard Survey and the Environmental Protection Agency indicate there are some 575,000 chemicals and mixtures in America's workplaces. The Bureau of Labor Statistics (BLS) estimates that 14 million workers are employed in the 320,000 manufacturing firms that would directly benefit from the proposal. If each of these workers is exposed only once every two weeks, there would be 360 million exposures annually. Obviously not every exposure or even series of exposures leads to injuries and illnesses. Nonetheless, the cost in lost production and medical expenses attributable to chemically induced illnesses other than cancer amounts to a staggering $1.5 billion, according to BLS and other Department of Labor data. The associated medical cost of lost workdays due to chemical illness or injury is $3.19 million annually. In addition, using Department of Labor data and adjusting for double counting, chronic illnesses account for another $1.3 billion in annual losses due to chemical exposure.

Disagreement Over Cancers. There is significant underreporting of chronic illnesses due to chemical exposures. A National Institute for Occupational Safety and Health study claims it is by a factor of 50, but we applied a much more conservative underreporting factor of 10 in our analysis. Over and above chronic illnesses there is cancer. There is controversy regarding the percentage of cancers attributable to workplace exposures.

There is disagreement regarding the percentage of cancer due to occupational exposures and uncertainty as to the exact degree of reduction our proposal would achieve. The National Cancer Institute and HEW have estimated that from 20 to 40 percent of *all* cancers were occupationally related, while at the other extreme two British researchers (Doll and Peto) claimed the proportion might be as low as from 4 to 6 percent. At OSHA's cancer policy hearings, a representative of the American Industrial Council (industry-funded) estimated that from 10 to 33 percent of *all* cancers are occupationally related. OSHA used an estimate of 10 percent for its baseline. Of that, it estimated that less than half are chemically induced.

There is widespread agreement, however, that even a 1 percent reduction in all cancers can save as much as $2.3 billion over a 40-year period.

Existing Communication Systems. Although there is already about 60 percent voluntary compliance in industry with some of the requirements of the OSHA proposed standard, this refers to limited labeling and not to data sheets on types of hazards and preventive measures and education and training on the use of labels and safety sheets. For example, OSHA cost estimates include the assumption that current compliance with the data sheet requirement to be only 30 percent. The growing body of research and industry evidence suggests that all of these components are necessary to achieve an effective health and safety program.

It has also been argued that current OSHA standards for high-risk substances already require labeling. *Current OSHA rules, however, require labeling for only 420 substances out of the estimated 575,000 chemical products. There are many substances which pose "significant risks" which remain unregulated.* Furthermore, most current labeling is for physical not health hazards.

State and Local Regulations

Much of the current labeling is the outgrowth of state and local legislation. Private mechanisms in places such as the worker's compensation system and market competition often provide disincentives to the accurate disclosure of information.

Nine states and 2 municipalities that have thus far issued their own chemical hazard regulations have done so only after it seemed apparent to them that a federal standard was not forthcoming. Many more states and localities have similar regulations in process. For companies that ship products across the country or that have plants in several states, the prospect of many different chemical hazard regulations is both a safety and a financial disaster.

The state laws governing hazard communication differ in their scope and approach. The two significant areas where actual conflicts arise involve the scope of the hazards covered and the information required in the labels. The practical consequence of this is that an employer may have to disclose information about a chemical in one state but not another, characterize a chemical as a carcinogen in one state but not another, and provide one label for a chemical in a particular state and a different label in another. As each new state or locality enacts a new law, the problem of conflicting requirements becomes compounded. As a result, companies will be forced to adopt the most stringent state requirements as their nationwide policy or comply with the different requirements in each state. Company policy will have to be reevaluated and possibly changed each time a new state law is passed. The following state laws on chemical hazards illustrate the potential problems of having to comply with many separate regulations.

Scope of Hazards

- *Connecticut* covers "carcinogenic substances" only.
- *California* requires the state Director of Industrial Relations to issue a list of "hazardous substances" drawing on lists developed by the International

Agency for Research on Cancer, EPA, California OSHA, and the state Food and Agriculture Department. This list has just recently been issued.

- *Maine* covers all substances listed in the Department of Transportation Hazardous Materials Table or required to be labeled by OSHA.
- *New York* covers any substance listed in the NIOSH Registry of Toxic Effects or which has yielded positive evidence of acute or chronic health hazards.

Labels

- *California* labels must have chemical or common name (not trade name only), signal or warning words ("DANGER," "WARNING," "CAUTION"), hazard and caution phrases; size and format regulated.
- *Maine* labels must have chemical or common name for workplace containers, and chemical name only (no trade secret protection) for containers sold or distributed in commerce.
- *Massachusetts* labels must have chemical, common or recognized generic name (not trade name only), the signal word "DANGER" and the word "POISON," and affirmative statement of principal hazard or hazards; typography and location of warning text specified.
- *Washington* labels must have name and place of business, chemical, common or generic name (not trade name only) of each hazardous component, a signal word in order of diminished severity ("DANGER," "WARNING," or "CAUTION"), affirmative statement of principal hazard or hazards, precautionary measures, instructions as to first aid treatment, the word "POISON" for poisonous substances, poison antidote, and handling and storage instructions.

A preliminary Department evaluation of the cost of compliance with state and local regulation indicates an expected initial cost of $2.4 billion and an expected present value of the cost of $18.7 billion. By contrast, the expected initial cost of the proposed OSHA standard is $0.6 billion and the expected present value of the costs is $2.6 billion. Industry estimates of the cost of compliance with state and local regulation, especially in light of the list of references recently issued by the State of California, indicate that this Department estimate may be too low.

Costs and Benefits Associated With Proposal

The most important point is, of course, that the proposed standard would reduce chemically induced illnesses and injuries and would do so in a cost-effective manner. It is our assumption that a 1 percent per year reduction in injuries and illnesses would occur in the workplace over a 20-year period. Even though the OSHA Act has been interpreted by the Supreme Court to preclude our setting health standards on the basis of cost/benefit considerations, our analysis of the hazard communication proposal shows that the discounted present value of benefits would be at least $5.2 billion in savings in lost production time and medical costs; over that same period the costs of the standard would be only $2.6 billion compared with the Carter administration $22.9 billion. (These estimates have been calculated at a discount rate of 10 percent over a 40-year period. We have consistently used the most conservative assumptions in our estimates in order to leave little doubt as to the validity of our conclusions.) This means that the proposal would cost $16 per worker annually compared to $89 per worker under the Carter administration proposal.

In sum, the current proposal costs are about one-tenth of those estimated for the proposal sponsored by the Carter administration. The current proposal also costs less than most of the industry alternatives.

Impact on Small Business

Reduced Competition. OMB suggests that a Federal hazard communication standard is supported by large chemical companies because it would impose a competitive disadvantage on small companies. This assumes that it would cost less for a large company to come into compliance than a small one.

- In fact, OSHA's regulatory analysis indicates that, on a per establishment basis, the average initial cost for a company in the 250 + employee category would be nearly *50 times* that of a company in the under 19 employee category ($19,058 vs. $403); the costs for the 250 + employee establishment would be almost *14 times* that of a company in the 20–99 employee category ($19,058 vs. $1,427).

- This greater incidence of cost for the large employers is intentional. The hazard communication standard is designed to minimize the impact on small businesses in two significant ways.

    The performance orientation of the labeling and training requirements permits employers to scale their hazard communication systems to the size and sophistication of their operation.

    The compliance dates are staggered for small entities relative to large (the small chemical manufacturers would have an additional one year to comply). This effectively assigns much of the evaluation of the chemical hazards and the development of appropriate information sheets to relatively large chemical manufacturers. The hazard information will then be made available to the smaller chemical manufacturers and to chemical users (many of whom are also relatively small) via chemical container labels and information sheets before these employers are required to be in compliance with the standard.

- Duplication of effort and hence cost is thereby avoided in a manner consistent with the Regulatory Flexibility Act.

- By contrast, in the absence of a standard, small chemical users who want to develop hazard communication systems are at a disadvantage because they do not have the market power to extract the necessary information from large chemical suppliers.

Reliance on Chemical Industry for Evaluation. It is no doubt true that chemical users would support OSHA's proposal to shift the cost of hazard evaluation and communication upstream onto the chemical manufacturers. There is, however, nothing insidious about this. From a market perspective, such a shifting of costs makes eminent sense; it is far more efficient for the chemical manufacturer, who is in the best position to know about the hazards of its products, to provide that information than for each of many industrial users, who are not necessarily even in the business of producing chemicals, to find out this information for themselves. Moreover, Congress, in the TSC Act, itself recognized that the cost of developing data on the hazards of toxic substances should lie with their manufacturers and processors. Thus, OSHA intentionally structured its proposal to produce the effect of having hazard-related information originating with the chemical manufacturer and flowing downstream.

Small Businesses Support the Rule

While it is true that CMA does not adequately represent small chemical manufacturers much less user industries, it is not true that the need for a Federal hazard communication standard is espoused only by large companies. For instance, the National Paint and Coatings Association (NPCA), which represents mostly small companies, has been among the strongest proponents of a Federal standard. The National Association of Printing Ink Manufacturers and the Adhesive Manufacturers Association, both of which also represent mostly small companies, have endorsed the NPCA approach and the concept of a Federal standard. The NPCA's Hazardous Materials Identification System, if adopted as a Federal Standard, would cost at least as much as the OSHA proposal.

The Relationship Between the Records Access and the Hazard Communication Standard

OSHA's records access standard complements but does not displace the need for a hazard communication standard. The records access standard generally assures employees' access upon request to records indicating the identity of toxic substances and harmful physical agents to which they are exposed, as well as access to other exposure and health information if such information has been recorded by the employer. The access standard does not, however, require the creation of such records. The hazard communication standard, therefore, will significantly add to the information provided to employees by affirmatively assuring that employers will establish hazard communication systems within their workplaces. Furthermore, unlike the access standard, the hazard communication standard is designed to assure that hazard information will flow from the manufacturers to downstream employers, who are themselves often unaware of the identities of hazards posed by chemicals in their workplace. Once a hazard communication standard is issued, OSHA will be justified in eliminating the current requirement on the records access standard to keep, and make available, any record indicative of toxic substance identity for 30 years, since the container labels and data sheets will be a more effective means of making that information available to employees.

TSCA and the Hazard Communication Standard

The Toxic Substances Control Act (TSCA) declares that "it is the policy of the United States that adequate data should be developed with respect to the effects of chemical substances and mixtures on health and the environment and that the development of such data should be the responsibility of those who manufacture and those who process such chemical substances and mixtures." It further declares that "adequate authority should exist to regulate chemical substances and mixtures which present an unreasonable risk of injury to health or the environment."

To carry out these statutory purposes, a manufacturer must submit health and safety data to EPA prior to the manufacture or significant new use of a chemical, as well as lists of health and safety studies and information on substantial risk concerning existing chemicals. In a select number of cases, EPA can require the testing of a chemical. It also has the authority to prohibit, limit, require labeling, or otherwise regulate chemicals which present an unreasonable risk or injury to health or the environment.

While TSCA should undoubtedly result in much more health and safety data regarding chemicals being developed, it is in the main merely a reporting statute, in the sense that it requires only that this information be transmitted to EPA. There is no provision that requires that this information be made available directly to employees or the public. Furthermore, it is unrealistic to expect that very many of the thousands of chemicals about which *adverse* health and safety data will be generated will ever be the subject of regulation, including EPA labeling requirements, in the foreseeable future.

The OSHA hazard communication standard would make much of the data generated by TSCA directly available in a relevant form to workers, who bear the brunt of society's exposure to these toxic substances, as well as to downstream chemical users. The effective implementation of TSCA can therefore only enhance the benefits of the OSHA standard. On the other hand, since TSCA requires that this information be generated anyway, the incremental costs of the OSHA standard should be viewed as correspondingly diminished.

Conclusions

- There is broad-based support for a Federal standard—support from business, from labor, from Congress, and from the states. In fact, for once we have virtually no opposition to regulation in this area. We have met with groups representing more than 18 million members of labor unions and with associations representing more than 2 thousand companies, many of which are small businesses. They have all indicated their support for a national standard. Associations which represent small businesses are particularly enthusiastic since they understand that our proposal will eliminate the confusion and costs of the many different chemical hazard regulations which now exist and are in the pipeline. There has seldom, if ever, been a situation more ripe—politically and economically—for a Federal standard to be proposed.

- There are good reasons for this support. The hazard identification requirements would only apply to the 11,000 manufacturers of chemicals, but the benefits would extend to the employees of some 320,000 firms that are supplied with chemicals by these companies. The proposal would allow employers to provide and use information in a market-oriented manner, suited to their own workplace situation and the varying needs of their employees. As noted, it would also serve to discourage a proliferation of differing state and local requirements that would hinder the efficient flow of commerce.

- Our proposal is market-oriented. Unlike the proposal of the previous administration, it relies on performance rather than specification, and on communication of hazards rather than identification of technically complex chemical contents. It employs an information approach that avoids OSHA's usual command-and-control methods that in the past have so alienated the business community. Our proposal represents a general approach to the problem—with uniform requirements, kept to a minimum, that would apply nationwide—rather than the fragmented, state-by-state and city-by-city approach that seems to be gaining ground, not by design, but by default.

- We believe that with training, education, and information workers and employers will be able to reduce chemically related workplace injuries and illnesses substantially. While some benefits will occur right away, benefits will grow over time because of long latency periods for chronic illnesses and cancers. In addition, benefits will be forthcoming over time because of the natural gestation period for new ideas and habits and the continuing introduction of new chemicals. To us it seems like common sense that if employees are informed about a hazard, especially one that is not pleasure-giving or addictive (like cigarettes or drugs contrasted with workplace hazards), that the employees will try to avoid the hazard. Where avoidance takes effort, such as in choosing to wear personal protective equipment, the employer's interest in reducing injuries and illnesses and in continuing training and education programs will provide the added stimulus necessary. (This added stimulus is absent in the case of using automobile seat belts.)

- Our conclusion is that we need this standard and we need it now. The necessary information is not being provided by the marketplace. In the record of the public hearings on the proposed standard, trade association after association, company after company testified that the information market was not functioning adequately—that without a uniform requirement for the disclosure of the identity of chemical products from all manufacturers of such products some companies, fearing possible competitive disadvantage, would not provide the requisite information.

- Considering the groundswell of support for a national standard, it is not feasible or expedient to opt not to regulate at all. We are only proposing a standard, not a final regulation. This is only a starting point. The details of a final standard are subject to public hearings and negotiation. For 11 months organized labor has been saying that we were not coming out with a new proposal, and we have been saying that we are. We withdrew the Carter administration's costly, ill-conceived midnight regulation in February. Labor has not yet been given a cudgel with which to beat this administration. Failure to act on this matter will provide one. Recent articles point to the Democratic Party's efforts to rebuild its ties to the labor movement by painting this administration as anti-worker. Let us not ignore political reality.

10. *Letter*, Kip Viscusi to Thorne Auchter (OSHA), January 29, 1982

Duke University
DURHAM
NORTH CAROLINA
27706

THE FUQUA SCHOOL OF BUSINESS
CENTER FOR THE STUDY
OF BUSINESS REGULATION

W. KIP VISCUSI, DIRECTOR
TELEPHONE (919) 684-5074

January 29, 1982

Mr. Thorne Auchter
Assistant Secretary of Labor
 for Occupational Safety and Health
U.S. Dept. of Labor
Room S2315
200 Constitution Ave.
Washington, D.C. 20210

Dear Mr. Auchter:

I have reviewed the latest draft of OSHA's chemical labeling proposal and the conflict surrounding it. As you know, I first became involved in this policy several months ago while serving in a minor capacity as an economic advisor to OSHA on the economic merits of hazard communication. OSHA selected me for this task since I am the only economist who has addressed the conceptual and empirical aspects of the process by which workers learn about risks, which in turn affects their subsequent behavior. I have published research on these topics in most of the leading economics journals and have also published a major book on these issues, *Employment Hazards: An Investigation of Market Performance* (Cambridge: Harvard University Press, 1979), which was awarded Harvard University's Wells Prize for the best economics dissertation in 1975–1976 and has also been selected by Princeton University as an "outstanding book in labor economics."

I became involved in chemical labeling with some reluctance. The original labeling proposal by Eula Bingham was fundamentally ill-conceived, as it would have imposed major burdens on firms and provided few benefits to workers since the information provided was in terms of a polysyllabic chemical description rather than a series of understandable warnings. I was relieved to see that OSHA had abandoned this approach and was pursuing a much sounder policy.

Much of my enthusiasm for a chemical labeling standard derives from the strong economic basis for such a regulation. The justification is twofold. First, unlike safety risks, the health hazards that workers face are often not well understood so that market forces cannot function effectively. A meaningful hazard communication system can address this problem directly by making workers' perceptions more accurate, enabling workers to take precautionary safety-enhancing actions and to select their jobs more wisely.

In some cases, such as the paint industry, it is in the self-interest of firms to use such a system in order to reduce their accident costs and insurance premiums. Despite these exceptions, market forces will tend to provide too little risk information for a variety of reasons. Most important is that the employer has a vested interest in the use of the information. Once workers are aware of the risks posed by their jobs, they will require a higher wage to work a hazardous position or they may quit their job altogether, thus providing a financial disincentive to firms even in situations in which the benefits to society exceed the costs. Many of the classic problems associated with information, such as its status as a public good, also tend to discourage firms from providing sufficient risk information. In my *Employment Hazards* volume, I explore these and other problems with information provision, where in each case market inadequacies lead to too little hazard information.

A second attractive feature of a hazard communication effort is that this policy works through existing market forces, complementing the powerful economic incentives for safety that already exist. In contrast, rigid standards attempt to supercede the market by mandating enterprises' technological choices irrespective of the costs of compliance and the benefits to workers at that particular firm.

A sound labeling system should have the general character of that proposed by OSHA. It should promote operationally-oriented labels (e.g., flammability warnings, not detailed chemical breakdowns); it should provide leeway to firms to select the most desirable labeling system for the particular situation; and it should make material safety data sheets available and sufficiently accessible to deal with medical emergencies.

The present debate between OSHA and OMB is not so much over the structure of the policy but over the benefits associated with it. I too was concerned with the overstatement of the benefits in the Jan. 1981 proposal, and OSHA has since lowered these estimates and indicated how the results would change if the assumptions were altered even more. OMB in effect is taking OSHA's sensitivity analysis even further by maintaining that under other assumptions that are possibly correct the benefits may be quite small. The difficulty is not that the analysis is methodologically unsound but that the numbers used in these calculations are questionable.

I would like to focus on the two greatest problems—i) the lack of precise evidence regarding the relationship between employment and cancer and ii) the uncertain link between hazard communication and worker behavior. The imprecision of our knowledge regarding the job-cancer link is largely responsible for the disparity of OSHA's and OMB's views. Quite simply, the magnitude of these relationships is difficult to assess precisely because of the long time lags involved, the low levels of the cancer risks, the multiple causes of cancer, and the wide variety of individual activities and exposures that affect the cancer risk.

While these factors make OSHA's attempts to assess benefits imprecise, they create insurmountable problems for the worker. Individuals seldom have a reliable basis on which to judge the degree to which they are facing a cancer risk, and it is difficult for them to distinguish when to exercise special care. The same ambiguity that has generated the OMB-OSHA controversy is the primary reason why a regulation is needed. If instead OSHA were to focus only on those policies whose benefits could be quantified with precision, it would emphasize regulation of readily monitorable safety hazards rather than dimly understood health risks. This emphasis would be the opposite of what should be done.

The second matter of concern is the effect of the hazard communication system on worker actions. The labor market evidence we do have suggests that there will be a response. My analysis of workers' perceptions did not address labeling *per se,* but I did determine that risk perceptions were strongly influenced by worker observations regarding their work environment, their injury experiences, and other factors one would expect to contribute to a sound learning process. These perceptions in turn affected workers' quit decisions and the wage rates workers required to work the job.

Hazard communication also has an apparent beneficial effect since the paint industry adopted it voluntarily. The industry's representatives have noted that the savings in insurance costs, accident costs, and liability costs led to their decision.

The uncertainty on these issues could easily be resolved by monitoring the performance of the labeling systems adopted, which I hope OSHA will do. Given the degree of our uncertainty, it is especially desirable that the draft OSHA proposal permits a diversity of approaches so that firms can discover the most effective communication policy.

I should emphasize that my enthusiasm for hazard communication does not stem from a personal bias in favor of OSHA's traditional approach. As you may know, I have been a long-time critic of OSHA. My views stemmed from my academic work, which is one of the principal empirical assessments of the failure of OSHA policies to promote worker health and safety in the 1970's.

More recently, I gave a speech on health and safety regulation at the AEI Public Policy Week. My commitment to regulatory reform is apparent, as I endorsed the general spirit of the efforts by OMB and urged them to be even more zealous in undertaking sunset actions. In my former capacity as Deputy Director of the Council on Wage and Price Stability, I also attempted to promote efficient regulations, though with less success than the Reagan Administration has had. In my AEI speech I also advocated that OSHA take a more active role by de-emphasizing safety and by emphasizing health risks. More specifically I advocated a chemical labeling system, which I viewed as possibly "the best OSHA policy ever." I have made similar proposals in my academic work, most recently in my book *Risk by Choice*, which will be published by Harvard University Press later this year.

The reason I have placed so much emphasis on a hazard communication policy is that this approach would establish a new direction for OSHA policies. Instead of mandating standards for readily perceived safety risks, OSHA would be attempting to augment market forces to promote more efficient levels of health risks. If the administration fails to pursue some form of chemical labeling policy because the benefits are unclear, in effect it will be establishing a bias against all innovative efforts which, by their very nature, tend to have uncertain effects precisely because of their novelty.

Sincerely,

W. Kip Viscusi
IBM Research Professor

WKV:ks
cc. Mary Ellen Weber

OSHA CCU # 21781

11. *Letter*, Kip Viscusi to Mary Ellen Weber (OSHA), February 1, 1982

Duke University
DURHAM
NORTH CAROLINA
27706

THE FUQUA SCHOOL OF BUSINESS
CENTER FOR THE STUDY
 OF BUSINESS REGULATION

W. KIP VISCUSI, DIRECTOR
TELEPHONE (919) 684-5074

February 1, 1982

Dr. Mary Ellen Weber
Director, Regulatory Analysis
OSHA, U.S. Dept. of Labor
Room N3657
200 Constitution Ave., N.W.
Washington, D.C. 20210

Dear Mary Ellen:

   I am writing to express a major complaint about the chemical labeling analysis and, more generally, about the risk regulation analyses in the Federal Government. As you know, the chemical labeling analysis that your office performed included many of the monetary benefits of the chemical labeling standard. These included lost income, lost production, and medical costs that would be averted if worker accidents and illnesses were reduced. Both OMB and OSHA seem to be talking about these numbers as if they represent the benefits of the chemical labeling standard. They do not. These entries comprise but a small portion of the total benefits of risk reduction since they totally exclude the individual worker's willingness to pay for risk reduction that is not included in these statistics. My own research has indicated that the value of life and the value of injuries is several times higher than the results one would obtain using earnings and income statistics such as those used by OSHA. Usually, the willingness-to-pay numbers are about ten times greater.

   What seems to have happened is that rather than offend peoples' moral sensitivities by using a number for the value of life or the value of accidents, OSHA instead has used less controversial proxies for these values. These partial estimates of the benefits in turn have become used in policy discussions in a manner that would suggest that everyone regards these numbers as reflecting the total benefits. By failing to place an appropriate value on life OSHA may have unwittingly made its chemical labeling proposal look much less attractive than it actually is.

192

I see two ways out of this bind. First, OSHA could actually go out and place a dollar value on the saved lives, prevented cancers, and reduced accidents that will result from this standard. The overall regulation will then be evaluated much more accurately and will look much more attractive than it now does. Second, OSHA could follow the opposite approach and net out all of the benefits that it has already calculated from the cost and call this figure the net cost of the proposal and then figure out what the net cost is per life saved or per cancer prevented to try to figure out whether the cost per unit of these non-qualified health benefits is too great. I did not suggest this before because the net cost was negative under OSHA's assumptions. For OMB's assumptions, it is positive.

If your staff needs any assistance in performing these calculations, let me know.

Sincerely,

W. Kip Viscusi
IBM Research Professor

WKV:ks

12. NPRM. Hazard Communication, 47 *Federal Register*, 12,092, March 19, 1982

DEPARTMENT OF LABOR

Occupational Safety and Health Administration

29 CFR Part 1910

[Docket No. H–022]

Hazard Communication; Notice of Proposed Rulemaking and Public Hearings

AGENCY: Occupational Safety and Health Administration, Labor.

ACTION: Notice of proposed rulemaking and public hearings.

SUMMARY: The proposed standard requires chemical manufacturers to assess the hazards of chemicals which they produce, and all employers having facilities in the manufacturing division, SIC Codes 20–39, to provide information to their employees about these hazards by means of hazard communication programs including labels, placards, material safety data sheets, information and training, and access to written records. OSHA has determined that this standard is necessary because many employers and employees are not aware of the presence of hazardous chemicals in their workplaces. The proposed standard provides for hazard determinations to be conducted to identify these hazards, and for subsequent communication to employees of the hazards thus identified. These activities should serve to alleviate the lack of awareness concerning hazardous chemicals, and should provide an impetus for employees and employers to devise better means of protection from these hazards. Public hearings are being scheduled to provide interested parties the opportunity to orally present information and data related to the issues raised by this proposed rule.

DATES: Comments and notices of intention to appear at the public hearings must be received on or before May 18, 1982. Statements and any documentary evidence to be presented at the hearings must be submitted by June 1, 1982.

The hearings will begin on June 15, 1982 in Washington, D.C. and at subsequent times and locations as provided in a separate notice to be published shortly.

ADDRESSES: Comments should be submitted in quadruplicate to the Docket Office, Docket H–022, U.S. Department of Labor, Occupational Safety and Health Administration, 200 Constitution Avenue, NW., Room S6212, Washington, D.C. 20210; (202) 523–7894.

Notices of intention to appear at the hearings, statements and documentary evidence should be submitted to Mr. Tom Hall, Division of Consumer Affairs, U.S. Department of Labor, 200 Constitution Avenue, NW., Room N3635 Washington, D.C. 20210; (202) 523–8024.

The location of the June 15, 1982, hearing will be announced at a later date.

Written comments received and notices of intention to appear will be available for inspection and copying in the Docket Office, Room S6212 at the above address.

FOR FURTHER INFORMATION CONTACT:
Proposal: Ms. Jennifer Silk, Office of Special Standards, Occupational Safety and Health Administration, 200 Constitution Avenue, NW., Room N3663, Washington, D.C. 20210; (202) 523–7166.
Hearings: Mr. Tom Hall, Division of Consumer Affairs, Occupational Safety and Health Administration, 200 Constitution Avenue, NW., N3635, Washington, D.C. 20210; (202) 523–8024.

I. Background

A. History of OSHA's Proposed Hazard Communication Standard

OSHA's involvement in the identification and communication of hazards in the workplace began some years ago. In 1974, the Standards Advisory Committee on Hazardous Materials Labeling was established under section 7(b) of the OSH Act to develop guidelines for the implementation of section 6(b)(7) of the Act with respect to hazardous materials (1). On June 6, 1975, the Committee submitted its final report which identified issues and recommended guidelines for categorizing and ranking chemical hazards (2). Labels, material safety data sheets, and training programs were also prescribed.

The National Institute for Occupational Safety and Health (NIOSH) published a criteria document in 1974 which recommended a standard to OSHA (3). The document, entitled "A Recommended Standard * * * An Identification System for Occupationally Hazardous Materials," included provisions for labels and material safety data sheets.

In 1976, Congressman Andrew Maguire (New Jersey) and the Health Research Group petitioned OSHA to issue a standard to require the labeling of all workplace chemicals. The House of Representatives' Committee on Government Operations in 1976 and 1977 recommended that OSHA should enforce the health provisions of the OSH Act by requiring manufacturers to disclose any toxic ingredients in their products, and by requiring employers to disclose this information to workers (4, 5 and 6).

On January 28, 1977, OSHA published an advance notice of proposed rulemaking on chemical labeling in the **Federal Register** (42 FR 5372). The notice requested comments from the public regarding the need for a standard that would require employers to label hazardous materials. Information was also requested regarding the provisions to be included in such a standard to assure that employees are apprised of the hazards to which they are exposed.

A total of eighty-one comments were received from a variety of federal, state, and local government agencies, trade associations, businesses, and labor organizations. In general, there was support for the concept of a hazard communication standard. A number of commenters said that such a standard should be comprehensive in scope, but not too complex in design. Many expressed the opinion that OSHA's standard should be compatible with the standards of other regulatory agencies with labeling authority, such as the Department of Transportation (DOT), and with existing voluntary labeling standards, such as that of the American National Standards Institute (ANSI). A few commenters expressed concerns about protection of trade secret information and about labeling chemical intermediates.

Various suggestions were put forth for determining which materials should be considered hazardous and thus covered by such a standard. Some commenters thought that chemicals that meet specified definitions or other classifications should be regulated. Others preferred that a list of substances to be regulated be provided, for example, those substances in 29 CFR 1910.1000 (OSHA's list of air contaminants), in the NIOSH Registry of Toxic Effects of Chemical Substances (RTECS), or in the DOT hazardous materials list.

Virtually all commenters recognized the need for labels in the workplace, and for inclusion of warnings and descriptive information. However, opinions varied as to what form these labels and information should take, or whether an existing system should be adopted. Similarly, there was general recognition of the need to inform employees of the hazards to which they are exposed by means of data sheets and training programs, although suggestions as to content and format varied.

Bibliography

BOOKS

Ball, Howard. *No Pledge of Privacy: The Watergate Tapes Litigation, 1973–1974.* New York: Kennikat Press, 1976.

_____; Krane, Dale; and Lauth, Thomas. *Compromised Compliance: The Implementation of the 1965 Voting Rights Act.* Westport, CT: Greenwood Press, 1982.

Bardach, Eugene, and Kagen, Robert A. *Going by the Book.* Philadelphia, PA: Temple University Press, 1981.

Bell, Griffin B. *Taking Care of the Law.* New York: William Morrow and Co., 1982.

Califano, Joseph, Jr. *Governing America: An Insider's Report from the White House and the Cabinet.* New York: Simon and Schuster, 1981.

Carter, Jimmy. *Keeping Faith: Memoirs of a President.* New York: Bantam Books, 1982.

Clark, Timothy, et al. *Reforming Regulation.* Washington, D.C.: American Enterprise Institute, 1980.

Congressional Quarterly. *Federal Regulatory Directory, 1980–1981.* Washington, D.C.: Congressional Quarterly Press, 1980.

_____. *Nixon: The First Year of His Presidency.* Washington, D.C.: Congressional Quarterly Press, 1970.

Cooper, Phillip. *Public Law and Public Administration.* Palo Alto, CA: Mayfield Publishing Co., 1983.

Cronin, Thomas E. *The State of the Presidency.* Boston, MA: Little, Brown, 1975.

Davis, Kenneth C. *Administrative Law and Government.* St. Paul, MN: West Publishing Co., 1975.

Edles, Gary J., and Nelson, Jerome. *Federal Regulatory Processes: Agency Practices and Procedures.* New York: Harcourt Brace Jovanovich, 1981.

Edwards, George C., III. *Implementing Public Policy.* Washington, D.C.: Congressional Quarterly Press, 1980.

Evans, Rowland, Jr., and Novak, Robert D. *Nixon in the White House: The Frustration of Power.* New York: Random House, 1971.

Fisher, Louis. *The Politics of Shared Power: Congress and the Executive.* Washington, D.C.: Congressional Quarterly Press, 1981.

Ford, Gerald R. *A Time to Heal.* New York: Harper & Row, 1979.

Fritschler, A. Lee, and Ross, Bernard. *Executive's Guide to Government.* Cambridge, MA: Winthrop, 1980.

Funderburk, Charles. *Presidents and Politics: The Limits of Power.* Monterey, CA: Brooks-Cole Publishing Co., 1982.

Heclo, Hugh, and Salamon, L. M. *The Illusion of Presidential Government.* Boulder, CO: Westview Press, 1981.

Hess, Stephen. *Organizing the Presidency.* Washington, D.C.: Brookings Institution, 1976.

Kessel, John H. *The Domestic Presidency: Decisionmaking in the White House.* North Scituate, MA: Duxbury Press, 1975.

MacAvoy, Paul W., ed. *Unsettled Questions on Regulatory Reform.* Washington, D.C.: American Enterprise Institute, 1978.

MacKenzie, G. Calvin. *The Politics of Presidential Appointments.* New York: Free Press, 1981.

Miller, James C., and Yandle, Bruce, ed. *Benefit-Cost Analysis of Social Regulations.* Washington, D.C.: AEI, Inc., 1979.

Nathan, Richard P. *The Plot That Failed: Nixon and the Administrative Presidency.* New York: John Wiley & Sons, 1975.

Neustadt, Richard E. *Presidential Power.* New York: John Wiley & Sons, 1980. D.C.: U.S. Government Printing Office, 1980.

———. *Presidential Power.* New York: John Wiley & Sons, 1980.

Nixon, Richard M. *RN: The Memoirs of Richard M. Nixon.* New York: Grosset and Dunlap, 1978.

Price, Raymond. *With Nixon.* New York: Viking Press, 1977.

Ripley, Randall B., and Franklin, Grace A. *Congress, the Bureaucracy, and Public Policy.* Homewood, IL: Dorsey Press, 1980.

Rourke, Francis E. *Bureaucracy, Politics, and Public Policy.* Boston: Little, Brown, 1976.

Stone, Alan. *Regulation and Its Alternatives.* Washington, D.C.: Congressional Quarterly Press, 1982.

Thompson, Frank J. *Classics in Public Personnel Policy.* Chicago: Moore Publishing Co., 1979.

Warren, Kenneth. *Administrative Law in the American Political System.* St. Paul, MN: West Publishing Co., 1982.

ARTICLES

Aberbach, Joel D., and Rockman, Bert A. "Clashing Beliefs within the Executive Branch." 70 *American Political Science Review,* No. 2, June 1976.

Benze, James G., Jr. "Presidential Management: The Importance of Presidential Skills." 11 *Presidential Studies Quarterly,* No. 4, Fall 1981.

Breyer, Stephen. "Analyzing Regulatory Failure." 92 *Harvard Law Review*, No. 3, January 1979.

Bruff, Harold H. "Presidential Power and Administrative Rule-Making." 88 *Yale Law Journal*, No. 3, January 1979.

Campbell, Alan K. "Civil Service Reform: A New Commitment." 38 *Public Administration Review*, No. 2, March–April 1978.

Clark, Elias. "Holding Government Accountable." 84 *Yale Law Journal*, No. 4, March 1975.

Clark, Timothy. "OMB to Keep Its Regulatory Powers." *National Journal*, March 14, 1981.

_____. "Do Benefits Justify Costs." *National Journal*, August 1, 1981.

Couric, Emily. "Altering the U.S. Regulatory Map." *Legal Times*, November 24, 1980.

Cutler, Lloyd N., and Johnson, David R. "Regulation and the Political Process." 84 *Yale Law Journal*, No. 7, June 1975.

DeMuth, Christopher. "A Strong Beginning on Reform." 6 *Regulation*, January–February 1982.

Fisher, Louis, and Moe, Ronald C. "Presidential Reorganization Authority." 96 *Political Science Quarterly*, No. 2, Summer 1981.

Garner, Les. "Management Control in Regulatory Agencies." 34 *Administrative Law Review*, No. 3, Summer 1982.

Gilmour, Robert S. "The Congressional Veto: Shifting the Balance of Administrative Control." 2 *Journal of Policy Analysis and Management*, No. 1, 1982.

Greider, William. "The Education of David Stockman." *Atlantic Monthly*, December 1981.

Hoffman, Dianna. "President May Regret Barely Qualified Appointees." *Legal Times*, June 29, 1981.

Kahn, Alfred E., and Roach, Michael. "Commentary: A Paean to Legal Creativity." 31 *Administrative Law Review* 1979.

Kirschten, Dick. "President Reagan after Two Years." *National Journal*, January 1, 1983.

Kosters, Marvin H., and Eisenach, Jeffrey A. "Is Regulatory Relief Enough." *Regulation*, March–April 1982.

Lasko, Warren. "Executive Accountability: Will SES Make a Difference." 9 *Bureaucrat*, No. 3, Fall 1980.

Lauth, Thomas P., Jr. "ZBB in Georgia State Government: Myth and Reality." 38 *Public Administration Review*, No. 5, September–October 1978.

Long, Norton E. "The S.E.S. and the Public Interest." 41 *Public Administration Review*, No. 3, May–June 1981.

Masters, Kim. "Judicial Conference Report Slows Action on Regulatory Reform Bill." *Legal Times*, July 27, 1981.

Miller, James C., III. "Lesson of the EIS Program." *Regulation*, July-August 1977.

Nager, Glen D. "Bureaucrats and the Cost-Benefit Chameleon." 6 *Regulation*, September–October 1982.

Newcomer, Kathryn, and Kamber, Glenn. "Changing the Rules of Rulemaking." 11 *Bureaucrat*, No. 2, Summer 1982.

Note. "Delegation and Regulatory Reform: Letting the President Change the Rules." 89 *Yale Law Journal,* No. 3, January 1980.

Note. "Regulation and the 1983 Budget." *Regulation,* March–April 1982.

Note. "Regulation and the 1982 Budget." *Regulation,* July–August 1981.

Note. "The Supreme Court, 1979 Term." 94 *Harvard Law Review,* No. 1, November 1981.

Pierce, Neal R., and Hamilton, Jay. "Flypaper Federalism." *National Journal,* September 12, 1981.

Randall, Ronald. "Presidential Power versus Bureaucratic Intransigence: The Influence of the Nixon Administration on Welfare Policy." 73 *American Political Science Review,* No. 3, September 1979.

Robinson, Glen O. "On Reorganizing the IRAs." 57 *Virginia Law Review,* No. 6, September 1971.

Rosen, Bernard. "Uncertainty in the Senior Executive Service." 41 *Public Administration Review,* No. 2, March–April 1981.

Rosenberg, Morton. "Beyond the Limits of Executive Power." 80 *Michigan Law Review,* No. 2, December 1981.

_____. "Presidential Control of Agency Rulemaking." 23 *Arizona Law Review,* No. 4, 1981.

_____. "Report on Executive Order 12,291." *Congressional Research Service, Library of Congress,* reprinted in *Legal Times,* June 29, 1981.

Rosenbloom, David H. "Public Administrator's Official Immunity and the Supreme Court." 40 *Public Administration Review,* March–April 1980.

Scalia, Antonin. "Back to Basics: Making Law without Making Rules." *Regulation,* July–August 1981.

_____. "Deregulation HQ: An Interview on the New Executive Order with Murray L. Weidenbaum and James A. Miller III." *Regulation,* March–April 1981.

_____, ed. "Regulation: The First Year." *Regulation,* January–February 1982.

Shane, Peter M. "Presidential Regulatory Oversight and the Separation of Powers." 23 *Arizona Law Review,* No. 4, 1981.

Sohn, Michael, and Litan, Robert. "Regulatory Oversight Wins in Court." *Regulation,* July–August 1981.

Stewart, Joseph, Jr.; Anderson, James E.; Taylor, Zona. "Presidential and Congressional Support for IRCs." 35 *Western Political Quarterly,* No. 3, September 1982.

Sunstein, Cass R. "Cost-Benefit Analysis and the Separation of Powers." 23 *Arizona Law Review,* No. 4, 1981.

"The Supreme Court, 1979 Term." 94 *Harvard Law Review,* No. 1, November 1981.

Thomas, Norman C. "Politics, Structure, and Personnel in Administrative Regulations." 57 *Virginia Law Review,* No. 6, September 1971.

Thompson, Frank J., and Davis, Raymond G. "Personnel Reform: The Malek Manual Revisited." 6 *Bureaucrat,* No. 2, Summer 1977.

Vernon, Charles W. "The IIS Program: An Assessment of the First Two Years." 26 *American University Law Review,* 1138, 1977.

Weiss, Laura. "Markups Slated for Regulatory Reform Bill. *Congressional Quarterly,* June 20, 1981.

_____. "Reagan and Congress Planning Regulatory Machine Repairs." *Congressional Quarterly,* March 7, 1981.

White, B. Ward. "Proposals for a Regulatory Budget." 1 *Public Budgeting and Finance,* Autumn 1981.

Whitney, Kevin. "Capitalizing on a Constitutional Void: EO 12,291." 31 *American University Law Review,* No. 3, Spring 1982.

Wines, Michael. "Reagan's Reforms Are Full of Sound and Fury, But What Do They Signify?" *National Journal,* January 16, 1982.

_____. "Regulatory Writing in Washington—Making Days Stretch into Years." *National Journal,* November 13, 1982.

_____. "They're Still Telling OSHA Horror Stories, But the 'Victims' Are New." *National Journal,* December 7, 1981.

Witter, Lee F. "Legislative Veto." 9 *Bureaucrat,* No. 2, Summer 1980.

Wyszomirski, Margaret J. "The De-Institutionalization of Presidential Staff Agencies." 42 *Public Administration Review,* No. 5, September–October 1982.

Index

About the Author

HOWARD BALL is Professor and Chairman of the Department of Political Science at the University of Utah, Salt Lake City. His numerous writings include two books previously published by Greenwood Press: *Compromised Compliance: Implementation of the 1965 Voting Rights Act* (1982) and *Judicial Craftsmanship or Fiat?: Direct Overturn by the United States Supreme Court* (1978).